Garud Puran

(With detailed Introduction)
Roman script with English Translation

By Hira Ballabh Joshi

M.A, M.Phil, Jawaharlal Nehru University, New Delhi

M.B.A, Manipal University

Courtesy-
Hindu Purohit Sangh
http:// www.hindupurohitsangh.com
www.facebook.com/hindu.purohitsangh

DIAMOND BOOKS
www.diamondbook.in

© **Author**

Publisher : **Diamond Pocket Books (P) Ltd.**
X-30, Okhla Industrial Area, Phase-II
New Delhi-110020
Phone : 011-40712100, 41611861
E-mail : sales@dpb.in
Website : www.dpb.in
Edition : 2017
Printed by : Repro Knowledgecast Limited, Thane

Garud Puran
By : *Hira Ballabh Joshi*

THE UNIQUENESS OF
TERMS AND CONCEPTS

Various terms in English and other European languages convey specific meaning as they are concerned with Abrahmic religions and are therefore alien to Dharma traditions. To overcome this shortcoming, certain original or more appropriate terms are referred in this translation. Some of them are as follows:

1. **Shradhaanjali** (homage) **to the departed**: The word used for homage in Sanatan Dharma is "**Sadgati**" (Speedy Elevation to Truth) or "**Paramgati**" meaning "Wish this Atma attains **Mokshya**. Each follower of Sanatan Dharma is on a journey towards Mokshya. Thus, we wish the departed Atma speed in its journey to Mokshya and not take rest or peace. This is parallel to the wish of "Rest in Peace" (RIP) for those who are buried and wait in their graves for the Day of Judgement.

2. **Work as Offering:** For a Sanatan Dharma follower, work is as an offering (every act should be treated as offering to Ishwara (God), including intake of food), thus, work is not treated worship. Therefore, one should start every event or other things with Om Ganeshai Namah.

3. **I am Dharmik:** For a Hindu, the Ishwara is kind, compassionate and loving in all circumstances and not something to fear. Ishwara is everywhere and we are also part of It. It is present in us as Atma. "I am Dharmik" is to be used in place of: "I am God fearing." Similarly, the expression like "He/She is like Bhagwan (God) to me" is alien to Sanatan Dharma as Bhagwan is within you.

4. **Dharma and Philosophy:** Dharma promotes logical thinking. Dharma is Darshan, i.e., what was seen by seers. Therefore, unlike Abrahamic religions, there is no place for Dogma in Dharma traditions.

5. **Atma of a person:** "Atma" of a person is eternal and part of Brahmn, i.e., Ishwara. Therefore, Atma is different from 'soul' which has nothing to do with Ishwar and soul dies with the death of a person. Further, it is also not spirit as the spirit can have negative and positive meanings, whereas Atma is always divine.

6. **Treat Ramayana and Mahabharata as Itihas** (historical): Do not use the word "mythology" for our historic epics Ramayana and Mahabharata. Shri Rama and Shri Krishna are historical Avatars and not mythical characters.

7. **Temples are not prayer halls**: Temples are "Devalaya" (abode of Ishwara) and not "**Prathanalaya**" (prayer halls).

8. **Religion as Dharma:** Dharma broadly refers to conduct that is perfectly in accordance with the cosmic order of universe. Dharma has both social as well as individual aspects to it, relating to natural order, public morality, righteousness, Karma, justice (14.46), social harmony, religious duties, right behaviour and virtuous conduct towards all creatures, earth and the entire creation whereas Religion denotes to the belief system and following of divine commands. **Dharma is actually the most splendid crown jewel adorned by a Sanatan Dharmi.** A follower of Dharma tradition can never become Dharma-nirpeksha (secular) as Dharma denotes all the good and righteous ways.

9. **Thirty Crore Devi-Devta**: There is only one ultimate reality among Hindus which is known as "Brahmn" (not Brahma, who is a deity). It is neither male nor female, therefore, referred as '**Tat**' (meaning 'It' being gender neutral). The Brahmn (Ishwara) is everything including the universe itself. It is the source of all creation including the Devi-devtas (deities) who maintain and run the creation. Brahmn has created **33 Devi-Devtas** to oversee the various aspects of creation and having different responsibilities. Indra, Surya, Vayu, Agni, Yama, Varuna are some of the functional designations of the 33 category (not 33 Crore) of deities. These are eight Vasus, eleven Rudras, twelve Adityas, plus Indra and Prajapati Brahma. Each of these 33 Devi-Devta is manifested in nature such as Air, Water, Energy, Life, and Light and so on. It is through Devi-Devtas that the Ishwara touches and nourishes its creation every moment and is visible to the creation. The words Ishwara or Bhagwan are synonym of Brahmn and denote the state of opulence.

10. **Murti Pooja**: Murti or Vigraha worship has a deeper meaning and it is not merely idol worship. This is a process to bring the abstract reality to a concrete form so as one can connect with

the abstract and to internalise it. Murti is a link between Atma and Parmatma. Just like the relationship between body and Atma.

11. **Prefix "Shree" and correct pronouncement**: Always use prefix Shree or Shri for Bhagwan Shree Ram, Shree Krishna, Bhagwan Shiv, Bhagwati Shri Durga. Please don't refer to Shree Ganesh and Shree Hanuman as "Elephant god" and "Monkey god" respectively. It is necessary to pronounce the holy name of Bhagwan, holy places and other terms correctly. We must not pronounce Shri Raam as Raamaa, Shree Krishna as Krishnaa and Bhagwan Shiv as Lord Shivaa. Similarly, the holy river is called Ganga and not Ganges.

12. **Wishes for Auspiciousness:** Most of the Hindu festivals are occasions for spiritual awakening, therefore, we should wish auspiciousness to others. But instead of saying, for example, "Happy Diwali" a wish should rather be expressed as "Shubh-Diwali" or 'Wish you auspicious Diwali'.

13. **Agni** (Fire) **is manifestation of a Devi:** Don't throw impure material on the divine **Agni Devta** (fire). Instead, ask them to pray: "Oh divine fire, lead me from darkness to light" (Tam so ma Jyotirgamaya) by lighting a lamp. These are all strong images that go deep into the psyche.

14. **The entire creation is Divine:** Please avoid using the words "spirituality" and "materialistic". For a follower of Sanatan Dharma, everything is divine. The words spirituality and materialism came to India through evangelists and Europeans who had a concept of Church v/s State or Science v/s Religion. On the contrary, in India, Rishis were scientists and the foundation stone of Sanatan Dharma is Science. Here, all is also divine.

15. **Paap and Punya**: "Sin" as understood in Abrahmic religions is an act of offence against God i.e., not following word of God is sin. We use the word Paap which is Adharma and is an offence against oneself as it impacts one's karma. The opposite of Paap is Punya and there is no parallel word for it in English.

16. **Do not distort the terms:** Salvation, Hell and Heaven, Demon, Samaritan, etc. are inadequate to describe the concepts of Dharma traditions as they are Abhramic concepts and convey different meaning. Do not use the word meditation for "Dhyana"; 'breathing exercise' for "Pranayama"; King of Justice for Dharam-raaj; Gift in place of Daan and so on. Similarly Swarga does mean heaven and Narak is different from hell as Swarga and Narak are only transitional phases for experiencing the returns of Karma and means of purification. Maya is different from delusion, Kathaa is not story telling. Further, the words Pavitra is not pure, Sudhh, Saatvik, Sansaar, Purusharth, Karma, Sat-Asat convey different meaning altogether. Rishis were seers or divine logicians and not saints. Vivaah is not same as marriage as it is a sacrament and not a contract. Upavaas and Vrit (vow) are the means to realise Ishwara, coming near self and fasting is only a way to prepare body for that Saatvik state of mind; fasting (Niraahaar) is to purify the body for the purification of Mana and Chitta (mind and intellect). There are no parallel words for Brahmn, Bhajan, Kirtan, Japa, Sanskar, etc. as these practices do not exist in other systems of faith.

Therefore, the use the original words should be resorted so that these terms become part of vocabulary of English and other languages and better understanding of Dharma is promoted.

17. **Importance of concluding chapter:** Like in many other scriptures, the last chapter of Garud Puran also deals with the deeper spiritual knowledge. Further, the Chapter 16 is not directly related to the main subject matter of Garud Puran. However, you have to graduate through various chapters so as to properly grasp the deeper knowledge of the last chapter.

✳ ✳ ✳

CONTENTS

	Topic	Page No.
Introduction.	An Unique Scripture, Deeper Question Asked, Dharma- the Crown Jewel, Monotheistic Advait Darshan, Re-birth, Maya, Mokshya, Swarga and Narak, Sad-gati, Divine Law of Karma, Praarabdh and Purushaarth, Karma Yogi, the Most Ancient and the Most Modern Dharma, Paap and Punya, Daan - an act of Compassion and Equality, Healthy Body, Life Mantra, Call to the youth, etc.	X-LXXXIV
Invocation	Invocation for successful recitation of Garud Puran	1
Chapter 1.	The deeds leading to Swarga and Narak, offering of Pind and formation of body, an account of the terrifying torments experienced by the Paapi (sinner) during journey to Yama-lok (realm of Yama) and narration of miseries of the Paapis on this earth and in the Parlok (other-world) and so on.	2-10
Chapter 2.	Entry into the sixteen Puris (cities) leading to Yam-lok, the agonizing Vaitarnee river, torments of Yam-lok, offering of Pind, etc.	11-21
Chapter 3.	An account of torments of Yama, briefing to Yama by Chitragupta and feedback from Shravana, Dharm-raaj delivers the judgment.	22-30

Chapter 4.	How Paapi (sinner) fall into Vaitarnee river, four gateways leading to the city of Dharm-raaj, truth seekers and their company, consequences of good and bad deeds.	31-39
Chapter 5.	Various births according to Karma of individuals; description of different diseases and so on.	40-47
Chapter 6.	Formation of embryo, evolution of Jeev (creature), sufferings in the womb, the bad Karma of human beings and their consequences.	48-54
Chapter 7.	Ways to escape Narak, importance of descendents for proper transmigration; Aurdhva-dehik Kriya (higher bodily rite) performed by a king and emancipation of Pret.	55-65
Chapter 8.	Daan (donations and virtuous gifts), Punya (meritorious deeds), Dharma, Karma, duties of the offspring and Daan for the departed.	66-81
Chapter 9.	What should a dying person do during last hours and the required observances; importance of Tulsi, Saaligram and others.	82-88
Chapter 10.	Divine emotional homage to the departed, post death rites, Pret condition, collection of the mortal remains and their immersion, Narayan Bali, Panchak, rewards of Pind Daan.	89-102
Chapter 11.	Inescability of death, death no reason for sorrow, the Dashgaatra karm, competency to perform the Kriya (Rites) and the procedure (Vidhan).	103-108

READ!

READ!

READ!

Chapter 12.	Ekaadash Karma (eleventh-day rites), Daan (donations, charity), Varsho-utsarg (rites for release of the bull), Uttam Shodashi, Sapindikaran, Narayan-Bali, etc.	109-116
Chapter 13.	Sutak (impurity) period, Sapindi Shraaddh, Gaya Shraaddh and importance of Daan (donations and charity).	117-132
Chapter 14.	The grandeur of Yamlok, an account of the castles of Chitragupta and others, architecture of the assembly of Dharmraaj, welcome of virtuous in that assembly.	133-142
Chapter 15.	Birth of the Dharm-atma, Shath-Chakra, Yoga-Dhyan, devotion to Ajapaa, meditation of Sri-Guru and so on.	143-156
Chapter 16.	Maya (delusion), Trishna (longing), Pragya (wisdom), Mokshya from Sansaar (world of change) and so on.	157-173
Shruti-phal	Listening of Garud Puran within ten days and the rewards obtained by the performer and Mokshya to the departed.	174-175
Shok Sabha (Model Speech)	Aim of Shraddhanjali, Dharma, Karma, Purusharth, Daan, Grihast should become Karma-Yogi.Emphasis on Good Deeds of departed, and Immortality of Atma.	176-180

INTRODUCTION

Om Vishnave Namah
Sri Krishnaay Namah

Ajam-ajaram-anantam gyaana-roopam, mahaantm
Shivam-amalam-anaadim bhoota-deha-adi-heenam;
Sakala-karan-heenam sarva-bhoota-sthitatm-tm
Harim-amalam-amaaym sarvagm vand-ekam.

(Mahagarudpuraan-1/1)

(the eternal, who is without birth and beyond aging, who is in the form of knowledge, is supreme, is without beginning and end; the auspicious, the merciful, bodiless, the one without physical organs of senses, the omnipresent, the one beyond Maya, the benevolent, ubiquitous and the one and only, I pray to that absolute).

The core principles of Sanatan Hindu Dharma can be summarized in the following points: (i) The Universe is cyclical in nature, not linear. (ii) It is not only the Creator who is divine but his creation is also divine (iii) The **Atma** (spirit of the individual) is a part of **Brahmn** (the ultimate reality, i.e., Ishwara); therefore, it is important and divine. (iv) Brahmn is limitless and it can manifest Itself in various forms. (v) The Cycle of Birth and Death and Rebirth are the process of transmigration of Atma. (vi) The alienation of Jeeva (living being) from Brahmn is due to Maya. (vi) The ultimate goal of life, for the adherents of Dharma tradition, is **Mokshya** (unity with divine by Mokshya from the **Sansaar,** i.e., endless cycle of birth and death). Thus, the aim is to merge with the same Supreme power from which the Atma has being separated. Here, death is treated as a transitional phase, and life as an opportunity to obtain Mokshya. Dharma is a means to achieve the goal of Mokshya. (vii) Human body is a carrier of the Atma, therefore, important. (viii) Eventually, everyone will achieve Mokshya. (ix) Swarga and Narak are only transitional phases in a long journey. (x) Karma (action through body, speech and mind) of a person determines the Destiny. (xi) The human being is not sinner rather potentially divine. (xii) Ishwara is loving and an ocean of compassion.

Dharma broadly refers to conduct that is perfectly in accordance and consonance with the cosmic order of universe. Dharma has both social as well as individual aspects to it relating to natural order, public morality, righteousness Karma, justice (14.46), social harmony, religious duties (religion is different from Dharma), right behavior and virtuous conduct towards all creatures and the entire creation. **Dharma is actually the most splendid crown jewel adorned by the Hindus.** The word Dharma is so unique that it conveys different but righteous meanings when used in varied contexts. The natural ways things happen and accepting them as a way of life is called Dharma. The one principle that makes Sanatan Dharma infinitely different from all other religions is its treatment of human being as **Amritasya Putrah** (children of immortality- **Sveta. Upanishad**). Thus, all humans have divinity in them and by striving on the path of Dharma, they can achieve Mokshya.(5.48,49). Dharma relieves from sorrow and makes life successful (8.96). Dharma alone is the companion of human being and it also shapes the Karma (8.101).

The goal of life in Sanatan Dharma is: Aatmano Mokshyartham Jagat hitaay Ch (for Mokshya- unity with divine- of individual self and for the well being of all on earth - *Rig-Veda*). The importance of Dharma in life can be gauged from the fact that even though non-violence is the principle component of Dharma, yet one is allowed to resort to violence as a last step for upholding of Dharma. The Avtaar of Shri Ram and Shri Krishna were aimed at establishment of the order of Dharma (Gita 4.7) and annihilation of wrongdoers and demonic forces (Gita 4.8) as Adharma (absence of dharma) leads to total destruction. (However, the Priest, Saadhus, Brahmins and Ascetic are not allowed to resort violence.) Sparing a life of others has been treated as highest virtue. *(Details on Dharma are at Page No. XLII)*

There are sixteen Sanskaar (sacraments) in Sanatan Dharma which are to be conducted as the milestones in the journey of life. The rituals of **Antyesti** (last rites), one of the sixteen Sanskaars, are very special as it is performed as the rite-de-passage for the **Sad-gati** (Speedy Elevation to Truth) of the departed. It is not only aimed at honoring the departed but also to receive blessings for a happy life. The rite also brings solace for the grief stricken family and is rooted in the Vedas, the hymns of tenth Mandal of Rig-Veda (tenth chapter of this scripture), recited during the cremation, speaks:

1. "O holy Fire! Lead this departed to forefathers. This, who is offered to you, is wandering around in all directions. O Jaat-veda (fire deity for cremation and oblation of the body), may this Atma get a new life, get eatables till old age, and get a new Vayabya (made of air) body." (10.26).

2. "O departed! Go and join your ancestors, the Yama and the Supreme in the sublime paradise. Return to your home leaving all your Paap (sins) behind, here in this world. May you be filled up with divine splendor and enter into a new body". (10.28).

3. "O Fire! Please take care, kindly do not burn, do not harm and scorch this departed, from all sides, do not throw flesh here and there; O Jaat-veda, when you reduce it to ashes, then send the departed to our forefathers, where there is no pain, where there is no death." (10.31).

4. (With reference to those being buried) "O Departed, go to the splendid and beautiful mother earth. The earth which has gifted you, will keep you safe from death, may the earth become like tender velvet." (10.33).

5. "O Earth! Rise up, do not put weight on him, quench him, please become a smooth refuge for him. O mother Earth! Take care of this departed the same away as the mother nurses her child in her lap." (10.34).

In case of untimely death of a child, the final rites of burial are also rooted in Rig-Veda where the hymns mourn the death of the child while praying to deity of death to "neither harm our girls nor our boys", and plead to earth to "protect the departed child as if covered in soft wool."

The rites of cremation are aimed at much more than just the disposal of the body; they are also intended to release the Atma from its worldly existence.

The practice of **Daah-sanskaar** (cremation) is treated as more appropriate for release of Atma from physical body as compared to burial. This is based on the belief that the "Astral Body" will linger on as long as the physical body remains visible. Therefore, if the body is not cremated, the Atma remains nearby for days or months. The dead bodies of children and Saadhus are buried as it is supposed that they are not attached to world of Maya.

Maharishi Veda Vyas compiled the eighteen Puraanas. Out of which Bhagwat-Puran, Vishnu-Puran and Garud-Puran are considered to be the more important in Kali-yug. Even out of these three, the glory of the Garud-Puran is exemplary. However, the same thread of narrative runs across all the Puranaas wherein the Darshan (what has been seen by Rishis) of Vedant is conveyed through contemporary mythological stories so that it becomes easy to communicate the very subtle Darshan. The message in all these Puranaas is to take the divine shelter of **Ishwara** (Brahmn or God) and follow the path of Dharma as the action or deeds of individuals decide his or her destiny. Garud Puran, which is abridged version of 'Maha Garud Puran', falls under the category of **Saatvik Puranas**. 'Maha Garud Puran' has two parts, viz., Purv-Khand and Pret-kalp (Uttr-Khand). "Pretkalp" is that part of Maha Garud Puran which deals with the **Antyesti** (last rites), **Shrddha** (a rite performed, with faith, for the elevation of ancestors as well as for the well being of offspring), **Sapindi-karan** (a rite by which departed leaves the condition of Pret and enters in the company of Pitr, i.e., ancestors), **Dash-gatra** (formation of ten body organs), **Karma-phal** (award for deeds), **Swarga** (heaven), **Narak**(hell), **Mokshya**(liberation), **Daan-Punya** (donations and virtuous deeds), **Punar-janmn** (rebirth) and Tapa (penance), etc. The Pret-kalp forms an important part of 'Maha Garud Puran' and is also the main reason for the popularity and uniqueness of this Puran.

In Pret-kalp, **Bhagwan Vishnu** (the manifestation of Brahmn or Ishwara, the abstract reality in physical form having attributes, is referred as Bhagwan. Shiv, Vishnu (Krishna, Ram) and Devi are Bhagwan or Bhagwati) is giving reply to His Vaahan Garuda (a mighty mysterious bird symbolizing Atma, is the chariot of Bhagwan Vishnu) on the topics like Karma, **Teerth** (pilgrimage), **Purusharth** (human endeavor), **Sansaar** (cycle of birth and death), rebirth, importance of human life, Daan, the terrible **Vaitrani river**, **Gau daan** (donation of cow) and various other matters. The questions like where does a departed go after death, what is the nature of **Narak**, what is role of **Karma** and **Maya** (delusion) and similar other mysteries are answered in various sections of this scripture. Types of Narak, rewards and punishments of Karma, fate of the Paapi, birth in different species are also the matters described. These replies, given by Bhagwan Vishnu to the questions posed by Garuda, were passed on to Rishi Ved Vyas by Garuda and through

Vyas, it reached to **Rishi Suta** who in turn narrated it to various other Rishis.

The sixteen chapters of Garud Puran can be divided into three parts. First to sixth chapter deals with offering of Pind and formation of body, **Yam-lok** (realm of Yama), torments of Yama, Vaitarnee River, rebirth based on Karma, etc. Chapter seven to fourteen deal with good deeds, rites for **Sad-gati** (Speedy Elevation to Truth, i.e., Swarga or Mokshya) of departed, the duties of dying person, Karma, Daan, divine assembly of Dharm-raaj and so on. In chapter fifteenth and sixteenth we find deliberations on mediation, worship and the philosophy of Maya, Trishna, Mokshya, etc. Chapters eight, nine and sixteen contain subtle **Darshan**. Chapter sixteen, the last chapter, is the most enlightening. In fact like in Ramayana and many other scriptures, the last chapters of Garud Puran, while departing from the main subject, is purely putting forward the Vedanta Darshan.

UNIQUE BOOK EVER: Interestingly, Garud Puran is the only written document, and a scripture at that, which deals with the mysterious and otherwise fearful subject of post-death. It is also worth mentioning that this is the only Puran which not only talks about what one should do but also what one should not do. Garud Puran is unique in the sense that it is a **Shrotbya Shaastra** (the scripture for narration and listening) and, therefore, a living scripture. This Purana is also narrated by Acharya within ten days of death of a Sanatani (followers of Sanatan Dharma). The idea is to instill Dharma, using the gloomy moments, so as to have deeper impact.

In addition, Garud Puran emphasizes the importance of Dharma, **Purushartha** (human endeavor), purity, piousness, truthfulness and devotion in life. It elaborates on the **Paap-Punya** (sins and virtues), morality, good conduct, **Sanskaar** (rite-de-passage), values, rewards and

XV

punishments. It tells us how the bad deeds lead to miseries and Narak whereas good deeds to Swarga and Mokshya. It vividly deliberates on the Journey of Atma after death of the body, the period under **Pret-Yoni** and subsequent release from that Yoni. How the Pret can inflict pain to their relatives is also highlighted. It says that even the thought process of relatives of departed can be affected by dissatisfied Pret.

According to "Matsya Puran", the Atma of departed remains near his residence and relatives till the twelfth day from the death. The spirit of the deceased also enters the body of the Purohit (priest) who is conducting last rites, as a preceptor. The spirit of deceased listens to the narration of Garud Puran with the aim to attain Mokshya. According to "Pitrimedh-sutra", as one achieves victory in life by observing the Sanskaar, similarly, the departed achieves Sad-gati upon conduct of prescribed rites.

Out of the sixteen Sanskaar of Sanatani Hindus, three are performed prior to birth, twelve during the life time and the last one is performed after death (funeral rites and other rites like Sapindi, Shraddh, etc.). But out of the above, it is mandatory to perform two rites : "**Jaat-karma**" (birth rites) and the "**Antyesti**" (last rites).

The 'Pret-kalp' of Garud Puran, describes procedure of rites to be performed by the offspring right from the day of death and thereafter.

There are numerous deliberations, sermons and teachings by Bhagwan Vishnu on the inter connectedness of this world with the other world. It is said that the narration of this Puran also plays a role for consolation to the relatives of the departed and helps them to overcome sorrow. Similarly, the cremation and Shraddh ceremonies bring together the relatives, friends and kinsmen and thereby giving strength to the bereaved to bear the loss.

Generally, Garud Puran is narrated and heard by the bereaved family but it is a misconception that it should not be narrated on other occasions. The narration and listening of this scripture is always a pious act as it increases the knowledge about existence; it destroys sins; is wish-fulfilling and bestows well-being in this as well as in the Parlok (other world). In this regard, the Garud Puran says:-

Puraanam gaarudam punaym pavitraam papa-naashanam,
Shranvataam kaamanaa-pooram shrotavym sarvadaiv hi.

(Shruti-phal -11)

Similarly, keeping this scripture at home is a virtuous act. The scripture is replete with the wisdom. Hence, it is stated in Shastra that everyone benefits from reading, narrating and listening of the Garud Puran.

According to this Puran, there are four occasions when human beings seriously contemplate on existential issues: while in the womb of mother; when suffering from disease; on the cremation ground and when listening to **Katha** (narration on the glory of Ishwara). But it is only when these thoughts get permanently enshrined in the human mind one is on the way for release from **Sansaar** (miseries of birth and death). Narration of this scriptures is not only intended for the well being of departed rather, it is far more important for the living ones so that they change their life by obtaining this deep knowledge. **Therefore, Garud Puran is a good choice for a gift to Ved-Pathi priests, teachers, Yogis, Sant-Mahatmas (so that they spread the wisdom further) and the people in general**.

In Garud Puran, the importance of Daan, offering of Pind and Shraddh Karma have been emphasized but the focus is actually on **Atma-Gyan** (knowledge of self) leading to **Sat-karma** (the actions that do not put you in bondage) so that the condition of Pret-yoni and Narak is avoided. It has been said that seeking the divine shelter of Ishwara is the simplest way of Atma-gyana. Garud Puran also says that a person can attain the ultimate

XVII

reality even without following the ritualistic path but simply by following the path of Dharma and **Gyana** (knowledge). This scripture also focuses on maintenance of social and ecological harmony. Similarly, it places emphasis on pre-eminent role of human body and the required care for it.

DEEPER QUESTION ASKED IN GARUD PURAN: The existential issues relating to birth and death have been vividly deliberated by Bhagwan Vishnu, in response to the queries raised by Garuda. Some of the queries raised are summed up in the following and other Shloka:-

Maanushatvm labhet kasmaan mrityum praapnoti tat katham,
Mriyate kah sura-shresth dehama-ashrity kutraa chitaa.
Kv yaanti indriyaaanyasy asprishyah s kathm bhavet,
Kv karmaaani kritaaneeh kathm bhunkte prasarpati.
Ati-vaaha-shareerm ch kathm hi shrayate tada,
Shavm skandhe vahet putro agni-daataa ch pautraakahaa.
Praapte kaale vai mriyate anityaa maanavaah prabho,
Chhidrm tu naiv pashyaami kuto jeevah s nir-gatahaa.
Kuto gachchhanti bhootaani prithivya-apo manas tathaa,
Tejo vadasv me naath vaayura-akaasham-ev chaaa.
Kutah karm-endriyaanaeeh panch buddhe-endriyaani ch,
Vaayavash chaiv panchaite kathm gachchhanti chaatyayamaa

(Shivraj Acharya Garud Puranam, 'Kondinnayayan', Chaukhamba Vidhyabhavan, 2004)

The above Shloka are translated as follow:
"How does one acquire the human form? Why one dies? O **Sur-shresta** (best of Suras)! Who is it that actually dies? Who resides in the body? Where do the sense organs go on death? How the dead body becomes impure? Where the human beings reap the fruits of their karma done during their stay in this world? How does spirit of departed take the refuge in **"Ativaahik" body** (a micro body for transmigration of the spirit to Par-lok i.e., other realm)? Why the son is supposed to take the body of departed parent on shoulders and why the grandson is supposed to ignite the funeral pyre? O Prabho ! Being mortal, every person dies in due course of time, but from where does the Atma depart on death? I am unable to find the opening from

where it goes. O Nath! Where do the five great elements which constitute the body- earth, water, fire, air, sky- and also the mind, go? Where do the five **Karmendriyan** (organs of actions) and the five **Buddhindriyan** (organs of intellect) situated in the body, go? How the five **Pran-vayus** (life breaths) are dissolved?"

Garuda further asks in some other Shlokas: "O **Jaanardan**! (Helper of people) where the five thieves-greed, attachment, longings, lust and arrogance- present in the body, go? Where do Dharma, Adharma and the good deeds and various donations, go? After seeing the vices of people a desire has cropped up in me, to ask few questions."

"What is death? How that strange thing happens? The one who dies natural death and his rites are also performed as per prescribed procedure, does not lead to **Durgati** (Speed to Untruth). This, I have heard as being commonly uttered by **Rishis** (seers). For special understanding, O Prabho, I ask these questions? What all rites need to be performed by a dying person? What is Daan? What is the procedure to be followed between death and cremation? What is the prescribed procedure for cremation? Does the Atma enters in the new body immediately or some delay is observed? What are the rites to be performed for departed in the ensuing year? What are the atonements for the person died unnatural death or died during **Panchaka**? O Divine grace! You are capable to dispel my ignorance? Do reply all the questions in **Lok-hitay** (public interest)?

MONOTHEISTIC ADVAIT DARSHN: The **Advaita** (not-two) is the mainstream **Darshan** (what was seen by the Rishis as against the philosophy which relates to contemplation) in the Sanatan Dharma. Advaita, a Vedantic Darshan, considers Brahmn as the ultimate reality and human **Atma** (spirit) as well as the material world being a part of Brahmn. In fact, it is the Atma which makes different people as unique individual personalities. The **Shloka** given at the beginning of this book is the very first Shloka of 'Maha Garud Puran', depicting oneness of **Brahmn** (Ishwara), toeing the Vedic Darshan. The Brahmn is described as the one without the second, incomparable (Chhand. Upn. 6.2.1). This principle of **"Eko-ham Bahushyami**- I am one but let me be many" is vividly expressed in this Purana.

The Brahmn is neither a male nor a female, therefore, referred as **'Tat'** (meaning 'it' being gender neutral). The Brahmn is everything including the universe itself (Taitireya Upn 3.1). It is the source of all the creation including the **Devi-devtas** (deities) who maintain and run the creation (Gita 10.2).

Ishwara (Brahmn) has created 33 Devi-Devtas to oversee the various aspects of creation (Brihda. Upanishad 3.9) and having different responsibilities. Indra, Surya, Vayu, Agni, Yama Varuna are some of the functional designations of the 33 category (not 33 Crore) of deities. These are eight Vasus, eleven Rudras, twelve Adityas, plus Indra and Prajapati Brahma. They are like ministers with authority appointed to run specific departments like Air, Water, Energy, Life, Light and so on. It is through Devi-Devtas that the Ishwara touches and nourishes its creation every moment and is visible to the creation. The words Ishwara or Bhagwan are synonyms to Brahmn and denote to the state of opulence. In fact, there are thousands of names used to call the ultimate reality and all of them denote to the various quality and attributes of the ultimate reality, with the exception of the word Brahmn, which is an abstract concepts. Bhagwan is used to refer to the manifestation of Ishwara with a form, i.e., Bhagwan Shiv, Bhagwan Vishnu (Shri Ram, Shri Krishna) and Bhagwati Devi.ॐ (Om) is the foremost name of Brahmn while in its physical manifestation, the Brahmn, having different attributes, is worshipped as Shiv or Vishnu or Devi. "Gayatri Mantra" is the supreme mantra of Brahmn or Ishwara and the mantra "ॐ (Om) Namah Shivaya" is prayer to Brahmn. Brahmn is manifested as **Nirgun** (formless) and **Sagun** (with form) just like the association of body and Atma (Swami Vivekananda). Since it is very difficult for a normal human mind to relate with an abstract reality or concentrate on nothingness or formless, therefore, forms have been ascribed to it. Shiva, Vishnu or Devi can be worshiped either as Sagun or Nirgun and the form one should worship depends on the disposition and the level of the evolved Atma of the worshipper.

The Bhagwat Gita tells us that all human beings are at different levels of spiritual evolution hence different people are able to perceive reality differently. We behold what we are and we are what we behold (Gita). One can choose one of the various forms or Mantras of choice for expression of devotion. Out of Trimurti of Brahmn, Vishnu and Mahesh (Shiva), only Shiva and Vishnu are Ishwara whereas Brahmn is a deity created by Vishnu. The Trimurti, representing the dynamic power of Brahmn is rather Devi, Shiva and Vishnu.

As far as the procedure of worship is concerned, Vishnu Puja generally involves strict prescribed procedure and use of Vedic Mantras but the worship of Shiva and Devi is often devoid of such strict discipline. Further, the manifestation in the form of Vishnu is shown as very sublime, beautiful, well adorned, and full of opulence whereas, Shiva is a cosmic Yogi, a renounce, One who represents the confluence of opposites. These are only the facets of Brahmn. Ultimately, all these forms are various manifestations of the one and only Ishwara who is capable to manifest in limitless ways, being all powerful. However, differentiation is rather from the point of view to devotees. Vishnu has been called "Hari" and Shiva as "Hara" and the meaning of both terms being the same, i.e., the one who releases from Sansaar (vicious cycle of birth and death).

Similarly, the meaning of Ram and Krishna is also the same i.e., charming, lovely or beautiful. Shiva and Vishnu are both **Ardh-nariswar** (half female and half male) meaning that the **Prakritior Shakti** (energy or matter) is not different from **Purush** (consciousness) or Ishwara. Thus, the consciousness is interchangeable between matter and creature. According to Vedant, there is oneness in the whole universe. The Modern Quantum Physics, which deals with interconnectedness of whole, came very near the Advaita Darshan. (Dr. B.M Hegde). Similarly, as Adi-Shankaracharya says: though the creation is not different from the creator yet it is beyond the capabilities of human mind to fully define Brahmn. Tulsidaas has described the attributes of Brahmn as followed:

Niraakaar-omkaar-moolam-tureeyam,
Giraa gyaan goteeta-meesham gireesham.

(It is formless, is the origin of Omkaar, pure consciousness, beyond speech, knowledge, senses, who is the giver of grace; the perfect one, Lord of time).

How he perceives the form of Bhagwan Rama, who is Brahmn in its human Leela (spectacle)? Goswami Tulsidas answered this by saying "**Raghuvar chhavi ke samaan raghuvar chhavi baniyaan**- Shri Ram is celestial hence his image can be compared with Shri Ram only". However, it is with the help of the form (an image or symbol) that one can reach the formless. Image or Murti is not the requirement from Brahmn, rather the human mind requires a symbol to concentrate. It is the one who is creator, who maintains and who transforms the entire universe; whereas the planet earth has a very limited sphere. Human birth, out of all other 8.4 millions births holds a pre-eminent position as it bears consciousness and it is the only birth during which good Karma can be accumulated leading to elevation (**Uddhaar**).

However, the prayers to Ishwara in any of the forms will reach to the one and only. Therefore, it is said:

Aakaashaat patitam toyam yathaa gachchhati saagaram. Sarv dev namas-kaarah keshavam prati gachchhati(As the rain falling from sky on various places ultimately reaches the ocean, likewise the prayers offered to all the Devas (deities) reaches to Keshava- the one and only Brahmn).

This also means that you need not worship various forms and different names separately. Whether you worship Shiva, Vishnu or Shakti or any other form, that is complete in itself. Yet, a person can have a presiding **Devta** (deity). A Sportsperson may take refuge of Bhagwan Hanuman or a student surrenders to Devi Saraswati. Similarly, remembering the different form of Ishwara like Shiva, Vishnu (Shri Rama, Shri Krishna), Devi separately is always beneficial as in that process one gets the chance to repeat the holy names again and again. Interestingly, all these names have the same meaning, they are personification of the eternal. Furthermore, these manifestations represent one universal principle and not the names or forms as such which means that you may call the Brahmn as Shiva, Durga, Krishna or anything else. It is our notion that is important, i.e what we feel when we remember Shiva or Devi. Therefore, in the worship of Maa Durga it is uttered that **Yaa Devi Sarv-bhuteshu Maatri-rupen Sansthita**": or "**Daya Rupen Sansthita**" or "**Shardha Rupen Sansthita**" or '**chetanetyabhi dheeyate**' (Devi who is residing in every person in the form of mother, in the form of mercy or in the form of faith, consciousness, we offer you Namaste). This prayer means that every human being becomes one with others with the above inherent qualities. Similarly, "**Sarva-roop-maayi Devi, Sarva Devi Mayam Jagat**" (all the forms belong to Devi Bhagwate and the whole world is absorbed in thee).

It is of utmost importance to understand the relation between Ishwara and His creation. The Ishwara has not created the human beings and the universe for his pleasures or to rule over them, rather it is out of love of

XXIII

creation as given in the answer by Rishis that creation is **Swabhaav** (nature) of Ishwara. Thus, it is the expression of self by Brahmn in the creation.

Similarly, the Ishwara is kind, hence in case you have no knowledge of scriptures and Mantras, then any other way to devotion, i.e., to perform Arti, prayer, or recitation with devotion, or just remembrance in any form gives the same reward (Gita).

BELIEF IN RE-BIRTH: Right from the Rig Veda to the subsequent Puraanic scriptures, the concept of rebirth remains an important precept. In this regard, the dialogue between **Nachiketa** and Yamraj, as mentioned in Kathopanishad, is educative. One of the three questions posed by Nachiketa to Yamraj was: "there remains a doubt about the fate of human beings on death; some say the existence of Atma continues but others say that the Atma ceases to exist after death. I want your guidance in this regard. This is my third and last wish." (Kathop.- 1.1.20).

Yamraj, though initially reluctant to speak on this subject, relents after seeing the selfless desire and firm determination of Nachiketa and says: **Na saamparaayah prati-bhaati baalm pramaady-antm vita-mohen moo ham. Aym loko na-asti par iti maanee punah punar-vashamaapadyate me**

(Kathop.- 1. 2. 6)

(Those, blinded and intoxicated by the attachments for wealth, etc., cannot aspire for larger objective of the Parlok (other realm) and they say this is the only life, only world we have, there is no other world; such people are trapped in the clutches of death (they are born again and die again).

Thereafter, Yamraj, while giving a rare sermon on the nature of Atma to Nachiketa says "**Na jaayate mriyate vaa vipshi-chinnaayn kutsh-chinn babhoov Kaschit; Ajo nityah Shashwatoyam puraanao n hanyate hanyamaane shareere** - For the Atma is neither born nor it dies. Nor having once been or does ever cease to be. The Atma is unborn, eternal, ever-lasting, deathless and primeval, the Atma cannot be slain)" (Gita-2/20).

Thus, the permanence of Atma is proved beyond doubt from the above reference. In the Advait Vedanta, the Atma is an **Ansh** (fraction) of Brahmn. Adi-shankara in "Nirvan-shaaktam" says "**Chida-anand-roop, Shivoham, Shivoham**- I am eternal consciousness and blissful. I am the eternal Shiva the auspicious one". Thus the Atma of individual is part of Brahmn. The difference being that the Atma moves from one body to another but the **Parmaatma** (Brahmn) pervades in the bodies of all creatures.

Thereafter, Yamraj tells about the destiny of those who die without acknowledging the Atma and says "**Yonim-anye prapadyante shareeratvaay dehinah Sthaanaum-anye. Anu-sanyanti yathaa-karm yathaa-shrutam**. - So many people achieve the body of a deity, of human, animal, bird, insects, etc., in that order of Karma and so many are born as Sthaawar (tree, plants, etc." (Kathop.-1. 2. 18).

Another Shloka from Garud Puran throws light on the subject of rebirth; **Vaasaansi jeernaani yathaa vihaay navaani grihnaati naro aparaanai Tathaa shareeraanai vihaay jeernaanyanyaani sanyaati navaani dehee" (9/ 47)**

(as a person puts on new garments giving up the old worn out ones, similarly the Atma enters into a new body discarding the worn out body).

There are many verses in the Gita which establish the link between this world, other world **(Par-lok)** and re-birth. In the second chapter Shri Krishna says to Arjun:-
Na tvevaahm jaatu naasm n tvm neme janaadhipaah, N chaiv n bhavishyaamah sarve vayamatah param.(Gita-2/12)

(neither was there a time when I did not exist, nor you, or all these kings; nor will there be so when any of us cease to exist).

Similarly "**Dehinoo asmin yathaa dehe kaumaarm yauvanm jaraa, Tathaa dehaantara-praaptir-dheerastatraa n muhyati.** (Gita-2/13). As the embodied Atma continuously moves in this body from childhood to youth and to old age, similarly the Atma passes into another body on death. The self realized person is not bewildered by such a change".

A very important, often repeated, verse of Garud Puran says: **"Jaatasya hi dhruvo mrityur-dhruvam janm mritasy ch.** - the words of Ishwara contains eternal truth: for the one who has obtained birth, death is certain; and for the one who is dead, birth is certain" (11.16).

MAYA AND INDIRYA: The **Indriya** (sense organs) are outwardly oriented and therein comes the role of Maya. Indriya are proficient in accumulation of outer knowledge. They distract one (Atma) from Parmatma and hence they have to be overcome. At the same time, there exist unlimited possibilities with the Atma to expand in inner or outer world. Further, there is deep relation between body and Atma, the Atma is functionless without a body and the body is motionless without an Atma.

MOKSHYA, SWARGA AND NARAK: In order to have a fair understanding of Sanatan Dharma, it is necessary to understand the concepts of Karma, Sansaar, Swarga, Narak and of Mokshya. In the Dharma traditions (the faiths that originated in Bharat like Jain, Budhism, Sikh and other smaller sects) the philosophy towards life is based on "cyclical view of creations". There is neither a beginning of creation nor an end; rather there is a continuous and endless circle of birth, death and re-birth. The death and birth are the part of the Sansaar Chakra (cycle of world).

After death, the departed will take re-birth, once the transitory phase is over. Thus, nobody remains in Swarga or Narak permanently. Swarga and Narak are the transitory phases. Thus, here, nothing is permanent, not even death. To prove this cyclical path, the Ishwara takes **Avatar** in His creation.(15.95). As Avatar, He, too, is to pass through this cycle of birth and death and all other vagaries of human existence. The incarnation of Bhagwan Shri Ram and Shri Krishna is not a onetime happening rather Ishwara appears in rotation through these forms, from age to age (Yug). They are not two but two facets of the same who incarnate in different age (time) according to the need of time with the basic aim of re-establishing Dharma (15.95).

The Kathopnishad and other scriptures define Swarga as a place where there is neither any fear nor any misery or aging. There exists a "**Akshya-patra**" (vessel which is never empty of commodities), a "**Kamdhenu**" (wish fulfilling cow) and a "**Chintamani**" (jewel that removes all anxieties), **Puspak Vimaan** (aircraft that flies as per wishes), **Kalpa-taru** (a Parijaat tree that fulfils all desires) and full of beautiful flowering gardens, rivers, chirping birds and sublime existence. The inhabitants of Swarga are not affected by hunger, thirst, grief and aging and have a blissful living. In Nasiketo-paakhyan, the city of Dharam-raaj has been described in very beautiful words-**Nadyaas-teere hyahm vipraa drichm-vaan mandiraanai ch, Teshu kreedanti manujaah sadaa dharmasy paalakaah. Sheeta-mand sugandhaiys-ch pavanaiah sevitaa naraah, Divy-roop-dharaa naaryah kreedanti nara-pungavaiah. Evem vidyaah striaayo ramyaa modante patibhiah sah, Pushp-odakayaas-teere te-naaryash-ch shobhanaah.**- "O thinkers! I saw beautiful temples at the river bank. In those houses, live the people of Dharma. I saw ladies with divine grace playing sports alongside the noble men. The cool breeze slowly blowing with fragrance while they play. Such ladies live with their husbands and they have blissful life in the shore of that Pushpo-daka river". Similarly, the amazing beauty of the city of Dharam-raaj is portrayed in Chapter 14 of this scripture which also puts light on the glory of Swarga. In comparison, the Narak is a place for the suffering of Paapi for their misdeeds.

Nasket says that he saw those sinful who adopt other's Dharma by discarding their own, falling in the Narak called "Tapt-baluk"-**Tasmin-loke mayaa drichmaa patitaas-tapta-vaaluke, Sva-dharmn ch parityajya para-dharma-rataa naraah.**

The Garud Puran narrates who will obtain Swarga or Narak. The pious obtain Swarga while the ones who are lustful, demonly, do not have reverence for scriptures, are not compassionate and so on, fall into Narak. In this regard, Shri Krishna tells us that the three doors of Narak are lust, anger and greed. (Gita 16.21)

The Garud-Puran tells us that there are 21 Narak which are situated in between the stars but a part of the Swarga and Narak are also witnessed on this earth itself. After death, the sinful-with a body made to experience the torments (which is replica of the physical body, but is made of a esoteric substance)-enters the Yam-marg (path to Yama). However, upon rebirth, one cannot remember the punishments one had gone through in Narak and the pleasures of Swarga yet the recognition that what is bad and good is retained at subconscious level. This remembrance of what is good and bad is actually the permanent gain one acquires from experience of Narak and Swarga. This sense leads to righteous path.

There are 8.4 million **Yonis** (varieties of births) in this universe. The departed, after facing the immediate returns for Paap and Punya in Narak and Swarga, will eventually take birth in one of the those Yonis, according to accumulated past karma. The cycle of re-birth is painful and relief from this endless cycle is only through obtaining Mokshya which is the prime objective of human birth. The dissolution of Atma in **Parmatma** (Ishwara) is the only permanent escape from Sansaara.

The world is full of Maya and one's name and image pertain to one's body and not of the Atma. The body, and whatever perceptible by senses (Indriya) is called Maya. The acts of Purusharth, Gyan, Jap, Daan and Mercy are the means for Mokshya. The rewards for good deeds and punishments for bad deeds are experienced in the Swarga or Narak respectively. The balance effects are experienced after obtaining the next birth on earth, on completing the stint at Swarga or Narak. The grievous Papis, after experiencing the torments of Narak, take birth in the **Sthawar** (plants) form.

The Paap committed during previous births are not completely destroyed in Narak; rather, part of them is passed on to next birth and their effect is visible in the disposition and status of a person. People born as human, after stint in Swarga, are evolved and are of righteous nature and good deeds. Thus, part of the effect of Karma are experienced in Swarga and Narak and part on earth. Narak, part of Yamlok, situated at the bottom of the universe, is the realm of the deity of death (Yam) where the **Paapi** enters after death. Similarly, the Swarga, also called Indra-lok, is situated in the universe beyond this solar system. The Ishwar has the ultimate authority over the entire galaxies and universe.

When life leaves the physical body, a **Tejas Sharir** (micro-body) or subtle body is taken out by the Yama-doots. Chitragupta, who is having divine sight, maintains the accounts of good or bad deeds of each being and assists Yama in pronouncing judgments. The Yama and Yami take final decision on the fate of departed being. (Yami is the twin sister of Yama, co-partner in the functioning of Yama).

On death, the Yama-doots take the departed to the court of Dharam-raaj (Yamraj is also called Dhram-raaj because he is completely impartial) where the Yama and Yami, depending on their Karma, send them to Narak or the Swarga.

This Tejas Sharir (micro-body) is converted to "Ativaahik Sharir", for a brief spell, for experiencing part of the karma. The reason to consign body to flames, among Sanatani Hindus, as a form of **Homa** (oblation)is because the fire is considered as pure. The second objective behind this practice is to ensure complete detachment of Atma from the body. It is to ensure that body is dissolved with the **Panch-tatva** (five elements), of which the body is composed of. Therefore, to ensure complete detachment, the articles that were used by departed should also be distributed among needy and leftover should be immersed in a river while immersing the ashes or buried. Barring the noble deeds of the departed, nothing else should be preserved as a memory of deceased (Swami Ramsukh Das). According to the Shastra, the **Smaadhi** (memorial) of the Sant, Mahatma, or any Hindu for that matter, cannot be constructed.

The **Parikarma** (circumambulation) and worship of human beings or creatures is not prescribed in the scriptures as it can mislead one from the path of Ishwara. Persons-who permit making of their statue or picture and allows their worship-they along with such worshipper, commit grave Paap (Swami Ram-Sukhdas). Therefore, instead of venerating a part, the complete (Brahmn) should be worshipped. Someone who was born as human being, must not be worshipped by making statues or any other form because they, too, were mortal travelers (Shri Ram and Shri Krishna being took birth as complete incarnations, therefore, they were not human being). The Sant should, therefore, be revered for their teachings and for carrying forward the Vedic knowledge. Worship is reserved for Ishwara only but the deities are the helpers of Ishwara,

XXX

therefore, their worship reaches to Ishwara (Gita 9.23). But only the supreme reality should be worshipped (Gita-9.25). Further, there is no **Avatar** (incarnation) of Ishwara other than those mentioned in Holy Scriptures. Therefore, no one should be declared to be a new incarnation (the last one being Gautama Buddha).

The very meaning of **"Aham Brahmasmi"** is that the Ishwara is present in all beings. Thus, everyone has the third eye of Shiva and all are the part of Brahmn though only a discerning one can further expand the Brahmn in her or him. The ability to open the third eye makes one worthy of divine blessings. The third eye destroys the darkness of human limitations and bestows ability to see things from a divine perspective.

Power of Ishwara can also be experienced and felt through the 33 category of Devi-devtas (deities). For example, the power of Ishwara is experienced every moment by sense organs through the energy and light of Sun, Moon, Indra, Agni, Yama, Varuna, Vaayu and other deities.

Every human being is potentially divine (Swami Vivekananda), and one should always remember that human beings are the best creation of Ishwara. Therefore, one should not give any chance to outer circumstance (Maya) to snatch away this opportunity.

Every human being should realize that in the entire universe, other than Ishwara, nobody is more important than oneself (Acharya Shriram Sharma). The other person can be more knowledgeable or elevated but can never be greater than oneself as both are part of the same Brahmn and are on separate journeys. The Ramcharit-manas describes this as follows: **"Ishwar ansh jeev avinaashee. Chetan amal sahaj sukh raashi"**.

Further, when we bow before a saint or offer Namaskar and Pranam to others, it is actually directed to the Brahmn which resides in him or her.

ATMANO MOKSARTHAM-JAGAT HITAY CHA: This Shloka of Rig-Veda declares that the motto of life is Mokshya for the self and the well being of all in the universe. Thus, ultimate aim of human life is to merge with Brahmn from whom we have got separated. Getting reborn as human shows that though one may have missed the Param-Gati but it also indicates that another opportunity toward achieving Mokshya is now available. It is only in the human birth where Purusharth (human endeavor) is possible and hence one can make the efforts for achieving Mokshya. All other births, including birth as Devi-Devta, is only **Bhog Yoni** (birth to experience the fruits of previous Karma). The concept of **Purusharth** (Dharma, Arth, Kama and Mokshya) actually provides a complete Darshan of life in Sanatan Dharma. Here, Dharma is the first & primary precept for leading a life involving **Arth** (economic well being, prosperity, happy family life) and **Kama** (sense gratification, pleasure, music, touch, taste, etc,) to be used for accumulating good karma through which one can achieve final salvation, **Mokshya.** The Mokshya has been called as "**Param** (supreme) **Purusharth**. Thus, the **three Purusharth** (Dharma, Artha and Kama) should be aimed at achieving **Mokshya.**

THE CONCEPT OF SHARIR-TRAYA (THREE OF BODY): To inculcate Garud Puran, it is necessary to understand the principle of Sharir-traya. The body has three components; **Sthool** (physical), **Sookshyam** or **Linga** (micro) and the **Kaaran** (causal) body. Sthool body is visible to eyes and it is this body which actually dies and gets cremated. The Atma takes along with it the Sookshyam and the Kaaran body on death. As the Sthool body is destroyed with death

XXXII

similarly the existing Sookshyam body is destroyed on achieving the next birth when a new Sookshyam body is created. Thus, Atma then attains a new Sthool body and a new Sookshyam body. But the Kaaran body remains intact meaning that it is not destroyed through the process of birth, death and rebirth. In this way, the Atma or **Jyoti** (light) transmigrates from the body upon death and is separated from existing body. Sookshyam or Ling Sharir is the vehicle used by Atma to travel from one body to another. The Sthool body is made of Panch-Tatva (water, air, fire, earth and space) while the Sookshyam body is made up of **"Panch-pran"** (Pran, Apaan, Samaan, Vyan and Udaaan), **Paanch Karmandriyan** (five elements of Karma), **Panch Gyanendriyan** (ear, eye, nose, skin, tongue) along with **Mana, Buddhi and Ahankaar** (mind, intellect and arrogance). The Sookshyam Sharira is also called **"Angust-maatra Sharir**- the thumb sized body" which is the carrier of Atma from one birth to another.

On death, the organs of senses, **Mana** (mind), **Sanskaar** (habits), **Paap-Punya** (sins and merits) are carried forward by the Sookshyam body to next birth. The memories of pre-death life, premonition, divine sight, third eye, **Vivek** (power of discretion), capacity to predict future and similar powers are achieved due to existence of this Sookshyam Sharer. Similarly, dreams during sleep also originate from it. This Sookshyam Sharir can be awakened through Yoga, Dhayan, Samadhi and Sadhna. There is some time interval between the death and acquiring the next birth. The Atma takes the help of Sookshyam Sharir, during this intervening period, for transition. Even after new birth, the new Sookshyam and existing Kaaran Sharir continue to remain in the Sthool body. The transmission of past life experiences is also through this Sookshyam sharer. The evil spirit is also dependent on this Sharir.

The Kaaran Sharir is the **Kaaran** (cause) for the formation and destruction of other two bodies. It is the seed and it determines the future birth. On death, the Kaaran and the Sookshyam Sharir depart together from the physical body. The Karm-phal of a person, accumulated through various previous births, is stored in the Karan Sharer. This Karm-phal is experienced by the physical body during life. Only Mokshya gives release from all the three bodies to become one with Ishwara.

The Sookshyam Sharir and the Sthool body experience rewards according to one's karma and stage of spiritual evolution. Your proximity with Ishwara depends on your level of purity and devotion acquired from the past. Therefore, one should make continued efforts to become ever pure in life and become Brahmn-leen. The foremost wish after death is to achieve Mokshya and the second level being to obtain status of deities in Swarga. The third level, in the descending order of importance, is to obtain Pitra-lok. The one who has achieved the status of deities or Pitr will be reborn once their store of Punya are exhausted. Next in the hierarchy comes human birth. The lower Gati after death is of Paapi to whom the body for **Yaatana Sharir** (body for torments), is given for experiencing the consequences of their bad deeds. This is to be kept in mind that it is not the Atma which suffers the reward or punishment of Karma, as the Atma is divine element, thus it is only the body of the departed which will face the consequences. The Shraaddh in Gaya and other holy places is performed with a view to get early release of departed from this Yaatana Sharir. There is a transitional waiting period from one birth to another which is spent not only in Swarga or Narak but also as plant and vegetation, worms, animals, etc. The **Achetan** (unconscious) creatures, as a matter of fact, are actually in the sinful waiting time subsequent to suffering the torments of Narak. The human Yoni is the only Chetan (conscious) yoni wherein the upliftment is possible.

SAD-GATI PRAPT HO (MAY YOU GET SPEEDY ELEVATION TO TRUTH) : The conditions acquired after death are known as "Gati" i.e., **Param-gati** (Mokshya), **Brahmlok-gati** (which is Param-gati), **Swarglok -gati** and **Pitralok-gati** respectively. Gati, because every individual is in the journey towards Mokshya and a speed in achieving the goal is wished for. It is for this reason that Sanatan Dharam is upon seeing a dead body, pay homage by saying "**Sad-gati Prapt Ho.** May you acquire Speedy elevation toward truth". Similarly, "**Param-gati Prapt Ho-** May you attain Swarga" or "**Swaragwasi Ho**"or "**Brahmlok Prapt Ho**" are the specific wishes. (10/ 19).This is also the wish in the Vedic prayers- "**Asato maa Sad-gamaya-Tamso ma Jyotir-gamayah, Mrityorma Amritam Gamayah**". Here, death is the only means of transition from one body to another, therefore, it is known as Dehaantaran (change over body).

TO ACHIEVE MOKSHYA: THE LIFE GOAL: Adi Shankar in his famous composition "Moh-Mudgar"says-"**Punar-api jananam punar-api maranam punar-api jananee jathare shayanam, Ih sansaare bahu dustaare kripayaa Paare paahi muraare** birth again and again and death again and again, suffering repeatedly by the miseries of being in the womb of mother. O Krishna! Get us across over this miserable world".

How to achieve Mokshya? Shri Krishna has answered this question in Gita by providing four paths: **Karma** (action, work, duty), **Bhakti** (devotion), **Gyan** (knowledge) and **Yoga.** Shri Krishna also says "**Sarv Dharmaan parityajy maam- ekam sharanaam vraj. Aham tvaam sarva-paapebhyah mokshayasyaami maa suchi** (Gita 18.66). discarding all the paths, come to me. I will lead you to Mokshya, redeeming from all sins".

Garud Puran states that whoever utters a Shloka of Gita or Bhagwat Puran during one's last moment goes to Brahm-loka (though this will happen only if the whole life is lived like that). Similarly, the reading of Vedas and Upanishads and Shiva & Vishnu Strotam, are also Mokshya-

Daayi (9/32-33). Those who have crossed all the stages of spiritual evolution do not go through the torments of Yamlok rather; they directly attain Mokshya or go to Swarga-lok.

An important Shloka on how to lead a life reads: **"Falgu kaarym parityajya satatm dharma-vaam bhavet, Daanam damo dayaa ch-eti saaramettraayam bhuvi** (8/93.1) leaving aside the meaningless deeds, one should follow Dharma, continuously. The combination of Daan, control over sense organs and mercy are the essence for life on this planet earth". Those who carry out welfare work and are always considerate of what is Dharma and Adharma, those who are into helping others and those who read Shastra regularly, they go to higher Gati.

It is through the human birth alone that one can make effort to get out of this miserable and vicious cycle of birth and death. Further, it is also not necessary for everyone to go through all the 8.4 Million Yonis before one gets human birth or Mokshya. Even in a single human birth, through good deeds, one can achieve Mokshya, Swarga or human birth once again.

When the account of good deeds and bad deeds are at equal proportion or the merits are higher than the sins, human birth will be obtained. The Karma accumulated from the past birth and from the good deeds of the present birth will bring Mokshya. Till Mokshya is attained, the Atma will have to take re-birth, time and again. The Atma remains immortal till Mokshya, thereafter it merges into Brahmn.

Therefore, there is lot of emphasis on making the human birth meaningful and not wasting it: **"Mahataa punaya-yogen maanusham janm labhyate-**(2/34) it is by great meritorious deeds, the human birth is acquired".

In Garud Puran, there is a message to refrain from bodily indulgence. It says that one who tries to find substance in the human body, which is like hollow trunk of banana log and is like bubbles which are perishable in moments, must be a thoughtless person. The body is made of five elements and if it dissolves back into the five elements due to the consequences of Karmas done by the same body, then why should one cry (10/57-58).

Ishwara is full of affection and Karuna (compassion) but is also judicious at the same time. Ishwara gives only that which one deserves on the basis of past Karma. Every moment one performs karma, either by body or by mind or by speech:-**Nahi Kashchit-kshanam-api jaatu tishthaty karma-krit**. Out of these countless karmas, the reward of some of the karmas is immediate while in some cases, in due course. It means some consequences will have to be experienced in the present life while some others will be passed on to the next birth. Those who come down to earth from Swarga, on exhausting good Karma, obtain birth in noble atmosphere (9.53) whereas those who are returning from Narak, after undergoing punishment, take birth in unfavorable life conditions.

LAW OF KARMA - A DIVINE LAW OF NATURAL JUSTICE: The word Karma is derived from the root "Kri" meaning "to do"; therefore, all action is Karma. We are doing karma all the time- listening, breathing, thinking- talking is also karma (Vivekananda).

Karma can be outer action (helping the weak, work in the farm or office, etc.) or Inner action (action by senses, speech, sight, mind, etc.) Thus all actions of body, mind and senses are karma.

The returns for accumulated Karmas will have to be experienced. Even Gautama Buddha had to experience the reward of Karma-phal of his past birth before he got Mokshya. Once a cousin of Buddha attacked him with a big stone, which broke a leg of Buddha. When the disciple asked as to why that had happened to him? He revealed that the attacker happens to be his cousin and in the previous birth he (Buddha) had also broken a leg of attacker.

The law of Karma is controlled by the principle of cause and effect. Every action will necessarily be followed by a reaction. It means that whatever good or bad you do in life will have good or bad repercussions. The repercussion can be in the form of life condition, impressions, mental frame in this or next life. The Karma will have to be compulsorily borne out: **Avashyam-ev bhoktavyam kritam karm shubhaa-ashubham.Naabhuktm-ksheeyate karm kalpa-koti-shatair-api** (5/57)

However, the law of Karma is not a blind law; rather it is guided by a divine intelligence as is also the law of natural justice. It is not necessary that all happenings are the result of previous Karmas; rather many of them are new happenings which will have consequences in future. It is also worth mentioning that the impact of bad karma can be changed by Purusharth (human endeavor) and also by **Ishwariya Kripa** (divine grace).

CLASSIFICATION OF KARMAS: The Karmas accumulated through previous births have been classified into three categories. The first is **Sanchit** (accumulated) Karma the rewards for which are reserved for next births. The second is **Praarabdh** (destiny) the rewards for which will be experienced during present birth while the third is **Kriya-maan** karma whose part consequences will be experienced during present birth and a part carried forward. **Praarabhdh Karma** is that part of accumulated Karmas which impacts current birth and acts as **destiny**.

Kriyaman Karma is the Karma in actual sense as they are performed by a person during the current life. Therefore, birth as human is called Karma-yoni where one can do Purusharth. As already stated, all other creatures (animals, birds and other) are in **Bhog-yonis** (birth for consumption of Karma). As they cannot do either good or bad deeds and whatever good or bad they seem to be doing, is actually their **Swabhav** (inherent nature).

The forthcoming life is decided by the Sanchit and Kiryaman Karma. Swami Ramsukh Das has described about what is good or bad karma in the following words: "The Kriyaman karma, which are performed on the lines as prescribed in scriptures are called good deeds and the one violating them lead to bad karmas." We get a complete guidance on this in Gita and also find the same message in Ramayan, Bhagwat Puran and other scriptures.

Kirymaan Karma has two aspects; **Drisht** (which are visible) and **Adrisht** (invisible). Drisht has also two dimensions -**Taat-kaalik** (immediate) and **Kaalaantarik** (deferred). The gratification obtained by taking food is immediate result of having food. But the food brings long life and health; this is deferred result of Drist Karma. Similarly, there are two category of **Adristkarma**, i.e., **Laukik** (worldly) and **Par-laukik** (other worldly). To perform **Yagya**, **Daan,** an act of help, meditation, pilgrimage, fasting, recital of mantra, Japs, etc., with a view to have rewards during the life time, is the Laukik reward of Adrisht. To perform the Yagya, Daan, act of welfare, etc., with a view to obtain Mokshya in next birth is the other worldly reward. Similarly, imprisonment during lifetime for an acts of theft, murder, etc. is the Laukik rewards of Adrasht and going to Narak after death and obtaining birth as birds, animals, worms and Pret yoni, etc., are the other worldly rewards of Adrisht.

The reward of Karma, already undergone in the present life, in the form of imprisonment, fine, humiliation, insult, etc., will not be transferred to next birth. But what was the quantum of the Paap of person and to what extent these have been experienced, i.e., whether full or part or more than required punishment of the sins, the leftover would be transferred or compensated in the next birth.

Therefore, that part of returns of sins committed, which has still not been experienced, is to be experienced either in this birth or next births.

There are two categories of **Sanskaar** component (inherited part) of Kriyaman Karma; **Pure or Pious** inheritances and **impure or impious** inheritances. The habits which are inherited by performing the Karma in accordance with holy scriptures are pure and pious and the one against prescribed code of conduct or those clearly forbidden ways or those that are against morality and law are impure and impious Sanskaar.

The good nature of a person is partially formed based on pure and impure inheritances of past and partially by his own efforts and the grace of Ishwara. Gyan and difference in the nature of people leads them to adoption of different ways and performance of different Karma.

FIRM (DRIDH), FLEXIBLE (ADRIDH), AND STOICALLY FIRM (DRIDHADI-DRADH) KARM: The returns of Firm Karmas cannot be modified through Bhakti and Purusharth or any other means. For example, death being a firm karma will have to be experienced. But the effects of Adridh (flexible) karma can be eliminated by taking remedial measure. The returns of stoically firm karmas will have to be experienced to some extent and some part can be modified. Therefore, person should focus on Purusharth, i.e., to achieve the Dharam, Arth, Kaam and Mokash. One should be industrious, creative, dutiful, laborious, courageous, and action oriented. Even doing Bhakti, involves doing Karma (**Yog-vashist**).

PRAARABADH AND PURUSHAARTH: That portion of **Sanchit Karma** (accumulated past Karma) which influences the present life is called **Praraabdh** (destiny) whereas human endeavors are called **Purusharth**. A question is often asked by people as to which of the two is more powerful. In this regard there are a number of references in Gita and other scriptures, which indicate that the **human endeavor can modify the Praraabdh**.

Ishwara has provided capability to human beings to overcome the limitation of impure part (attachment, hate, anger, lust, etc.), of Karma.

The Karma of previous births (Phal and Sanskar Part) remains stored in the conscience and are called **Sanchit Karma** (accumulated deeds). In that, the Praraabdh is formed by the **Phal Anksh** (reward part) and the **Sphurana** (pulsation) by **Sanskaar Ansh** (ethos or impression) part. Thus, Karma performed during current life and previous life impact the existence.

However, as already indicated, the adverse impact can also be eliminated by the Kripaa of Ishwara. The reward of "Praraabdh" karma comes before a person in the form of Life choices or circumstances.

Praraabdh can also be changed through **Purusharth** (human endeavor). The word Purusharth is made of **Purush** (human being) and **Arth** (object of desires). Thus Purusharth means goal of human life.

Therefore, when one is in favorable circumstances in life one should spend ones resources on charity and welfare activities and not so much on mindless consumption and enjoyment. Similarly, when in unfavorable circumstances, "one should think that these conditions have cropped up to destroy my past sins and pray to Ishwara to keep me alert and careful and not to indulge in sins in future and accept this situation as grace of Ishwara (so that the impact is lessoned) and at the same time involve in Purusharth".

When the Praraabdh is favorable, everything will be favorable. But when it turns unfavorable, it will impact not only life chances but also vitiate the thought process of a person. It will temporary create hindrances in the work. **Therefore, the affected person will have to put in extra labor during bad phase of Praraabdh.** For example, when a cyclist encounters rough patches in his track during a ride, he has to put in extra efforts to ride over that rough patch and is relaxed during smooth ride (Kirpalu Maharaj). Similarly, Aachrya Shri Ram Sharma had stated that one is not a slave of circumstances; rather one is its creator, controller and the lord. We are free to perform the karma but are not free to have the rewards. The ego and attachments with worldly objects and wealth will attract arrogance which results in sufferings. Attachment can only be destroyed by the Kripa of Ishwara.

Miseries have a positive aspect also in the sense that it brings people near to Ishwara (Kripalu Maharaj). But miseries will prove a hindrance in performing virtuous deeds.

Every human being is free to adopt right or wrong path but it is through right path that one can eliminate the impurities in life; one has free will and also power to discriminate, power to change one's own destiny. Therefore, it is said that you are the master of your own destiny (Swami Shivanand) and even you can influence the destiny of others through divine creation and endeavor. This freedom is given only to human being and not to other creature. All other creatures have to work according to their inherent nature and they cannot discriminate what is good or bad. Thus, giving fruit is in the nature of the tree and if we do not pick up the fruits, they will decay and give foul smell.

Everyone is free to become Karm-yogi or Bhakti Yogi. The person who has made his nature pure, his deeds automatically become pure. Attraction towards what is **Asat** (untrue) is the important aspect of human tendency. Due to this reason, human beings are in the grip of **Sansaar chakra** (cycle of birth and death) and go to lower and higher births time and again. But when one takes the refuge of Ishwara, while discarding **Ahankaar**(arrogance and ego), then one's nature is purified. Having a purified nature, one does not become Paapi even when performing deeds according to one's own nature (Gita-18/47). Taking the refuge in Ishwara makes one pure and affectionate towards all creatures (Gita-5/29). The one who surrenders to Him also develops the same divine qualities of Ishwara like being affectionate towards all creatures. (Srimad Bhagwat-3/25/21).

BE A KARMA YOGI: The human life is not meant for experiencing just the happiness and miseries as there is provision of these experiences in Swarga, Narak and the eighty four lakhs of Yonis. The human Yonis Karma-yoni; to perform action and do activity. This is a birth to perform action whole-heartedly and relentlessly. The human birth is the only means for advancing towards divinity, towards Mokshya. Therefore, Maanav-yoni is also termed as "Saadhan-yoni" (the birth as means to achieve Mokshya). The Isa Upanishad says that one must keep working till the last moment of life and treat work as Aahuti (oblation) to Ishwara. It is the treatment of Karma as oblation that makes any Karma as Yog. Further, any work one is doing is Su-karma provided the end as well as the means are not wrong.

Is there any relation between the position of planets in Kundali (horoscope) and Karma? As per Vedic astrology, the planets shown in the Kundali are symbolic. In fact, the stars present in our Kundali are reflections of our accumulated Karmas. The actual stars-Shani, Brihspati, Budh, etc., have no direct impact upon the destiny of a person rather it is the result of Karma that impact life and it is oneself who can change the destiny and not anyone else.

One should renounce inertia and attachment and become action oriented. The deeds of your past birth, which were of your own creation impact upon and control the present birth to some extent but the fate of next birth and the Mokshya are totally in our hands (Gita-3/8). Shri Krishna says that one should perform ones' prescribed duties. A person cannot even maintain physical body without work (Gita-2/47). One has the right to work only but never to its fruits; let not the desire for fruits of action be your motive, nor your attachment be the cause of inaction. Therefore, awake and renounce the meanness of heart (Gita -2/3). Sanatan Dharma gives equal importance for acquiring both, the Paraa (spiritual) and Aparaa (worldly) knowledge. But the worldly Karma should be guided by Dharma. Shri Krishna in Gita says that the ability to excel in work is called Yoga – **"Yogah Karmasu Kaushlam"** (2.50).

Similarly, one immediately gets peace by performing one's duty but becomes restless by non-performance and inactivity. However, one's desires may push towards **Paap Karma** (sinful actions). The real challenge is to control these desires and choose the path of Dharma. The accumulated Karma of previous births, the deeds and conduct of the present life and the grace of Ishwara together determine the future life of the human being. But the deeds and conduct also depend upon the **Kaamanaa** (desires). There may be many desires of human beings, some of those lead to path of Dharma and some to sinful way. One controls some of them but takes vows for the fulfillment of the other. Therefore, Adi-shankar, had stated that the Kaamanaayen are at the root of the Sansaar. Similarly, if one treats oneself as Atma then the one will be attached to Ishwara whereas if one treats oneself as body, then one will be attached to Maya. Therefore, do your Karma while remaining Niskaam (desire-less) and maintaining Saakshi-Bhav (to become witness of one's own action) (Gita). The Mana (mind) is always attracted by Maya. How to come out of this web of illusion is the real challenge. But it does not mean one should ignore the body. Vatsayan says **"Aatmano bhoga-ayatanm shareeram"** means the body is actually the place to experience rewards of good and punishment of bad deeds.

Similarly, **"One ruins the mind if he or she indulges in bad deeds and ends up in misery"** (Rig-Veda).

It is not possible to experience the karma without obtaining a body. But this body is decaying every moment and one should always keep this bitter truth in mind. Therefore, in Kathopanishad it is stated that "**Uttishthat jaagrat praapy varaan-ni-vodhat**- Arise, awake, think, control yourself, do not stop till the goal is achieved".

THE SHRUTI COMPLIANCE OF PURANA AND DESH KAAL: Garud Puran is one of the "Smriti" scriptures which came down through oral traditions. Therefore, during these thousands of years, some portion of the scripture got washed off from the memories and some got included in it deliberately or inadvertently. Unfortunately, some references that were inserted later into Garud Puranas are totally unconnected and therefore stand out and do not match with the spirit of Purana. Further these references are also not in accordance with the tenets of Shrutis (Vedas and its components like Samhita, Brahma-sutra, Aryanka and Upanishads, which are of divine origin). Hence it is necessary to present the Purans in the right perspective. All the scriptures of Sanatan Dharma should abide by the Darshan of Shrutis. The same thing has been mentioned by great poet Kalidas, in "Raghuvansh": "**Shruteriva-artham smritiran-va-gachchhat**" (2/2) meaning that the Puran should follow the path of Shruti. In other scriptures also, many Shlokas convey the message to follow the path of Vedas- "Itihaasa-puraanaabhyaan vedam samupabrinhayet. Bibhetyalpa-shrutaad vedo maamayam praharisyati" (Mahabharat Parv 1/267-268). In case of dispute between various systems of thoughts, Vedas will prevail. Pt. Baldev Upadhyay of Kashi (Puran Vimarsh-1987 page -530) and many other Pandits have agreed that some new Shloka got entry into Puranas during the subsequent periods. But, wherever a deviation is observed in the Puranas from that of Vedas, the Vedas should prevail; this is the rule **"Vyaas-okta-puraanaa- naam shruti-smrity-anu-saarena-aiv vyavasthaa yuktaa"**.

It is in fact easy to identify these Shloka as they do not fit in the basic philosophy, context, and thought process and spirit of the Purana. For example, the practice of Sati was a social evil which developed during a particular historical period due to socio-political reasons (that also in only some parts of Bharat) and this custom vanished subsequently due to change in those socio-political conditions. The practice had nothing to do with Sanatan Dharma but still few Shloka got entry in Garud Puran on Sati.

It is understood that because this custom cropped up in the society, particularly among the ruling classes in North India, there was pressure on the then priests (from the rulers) to insert provision in the scriptures for cremation and Shraaddh of the woman committing "Sati". As a result, some Shloka were added relating to the cremation of the one committing Sati. Therefore, in the present edition, the same have been dropped and replaced by the original and more meaningful Shloka from the original 'Maha-Garud Puran' or even Vedas itself. Here, diligence has been made to maintain the sanctity of the Garud Puran.

Vedic Darshan forms the core of Sanatan Dharma and in fact various Mantras used for daily prayers and for sacraments and rites are actually taken from Vedas.

Basically, the very purpose behind compilation of Puran and Itihas was to spread Vedic wisdom among the masses. Goswami Tulsidas has written that the Ramcharit Manas is various Ved, and Purana compliant. In fact, the Dharam-ratha context of Lanka Kand is based on Kathopanishad and the entire Uttar-kaand presents the abstract Darshan of Upanishads in an amazing way. Dr. Pandurang Vaman Kane, in his book titled "History of Dharamshastras" has mentioned that in the entire Vedic literature there is no reference of Sati. In some other Smritis, this custom is prohibited. In Paraasar-Maadhav, Sati has been treated as suicide, therefore, **Mahaa-paap** (grievous sin) (Pryaschit Kand, Page 46-47).

In a scripture, which says that the person who kills self never attains Mokshya, how can the Shloka recognizing Sati be authentic? Similarly, Vedic Darshan treats all people as equal; where there is no distinction between women, men, adult and child, higher and lower and so on. At the level of Atma, there is no differentiation between man and woman and all are the Ansh (fraction) of Brahmn. During the Vedic era, women had a high place in society and there was collective ownership of property. In Rig-Veda, people performing the Yagya and Pooja seek blessing and say "may we be blessed with daughter" (8/31/8). In Rig-Veda there is also complete gender equality regarding performance of Homa (worship). (1/113/19).

Similar distortion has also taken place with regard to caste. The system of superiority and inferiority solely based on ones' birth was not present in the society during the Vedic era. In the subsequent periods also, it was a social system and not religious. In the early era, the word "Shudra" was interchangeably used for the illiterate and the foolish. The concept of inequality between the persons does not fit in the overall Darshan of Garud Puran as well. Even there are Shloka in Garud Puran which are critical of Varna system calling it as hypocrisy (16.57). Moreover, it has also been told in these very scriptures that while implementing rules one should keep in mind the requirement of **Desh and Kaal** (time and place).

In fact, the Hindu society basically remained democratic and judicious during the entire known history. The basic idea behind Varna system was division of power between different sections of society so that there is no concentration of power in a few hands leading to the possibility of autocracy and dictatorship. This was basically a social structure aimed to maintain order in society though it is no more relevant today.

RESORTING TO EXAGERATIONS: Puran and Itihas scriptures were actually compiled to propagate message of Vedanta in easy language using a new narrative. The idea was to ensure easy understanding of the abstract concepts of Upanishads by masses. The Upanishads speak of universal principles only. Therefore, we find efforts being made to convey the subtle Vedic Darshan in the form, format and language which even an illiterate can also understand. Thus, the aim was to bring even the savage mind on the right path of Dharma. Thus, exaggerations such as "all of your Paap will be destroyed if you surrender to Ishwara even once," and so on. Taking help of simple anecdotes and examples is often intended to influence the simple, uneducated mind.

While some of the mythical stories are merely symbolic, some metaphors and allegories are imbued with a deeper meaning which are revealed only on repeated re-telling and repeated remembering. Thus, one must not try to understand the Vedic Darshan through mythology alone. As said above, the basic purpose underlying all this was to prepare people to listen/read and understand the universal principles of Upanishad. The stories and mythology are changeable according to time, space and culture hence the Puranas can be composed according to changing times but not the universal truth of Vedanta.

Thus, these repetitions and exaggerations need to be understood in this perspective and should not be taken as per their literal meaning. Further, the contexts and examples pertaining to the society which existed thousands of years back.

Similarly, in some of the available editions of Garud Puran, it is apparent that the then editors have made errors with regard to language. For example, in simple conversation, words like he, man, etc., not only denote the man but also woman. Likewise, there are limitations of languages because language, across various cultures, has tended to have a masculine slant. So, to present these interpretations with regard to males only is a serious mistake indications of which have also been made in Garud Puran itself (13/43). "In ancient and medieval (Hindu) scriptures, the word "man" is, actually, the representative of both men and women." (R. Prasad-Philosophy of Morals, 2008, page -125).

In 19th century, when the hand-written manuscript first started coming to printing press, special attention required to ensure authenticity of manuscript was somewhat missing which proved to be major mistake because the books were being published for mass circulation for the first time and these initial printed editions subsequently got accepted as original ones. Prior to this, handwritten books were in vogue. It is worth mentioning that there are around forty two version of **Manu-Smiriti**, a treasure house of knowledge, obtained from various parts of India but the one widely available in the market today is the Kolkata Version published in 18th century. Interestingly, there is variation in the content of various versions of Manu-smiriti. Some of them do not contain the often cited Shloka, which go against women and certain sections of society.

RENUNCIATION AND GREED: It is felt by some commentators that incorporation of few Shloka in Garud Puran point towards greed of the then priestly class. The incorporation of few such Shlokas is attributed to Pt. Naunidhi Ram, the Royal Purohit of the rulers of Jhunjhunu, Rajasthan who was the first to get an abridged version of Garud Puran published through a modern Press in the year 1888. This he did after carrying out few addition and deletions in the selections from Pret kalp. The popular editions available in market today are based on this version which has sixteen chapters with 1288 Shloka and known as "**Garud Puran Saarodhaar,**" whereas the original versions of Pret-kalp are having roughly 49 Chapters with 2896 Shloka. Again, there are more than one manuscript available from various parts of India and all of them have certain dissimilarities across them. However, it is important to note that there may be one or two Shloka in100 which could have been incorporated due to personal greed of the Purohit class. These Shloka are mainly on donation to Purohit and on supremacy of priestly caste and are easily identifiable as they are misfit in the Puranas. It is worth mentioning that being a royal priest, he mentions donation of precious items beyond the reach of common people. However, the edition compiled by Pt. Naundhi Ram is of a great significance because in that edition, the Shlokas from Vivek Chudamani of Adi-Shankara, Bhagwat Gita, Neeti Shastra, Vairagya-Shastra and other scriptures, have also been incorporated, as a result it becomes more discernible and cohesive for narration. As a matter of fact, the basic thread or narrative running through all the Puranas is the one and same and it is based on Vedanta.

Vishnu Puran provides that a person of poor means can perform Shraaddh by giving coarse grain, wild vegetable and fruits and minimum Dakshina. If that cannot be afforded, then one should give seven or eight sesame (Til) Anjali (oblation) with water to Priest and if even that is also not possible, one should just raise hands to Digpaals and Sun and say "O Prabhu! I have raised hand in air, may my Pitr be satisfied with my devotion". Therefore, the Vedic scriptures do not promote greed, as it diverts attention from Ishwara. As per this Darshan, passiveness promotes greed and puts one in bondage whereas Tyaag (renunciation) makes one free.

L

SOME OTHER IMPORTANT CONCEPTS

The word Dharma, Sapindi-karan, Daan, Shraddh, Divj, Vipra, Snaan, etc., have been referred frequently in Garud Puran. It is necessary to understand the meaning of these terms for better appreciation of Garud Puran.

DHARMA TRADITIONS: Sanatan Hindu Dharma denotes combination of faith, conduct and practices to be adhered to by all, as a way of life. Here, the word Hindu may, in a broader sense, refer to all those living in Bharat, whereas Dharma tradition denotes to all the oriental faiths like Sanatan Dharma, Buddha Dharma, Jain Dharma, Sikh Dharma and so on. The Sanatan Dharma is basically the oriental tradition and the word Sanatan means eternal.

Dharma, pronounced as **Dharam,** is one of most frequently used word in Garud Puran and also in the entire Bhartiya scriptures. Dharma is actually the most splendid crown jewel adorned by the people of Dharma Tradition. Dharma signifies holding a life that is perfectly in sync with the **Rta**, i.e., universal cosmic order. This is also an unique word which changes meaning with different context, viz., doing justice is my Dharma, impartiality, lack of jealousy, righteous conduct charity proper conduct of rites, proper care for one's body, etc., is Dharma of ruler (Raaj-dharma), wishing for the welfare of people is the Dharma of Purohit (priest) and Gurus, security of people is the Dharma of Soldier, protection of Dharma itself at all cost is the Dharma of one and all.

The main practices of Dharma are defined in various scriptures. Yagyavalikya defines Dharma with following attributes: Non-violence, truth, non-stealing, inner and outer cleanliness, control over sense organs, compassion, Daan (donation) and peace. Specific attributes are highlighted in various scriptures: Dharma is truth - (Brihad Upanishad). This entire world is upheld by Dharma (Atharva Veda); Dharma is impartiality (Garud Puran). The Golden Rule or the Ethics of Reciprocity that "do not behave the way you would not like for yourself" has been treated as the essence of Dharma in Padma Puran (Shiristi 19/357-58), and so on.

Manusmriti describes 10 principles for the observance of dharma: **Dhriti** (patience), *Kshama* (clemency), *Dama* (self control), **Asteya** (honesty), **Shauch** (cleanliness), *Indraiya-nigrah* (control of sense organs), **Dhi** (reason), **Vidya** (knowledge or learning), **Satya** (truthfulness) and **Akrodha** (absence of anger). Manu also writes that non-violence, non-coveting, purity and well being of body and mind are important part of dharma.

Devotion to the ultimate reality also finds a place in the precepts of Dharma in Gita, Ramayana and other scriptures. In fact, the first word of Gita is Dharma and Shri Krishna says that "for the protection of good people and destruction of wicked, and for the establishment of Dharma, He takes birth from age to age". However, even Nastik-non-believers and believers of all hues are part of Dharma, thereby making Dharma a more broader inclusive concept.

MOST ANCIENT AND THE MOST MODERN DHARMA: Rig-Veda is the oldest book of mankind, Vedanta is the oldest surviving Darshan and Sanatan Dharma the oldest Dharma and religion. However, the Vedic Dharma is not merely a belief system of dogmas rather, it asks for freshness through Viveka (discrimination) and Yukti. Thus, it also promotes rational thinking or reason. Vedic Darshan is, therefore, based on combination of Shastras (scriptures), Yukti, **Anubhav** (realization) and Karmas (spiritual practices). The scripture provide only a broad guidance yet the Vedanta has discerned to the finality on the notion of ultimate reality, i.e., Brahmn, where no further efforts are required any more though yogis are free to interpret on the elements of reality and argue on these subjects. The Vedas even say do not get fixed on us. The Vedas give us freedom but the wise, having good karma, will certainly choose the correct path. The Dharma of Vedas is ever evolving thus it could produce Adi Shankara, Madhavacharya, Ramanujan and in modern age Gurus like Dayanand Saraswati, Aurobindo, Srila Prabhupad, Narajanguru, Swami Vivekananda and many other luminaries. This ever evolving philosophy lets a Gautam Buddha, Mahavir Swami, Guru Nanak, Sant Kabir, Sant Basav, Ghosa, Meerabai, Akka Mahadevi and many Mahatmas and Gurus to come up and, due to its all encompassing worldview, different and differing paths including atheistic tradition of Charvak continue to exist even today - all of them however enfolded in the Dharma. This is because it treats the individual as divine Atma and has Ishwara reside in the individual and not in an unknown Swarga.

EKODISHT SHRADDH: Ekodisht is that Shraddh which is aimed at the release of single departed spirit, thus not linked with other ancestors. By performing Ekodisht Shraddh, the Pret (a condition of afflicted supernatural spirit acquired after death) is uplifted to the level of Pitr (a higher stage of dead ancestors just below Devta), which takes one year and thereafter the departed joins the Pitr. In Ekodist the **Vaiswa-dev**(offering of food to Pitr and deities) is also not required and the Shraddh is performed with single Pind, Single Arghya and Pavitrak. It means that for one year, the departed may remains in the form of a Pret. In this process, 16 Ekodisht Shraddh are required to be performed so that the Pret body gets protection from the torments of the Yammarg and is elevated. The last **(Antim) Shraddh** (after which the Pret becomes the Pitr) is called the **Sapindan rite**. (13.28,29,30).The first Ekodisht Shraddh is performed on the 11th day of the death. After that, 12 Shraddh are performed during every moon month in the year of death, two Shraddh are performed one day prior to each half yearly and two are performed on monthly dates. The last Shraddh is known as Sapindi-Karan Shraddh. After one year from the performance of Sapindi-karan, the departed, may acquire the **Karamyoni** (human birth) or **Bhog-deh** (body for experiencing Karma) - (Agnipuran-369/12-13).

LIII

However, the rights and elaborate Daans are not required in case of the departed having elevated Atma.

In between, on the 11th day Shraddh or on the day of the Sapindi-karan Shraddh or during any of the Ekodisht Shraddh, the rite of "Varshotsarg" (the release of a bull), is performed. On non-availability of a bull, an earthen bull or rice or kusha grass effigy is used as replacement.

SAPINDIKARAN OR SAPINDAN: Sapindan is that process by which the departed is initiated to the society of other Pitr, who are entitled to receive the Pind offerings. A Sanatani, from birth itself, owes three debts – **Pitr Rin** (Parental debt), **Dev-rin** (Debt of Deity) and the **Rishi Rin** (debt of Rishis). One repays the debt of Pitr Rin-the debt owed to parents- by having children of one's own who will perform the rites associated with Pitr Rin.

The four major rites under Pitr-Rin are:- Funeral rites, **Asti-Visarjan** (immersion of mortal remains), **Shraddh** and **Purohit Bhog** (feast to Acharya) and other. Garud Puran talks of the formation of body from offering of ten **Pindas** (made of cooked rice, barley, sesame seeds and ghee symbolizes a body). Thus ten **Pind** (one each for ten days), will be offered. In some other books, there is also provision of one Pind each for three days. Thus, offering of three Pind for three days and feast to uneven number of Purohits on fourth day followed by **Asti Sanchay** (collection of mortal remains), Shraddh and Ekodist Shraddh on Ekadas are prescribed for the followers of Vedic procedures. Similarly, offering one Pind each for three days (Yaagya-3.16) or offering of ten Pind in three days (three on day one, four on second day and three on third day) is also provided (Paaraskar). But those who are not strict adherent of Dharma should rather follow Garud Puran on this.

The collection of mortal remains with respect of **Agnihotiris** (who perform fire sacrifices) should be done on third day and that of other on fourth day (10.67). There is also a provision for any of the first, third, seventh or ninth day. Where there is no river, the mortal remains should be buried duly following the procedure as prescribed in **Grihsutra**. Therefore, the immersion should be done within 10 days in the water of Ganga (10.79) or any other holy river. Immersion in river signifies that the life flows on along the endless flow of river, just like a free Atma.(Yaagyavalkya-3.16).

The Vedic hymn which is recited at the time of collection of ashes, says "O Pret-Atma! Rise from here and get a new body, do not leave any of the elements of your body. Go, in whichever world you want to go. May **Savita** (Ishwara) establish you there. These are your ashes. May you attain divine prosperity. Fully developed with all parts of the body, may you be born pleasant-looking, be healthy".

THE PRET CONDITION AND SUTAK: Here, it is necessary to know the reason behind offering of the Pind. As soon as the dead body is cremated, the departed initially acquires an invisible **Vaayavya or Ativaahik body**(moving in the air) for transmigration of Atma from one body to another. Subsequently, this Ativahik body of Paapi is transferred to Pret body which is made of the three out of five elements of body- fire, air and sky. The other two elements i.e., earth and water remain underneath due to cremation and these three elements rise upwards. This Ativahik period is very miserable. This process happens with the human beings only, not with the body of any other creatures, because other creatures get re-birth in same or the other Yoni immediately after death hence other creatures do not go to Pret yoni. But those who could not receive the last rite (10/88) or who renounce the Dharma or who are most sinful or steal the wealth of religious places, who abandon their mother-father and relatives, and so on remain in Pret-Yoni for a long time (Varah Padama-Puran 172-49). The various factors leading to Pret Yoni are delivered in details in Garud Puran. The Pret body is less micro than the Ativahik body, but it is also esoteric and cannot be seen with naked eyes.

The Pret themselves suffer miseries and they may also torment others and their relatives. The Pret visit those houses, for obtaining food, where cleanliness is not maintained (Skand-Puran 6-18-22), "where there is always quarrel, "where the sound of Vedic hymns is not heard", "where women are not respected" (Garud Puran) and so on.

The one for who could not be cremated and the Paapi become Pret. Those who did not receive Pind, who did not perform **Sat-Karm** (virtuous deeds) during life-time, will have to suffer the entire torment period. It is only after receipt of ten Pind, the Atma acquires the Pret body, leaving the Ativahik Sharir which is even more miserable.

Body is formed by the Pind offerings. The head, eyes, nose, ears, chest, throat, womb, legs, delicate organs, bones, hairs, nails, rest of the organs of Pret are formed from first to ninth day's Pind and life and the sensitivity of the Ativahik Sharir dies and Pret body is born with tenth day's Pind. It is called "**Dash-gatra**" (formation of ten organs). The Pret receives the Pind offered on the eleventh and twelfth days as food. On completion of the process of formation of ten organs, they go to Swarga or Narak, in accordance with their deeds. The persons of great merits attain Mokshya or Swarga without undergoing Ativahik or Pret condition. Thus, a Pret body of the length of a hand is formed from the offerings of ten Pindas, which experiences the good or bad returns of Karma. The Ativahik phase generally continues for ten days. Therefore, the impurity and mourning period also extends during these ten days, though there are many exceptions as regards to impurity. Upon the death of a relative who is living in foreign country or on death of Sanyasis, one is purified just by taking bath (13/10-11), Gautam 14-42).The Sapinda impurity affects relatives upto seven generation. The priest is not affected by impurity (Shudhi Prakash-93). There are such other exception in which a person can perform duty during this period such as masons, service class, doctors, people involved in administration, armed forces and where it is important to continue duty for social order, etc. The one with great karma do not go through all this and may not require these rites but performing of these rites will always add value to life in this as well for other world.

Thus, Sapindi rites are performed to lift the departed to higher level and Sapindikaran is generally performed along with the first year's rites, but now-a-days due to time constraints, it is also being performed on the 12th day of death (Garud Puran) or even sometimes on 4th, 6th or 11th day of death.

In case someone dies while his father is alive, the Sapindi-Karan will not be performed till the death of the father. Sapindi is performed in sequence of father, grandfather, great grandfather (mother, grandmother, great grandmother). As against Ekodisht Shraddh, four Pinds are prepared for Sapindikaran-one for the departed, and three for other three ancestors. Thereafter, all four of these Pind are mixed together to make them one, so that the Pret is combined with Pitrin Pitr-Lok. After performing the Sapindi-karan and annual Sharadh, the departed-according to deeds-gets the position of a deity, Pitr, human or bird-animal in the descending orders of importance. In case the departed has acquired a status of a deity, the food offering of Shraddh becomes Amrit (nectar). The same Shraddh food becomes Bhog for the one who has acquired Gandharv Yoni, for the one in animal Yoni it becoming grass, in birds yoni it is received as fruit, in demon yoni as flesh, in Daanav Yoni as meat, in Pret-Yoni it becomes blood, and for humans it becomes grain, and so on.

TARPAN (OBLATION) TO A FRIEND: Like the Sapinda offspring, anyone else can also offer Tarpan (oblation) of water to a departed friend, sister, daughter, niece, mother-in-law, father-in-law, Guru, Priest and others. Even in normal days, after taking bath in the holy river and before "Sandhaya", Tarpan should be offered to the Deva, Rishi and Pitr. To praise the good deeds done by departed, when alive, and to pay homage as gratitude is also a part of last rites ceremony. From social perspective, it motivates a person for doing good deeds and also motivates the people towards doing virtuous deeds in their remaining life. It also paves way for formation of a divine society on earth (Gita 6.5). **Shrandhanjali** (condolence) meetings, **Bhajan, Kirtan** and sermons are also performed towards the same objective.

SHRADDH AND TARPAN:-The word "Shraddh" is derived from the word "**Shraddha**" (faith) because the basic object of Shraddh is based on faith. According to Brahmn Puran and Agni Puran the Homa, Pind-daan and **Tarpan** (oblation) performed for ancestors at the right time by right person, and place in accordance with due procedures as prescribed in the scriptures, is called Shraddh. During the Shraddh, the person performing rites for ancestors says: "May those of my Pitr, who are in the form of Pret be satisfied with the Pind made of sesame and barley. May also every power in creation from Brahma to the animate be happy with the **Tarpan** (offering of water) by me."

As the food consumed by a pregnant woman reaches to the embryo being developed in her womb, similarly, the commodities offered in the Shraddh, reach to the Atma of the departed. The spirits of the last three ancestors are able to receive the aroma or substance of the Pind of Shraddh even for fifty to hundred years after death, when they are roaming in the air, through their Vaayabya Sharir. Once satisfied with Shraddh ceremony they bestow better life (Yaagyavalkya), offspring, wealth, education and happiness to their decedents. The spirit of ancestors has access to every place just like Vasu, Shiv and Aditya. The objective of the Shraddh is also to worship the Ishwara keeping Pitr as an object. According to Vanu-Purana, the Shraddh performed with complete faith propagates not only the Pitr but also Jeeva, universe and the entire creation in addition to Ishwara.

In this regard, if one desires to invite Purohit for conduct of Shraddh, invitation may be given well in advance so that he or she is able to maintain Brahmcharya (self control). The next day, Purohit should perform the Pinda-daan and Tarpan to the ancestors of his **Yajmaan** (patron) as per prescribed Vedic procedure. If the son is minor and has not gone through **Upanayan**(sacred thread) Sanskaar, he may offer water and rest of the procedure will be done by the Purohit. Thereafter, Purohit may take meals. He should accept the invitation only of one Yajmaan at a time and take meal only in one house. After taking the offerings of Shraddh, Purohit should get himself purified by performing Gayatrari Japa, etc. (8.49). To accept **Dakshina** (donation) and to take meal of Shraddh from Yajmaan does not blemish a priest. But he should accept the meal of Shraddh and donations with the sole motive of the welfare of the ancestors of the host, not with selfishness. Therefore, it is also a form of denial on the part of priest.

GRATITUDE AND HOMAGE TO THE LOVED ONES: In addition, Shraddh is an occasion and opportunity for the offspring to remember their ancestors, relatives and friends who were their loved ones while they were alive. As per the scriptures, not only son but anyone can offer Shraddh to the one who's property, knowledge, love and affection, etc., one inherits. Thus, to offer food and donations to the friends, relatives, wise, Saadhu-sanyaasis, poor and needy is great tradition and is a noble cause (Dr. P.V. Kane: History of Dharam Shastras).

COMPETENCY TO PERFORM RITES: It is known from the various scriptures that the primary responsibility for performing last rites rests with the son; preferably the eldest son (11.21) because he is supposed to be in better position. The reason behind giving this task to son or the eldest son is due to their special status in the succession of inheritance under the Hindu Law (Manusamruti-9/132), (11.21). The women are normally exempted from the performance of the last rites but they are eligible to perform these rites.(Garud Puran 10/15,61). Right from Vedic era, women have been performing Antesti and other rites. We find that there were some practical reasons, rather than religious one, to grant exemption to the women. For example, cremation used to take place on river-banks, often far off places, and bodies being carried on shoulder, etc., during the earlier days. Most of those reasons exist no more and these days the daughters are being brought at par with sons with similar roles being performed by them. Further, size of families has also changed to nucleus ones. In the former times, the system of daughter moving to her husband's place, after marriage, also played a role. Because, the husband and wife have started residing at new home these days, therefore, the son's dominant position is now irrelevant. There are also references where the daughter can also be treated as son by treating her 'Putrika-putar- daughter as son' (Vashisht-17/16).

The wife and daughter are entitled to perform the **Antesti** (Garud Puran). Similarly, there is no restriction on women attending the cremation (10.55, 61).

In Brahmn Nirvan Tantara, Bhagwan Sadashiv gives direction that barring Varidhi Shraddh (the Shraddh to be performed by a man with the pregnant wife), the woman can perform all types of Shraddh. For this, the woman should wear a Janeu (sacred thread) from outside. Therefore, it has been said that **"Putra-abhaave tu patnee syaad dauhitro duhita-api vaa. Putroshu vidyamaaneshu vrishm na-anyen kaarayet**- In the absence of a son, the wife shall be competent to perform the Varsho-utsarg (release of a bull) and other death rites, or the son of daughter or the daughter herself shall be competent. But the others should not perform the "Vasho-utsarg" when the sons are there". (12/37, 11/13)

Further, this rule of Shraddh will be uniform for all the Sanatani Hindus (13/19). **"Dvi-vidhaa striaayo brahma-vaadinyah sadyo-vadhvy. Tatraa brahma-vaadinee naamunayaanaam agnondhann sva-grihe bhikshaa-charyaa ch. Sadyo-vadhoonaam to-opasthite vivaah-kaale vidupanayan kritvaa vivaah kaaryah** -The woman are of two types – Brahmn Vaadini (who deliver sermons of Vedas) and Sadyo-vadhu(who do not go for higher studies). Brahma-vadini wears Yagyaopavit (sacred thread), does Agnihotra (fire sacrifices), studies Vedas and acquires other education. The Yagyo-pavit is also necessary for a Sadyo-vadhu but that is performed at the time of marriage".(Harit Dharm-Sutra 21.20.24).

In this regard, it is said in some Shloka: **"Stree Va-ath puruchah kashchid ishtasy kurute kriyaam. Anaatha-preta-snskaaraat koti-yagya-falm labhet**- if a woman or a man perform the last rites of a destitute or an orphan, then the Punya (rewards) equal to ten Million Yagya is gained from the ceremonies done on behalf of that destitute" (18.18).Similarly, **"Putra-abhaave vadhooah kuryaad-bhaarya-abhaave ch sodarah. Shishyo vaa braahmnaasya-iv sapinadao vaa samaacharet**- In absence of a son, wife should perform the rites and in the absence of wife, the real brother should perform, in the absence of brother, the disciple, priest or the Sagotri (of the same Gotra) should perform the Sapindi rites" (11.13). Similarly, in subsequent chapters also, it has been said that, right from the cremation till the 10th day, the responsibility to perform these rites rests with son, grandson, great grandson, or brother or his offspring's. In the absence of wife, the younger brother, in his absence, the elder brother, in the absence of brother, his son will be eligible. If there is no offspring of the brother also, then an unmarried girl is eligible. In the absence of unmarried daughter, the son of a married daughter and so on. If there is no one in the daughter's family, then the mother's family is eligible. If there is no offspring in all the three families, then it would be the responsibility of the king (government). (7.42), Dharam-sindhu 370, Parashar Grahsutra (3/10/42-43). Thus, in no condition the performance of last rites be escaped. (11.17).

Further, it has been said that **"Asagotraah sagotro vaa yadi straaee yadi vaa pumaan. Prathame ahani yah kuryaat s dashaahm samaapayet** - in the absence of a son, **Asagotri** of another gotra or **Sagotri** (of the same Gotra, woman or man can perform but whosoever performs the first day rites of the Pret, will have to perform the rest of the rites, till 10th Day".(11/14).

Further, Garud Puran says that in the absence of son, the wife will perform the last rites of her husband (11/12-17), (12/51-53) and husband will perform the last rites of his wife (13/44). It is also said that"**Samparetasy yaa patyuah kurute cha-aurdhva-daihikam. Kchayaahm paakshikm Shraddhm saa satiety-uchyet mayaa** - the woman who perform annual and half yearly Shraddh of her departed husband, is called "Sati" (a truthful woman)" (12/52).

Similarly, some Shloka have come in Purana with regard to restriction during menstruation cycle. This is due to a Puranic story linking Brahmn-hatya (the killing of Guru by Indra). Knowing the relations of his Guru with the demons, Indra killed his Guru, as a result of which he was cursed. However, Indra went to Brahma for relief and Brahma distributed the curse among four sections: one part each to earth, trees, woman, and water. In earth, it is seen in the form of pits and trenches; in water it is seen in the form of foam; in trees, it is seen in the form of discharge, and in women this part appears as menstruation. Thus, nowhere else it is treated as impure. However, in Shrimad-Bhagvat, these four elements have not been linked with impurity whereas in some other Puranas, some restrictions have been placed on woman during the menstruation period. With regard to this story, one reference is worth mentioning, in which the women ask Brahaspati: "O Lord! The woman has been born to achieve Dharma, Arth (economic value), Kama and Mokshya. In case the woman take over one fourth Paap of Brahm-hatya upon herself, then she will be treated as Paapi and being procreator, many families will turn Paapi." Upon this Brahaspati said, "O Ladies! Do not be frightened from this part of the Paap. The part of Paap accepted by you will be provider of good rewards."

In this regard let it be clear that the menstruation has been treated as an ordinary process in Vedas and women were free to perform daily rites during menstrual period. In some scriptures, particularly in the Shaakta tradition the bleeding during the menstrual period has been treated as a form of pure fire. Therefore, there should not be any disapproving attitude towards menstruating woman. Possibly, the prime reason, to link the menstruation period with the Brahmn-hatya and impurity, was the concern for public hygiene, as it is not a spiritual topic. But now-a-days, sanitary pads, modern bathrooms (in place of bath in rivers) and various methods of hygiene are available; therefore, this issue has become obsolete. Arya Samaj, Sikh Panth and many Hindu sects have rejected the discrimination against menstruating woman saying that this practice is against the Vedic principle of Ekatma (universal Atma). In fact, the differentiation like men-women does not exist at subtle level of Atma. The Atma resides in physical body therefore the body can never become impure as a living being is always pure. Thus, says Shrimad Bhagwat: "Ishwara does not accept worship by a man who ignores his life partner" (3-29/24).

BALI VAISHVA-DEV: Bali Vasihva-dev denotes to offering of cooked food. Rishi Daksh (2/56) says that in the fifth part of the day, a householder should offer food, according to one's capacity, to Devta, Pitr, human beings, animals, birds, worms, insects and other creatures. Fruits, root vegetables or water can be offered, in the absence of cooked food. Vaishva-dev has special significance during the Shraddh. As per Anushasan Parv (17-16-18), on the day of Shraddh, Pitra-tarpan (offering of water to the fore-fathers) should be performed first and thereafter Vaishav-dev, wherein a part of the cooked food is offered to different Kuldevta (family deities) to direction, to Vegetations, etc. Any of the days when food for Vaishva-dev could not be cooked, then the household should observe fasting on that day.

PAAP AND PUNYA: Paap is an act by the individual which violets the Rit, i.e., the nature's momentum, cosmic order and moral behaviors of people (Dr. Kane). In other word not following Dharma or doing Adharma is Paap. Paap is not "Sin" as understood in Abrahmic religions. In those traditions as sin is an offence against God i.e., not following words of God is sin, whereas; Paap; is an offence against oneself, as it impacts one's karma. The opposite of Paap is Punya and there is no parallel words for it in English, as virtue and merit means to follow world of God, whereas Punya is to follow the Dharma. We find a number of Shloka on Paap and Punya in different scriptures. Vagbhatt in his Sutrasthan describes ten types of Paap Karma: Violence on others, stealing and adultery (are Paap done by body); speaking a lie, impoliteness, back bite (these are Paap done by speech); and give pain to others, take a vow to harm others, to see demerits in the virtues of others, to have ill feeling against innocents (are mental Paaps).

Garud Puran enumerates a number of grave and other Paaps which are as followed: (i) Brahmn-hatya i.e., Killing of human being particularly those absorbed in divinity-enlightened Brahmin, Saadhu, priest, etc., except when these killing are resorted for upholding of Dharma. (14.62) (ii) Lack of compassion towards the helpless, the people with disability, poor, orphaned and exploitation of the weak (iii) exploitation of women and children, selling of daughters,

LXIV

children (iv) Harassing a woman and killing of a pregnant woman treated as grievous Paap (v) Cheating, breaking the trust and killing by poisoning (vi) Polluting, the holy places, harming people devoted to Ishwara, disrespect to Vedas, (vii) Not devoted to Shiva, Vishnu, Durga, Ganesha and Surya. (vii) Not offering food and water to a hungry and thirsty and disrespect to a guest and parents (viii) Take away someone's livelihood and to take back donations; (ix) Brahmin who consume liquor, selling liquor, killing animal for selfish ends and eating forbidden food. (ix) Lustfulness and cheating husband or wife (x) Coveting with the wife of king or great person's wife or wife of Guru (xi) Giving wrong witness (xii) Destroying nature (environment, forest, rivers, gardens) (xiii) Breaking sanctity of a widow (xiv) Disregard to ancestors, attack on husband, wife and children, one who breaks relationship of husband and wife; illegitimate relation with daughter in law, daughter, sister and other family members, have illicit relationship with wife or husband of others. (xv) Rape (xvi) throwing bodily waste in Agni, water, garden, cowshed (xvii) Punishing the innocent and killing of mother, father, friend and old person; (xviii) one who destroys food stuff, (xix) one who keeps the company of Maha-Paapi.

Punya is a vast subject and is also deliberated in various chapters of Garud Puran: helping poor, orphaned, helping the people with disabilities, old, children, women and compassion towards other creatures, Daan whether small or great (8.112) (Daan given on behalf of mother is ten times greater than that given for father, sister and siblings is even higher) (8.115), to follow Dharma, carry out good deeds, construction of temples, water points (8.106), parks, forestation, etc., One should use wealth for earning Daan speech for truth, life for glory of Ishwara and Dharma, body for welfare of others, while keeping away from untruth (8.118).

It has been said: **"Ashtaa-dash-puraanaeshu vyaasasya vachana-dvayam, Paropakaaraay punayaay**

paapaay parapeedaanam - in all of the eighteen Purans, we get only two words of Ved Vyas, i.e., one gets **Punya** (merits) from **Paropkar** (welfare of others) and gets Paap from giving pain to others". Similarly, **Daan** (donation), **Dayaa** (mercy) and **Damo** (control over sense organs) have also been treated as important by Yagya-valkya. **"Deenaa-naatha-vishistebhyo   dadyaach-chhaktyaa   ch daksihnaam"** (8/45).

Daan leads to Punya and Daan is to handover the ownership of a thing, wealth, knowledge, service, love, food, utilities, wealth, etc, to others.

DAAN AN ACT OF COMPASSION AND EQUALITY: The act of Daan (donation) is inherent in Sanatan Dharma and is the divine path for establishment of a society which is egalitarian and caring. At the same time Daan is also a Mokshya-daayi (liberating) act from the point of view of donor. There is involvement of mind, heart and body in doing good deeds and it can be done through the act of speech, devotion of time, material, affection and service. **'Good deeds give divine happiness'** (Rig-Veda). As per Vishnu Dharma Sutra, to give donations to mother-father, knowledgeable, priest-purohit, Brahmin who is into study of Vedas, Guru, friend, person of great morality, noble person, poor people, orphan, destitute, deprived, people of special characters, people with disability, weak and so on, is rewarding and they are also eligible to receive the donation. Similarly the hunger of a hungry person makes him the most eligible for food (Swami Ramsukh Das). But, the deceitful, gamblers, thieves, cheat, non believers in Vedas, the Brahmins and Priest who do not follow the path of Dharma, are not eligible to receive the Daan. In Chhandogya Upanishad (5/10/5) it has been said:**'Vidyaavrittavate deyn moorkhe tann kadaachan. Samartho vedavrittaa hyas taaraGae taraGae Api ch**-that the people who perform Yagya, those involved in public welfare and give donation, they all scale to the

Chanderalok means they go to Swarga. Similarly, Gita says "Traayo dharm skandhaah yagyo, Adhyayann daanamati" (there are three shoulders of Dharma- Yagya (Pooja, Yagya), Swadhyay (self study, listening, preaching of scriptures and study of other good literature) and Daan (donation). Similarly, Manu-Smriti says: **"Svaadhyaaye nity yuktah syaadaivm ch ev karmanaa** - one should always be ready for Swadhyaya and the noble cause". To give water to the thirsty and food to the hungry, is also a donation (Brahmn-Puran-214-39). In today's context, the societies working for charity, the organization dedicated to the promotion of Sanatan Dharma may also be considered as eligible to receive Daan.

As per scriptures, any resourceful person should donate 10% of the profit, earned from legal means, for the glorification of Ishwara. **"Nyaay-opaarjit vittasy dasha-maashen dheematah. Kartavyo viniyogash-ch ishvara-preetyarth mev ch"** (Skand Puran).The wealthy persons should donate **Pachdha** (one fifth) of their profit (Shrimad-8-19-37). But the one who is very poor, does not spend unnecessarily and takes care of the whole family, the rule does not provide for Daan by such person (13/122). Not only this, but if a person with greed to earn **Punya** (reward), donates while mother, father, spouse, offspring remain deprived of life chances, then he (she) would earn Paap (sins) instead of reward (Manu-Smruti-11/1-10).

Scriptures say that the right to adorn the **Vyaspeeth** (the presiding priestly seat representing Guru Ved Vyas) for conducting rites and ceremonies rests with a married Acharya and not with the Sadhu and Sanyasi though sadhu-sanyasi are eligible for Daan and respect. The priest does not suffer for taking gifts of performing death rites and debt for acceptance of donations (8/65-66). The priest dedicated to Dharma, if accepts the donations for livelihood, will remain Nispaap (sinless) (8/49). By Japa of Gayatari Mantra, the priest is absolved from various types of debts including this one. Similarly, bath, Sandhya in the morning and twilight, fasts and vows also absolve one from the indebtedness. Here, it has also been said that a person should donate, according to his capacity, the best things to donate are the things which one treats most precious and which are coming from his heart with due reverence. There is divinity and fulfillment in the joy of giving. The Daan of gold (Valuable), has been said to be best donation (8/41-43).

The Daan should be made while keeping in mind the needs of receiver rather than the caste of a person (Vishnu Dharamottar). If the Daan is made secretly, it becomes much more rewarding. While offering Daan, there must not be the feeling of arrogance or superiority and it should not be made for selfish motives such as raising own reputation. Daan is not an alm giving or mercy but a duty. The giver should bend down and be humble with the receiver looking up. Therefore, Daan has been defined as distribution (2/66). Such type of devotional spirit brings the feeling of surrender and to attain Ishwara. That is a stage where Ishwara takes up the responsibility of devotee: **"Teshaam nityaabhiyuktaanaan yoga-kshemam vahaamyaham"** (Gita -9/22).

Affluence is the special blessing of Ishwara upon you and is the indicator of your past good deeds, your labor and endevour or the blessing of Ishwara. But one should not be mentally attached (Liptata) to the wealth; enjoy your wealth by renouncing it (Gita). Treat the wealth, which is beyond your requirement, as if kept in your trusteeship (Lok-sangrah, Gita) by divinity and the Ishwara wants you to serve fellow beings and creatures through this. You, in turn, will reap Punya (rewards) which will help you to achieve the objective of life. In case you feel pain when seeing someone in hardship, then it proves that Ishwara wants you to help that person or creature. Where the poor earns reward with deeds only, without making any Daan, the duties and responsibilities of affluent people are far more. The wealthy have been entrusted with more responsibilities by Ishwara. The crux of dharma lies at the welfare of others and relinquishment of selfishness. But detachment (Aliptata) does not mean relinquishment of worldly and family responsibilities. Upholding of Dharma and taking care of family and society and environment is the prime duty (8/106.2). The sense of inequality, superiority, attachment, exploitation (of creatures, environment) arrogance, greed and all these vices deviate one from the path of Dharma and Mokshya.

Sant Swami Ramsukh Das says that no divinity can come without the sense of **Karuna** (mercy), **Vaatsalya** (feeling of parental love for others), equality, tolerance, human sensitivity, humility and concern for poor, needy, weak, helpless, aged as these are also the divine qualities. "Samata comes when the pain of other becomes your own and happiness of others become your own happiness". Similarly, help of poor, weak, orphaned and people with disability are insisted upon. **"Deenaa-naatha-vashist-ebhyo dadych-chhaktyaa ch dakshinaam"** (8/45).

Sanathan Dharma advocates that all human beings are one and the same at the level of Atma; they are the sparks of same Brahmn and the difference is only of the physical appearance. There is oneness of whole creation; therefore, the concern for "universal self" is a defining attribute of followers of the Dharma.

Upon occurrence of pain in any part of one's body all efforts are made to relieve the pain, similarly, upon occurrence of pain or hardship to any human being, all efforts should be made to relieve that pain (Gita -6/32). Equality comes automatically when there is yearning in the heart as to how to make other happy (Rig-Ved, Varunsutra-2/28-29), how others are made comfortable? How they are benefitted? A feeling to ensure the welfare of all.

This starts from one's own home. A divine feeling in the heart that "there should not be any pain or hardship to anyone; may there be no harm to anyone; irrespective of my sufferings". Those who are devoted to the benefits of all, receive the **Kripa** (grace) of Ishwara. (Gita-12/4). The feeling of universal welfare takes one close to divinity whereas selfishness separates one from that power. One should not be extravagant and should use material objects for subsistence only, without any attachment. One must realize that all creatures have equal rights upon all the commodities available around (Ishopanishad-1). Your right on things is for your maintenance only and one who wants more than that, is a thief liable to be punished (ShrimadBhagwat-7/14.8). Sanatan Dharma propagates **Aadhyatmik-Manavtaa-vaad** (spiritual humanism) is the only philosophy wherein there is concern not only for each human being but also all things, animate and inanimate. Therefore, consumerism and hedonism are contrary to Vedanta. The wealth must be made a means of earning **Punya** (rewards) by utilizing it for Dharma. In this context, the earning of wealth becomes a noble cause only if it is used for noble purposes. Moreover, without wealth one is often handicapped in helping oneself as well as others.

Vedic Darshan preaches that one should extend helping hand to persons who are in need, whether material or spiritual. Providing food to the poor and also to other creatures, Japa-tapa, Homa and a life free of jealously are rewarding. To follow the Sixteen Sanskaar and perform Purusharth is also part of Dharma.

HEALTHY BODY, SATH-CHAKRA AND KUNDALINI JAGRAN: Care for one's body is essential because a healthy body is the only means of doing **Purusharth** (human endeavor) in this world as well as for Par-lok: **"Shareer maadynm khalu dharm saadhanam"**. There are many Shloka, in various scriptures, on taking proper care and maintenance of the body. Garud Puran says that no good deed can be performed without having a healthy body. Further, it says that you and you alone are responsible for the well being of your body. Adi Shankara has declared that the human body is a temple of divine Atma (Deha Devalaya), therefore, due care of this temple needs to be taken. The body must not be abused and misused. Therefore, the wealth in the shape of body must be protected as you can earn wealth, earn Punya and do everything else only if the body is protected and is healthy (16/17-19, 21-23). Various Yog-Mudras have been developed for the well being of body while Pranayam is intended for exercise of vital internal organs and the mind.

Charak defines disease as disharmony of the Dhatus. (Interestingly, Hyppocratic treatises, of which the Doctor takes oath, is nothing but a translated copy of Charak Samhita). There is a beautiful stanza which describes it all. **"Samadoshah, Samagnishcha, Samadhatu, Malakriyaha, Prasanna Atma Indriya Manaha, Swastha, ithya, videyathi** - When the Doshas and Dathus are balanced, when one has balanced diet, bowel motion, if one keeps mind, soul and senses pure; health is assured". The Vedic way to good health is to treat yourself and the entire creation as divine. One should love the family, neighbor, society, colleagues, superior, subordinates, customers and have respect for all the creatures around including environment. Be compassionate and giver; be enthusiastic, have a controlled life and be under the divine shelter of Ishwara. In fact the last word of Gayatri Mantra – **Prachodayat** - prays for making us lively and enthusiastic every day through igniting our minds. All this will relieve one from feeling of hate, anger, arrogance, greed, envy, etc., which are in conflict with the innate nature of human being. This will relive one from the tensions, stress, depressions, negative tendencies and also from diseases.

The philosophy of life should be based on **"Charaiveti Charaiveti** - one should be constantly in motion. Keep moving, keep moving on". (Aitareya Brahmana). This is applicable for the mind as well as the body. Further, the basic purpose of human body is welfare of other – **Paropakaa-raarth Edam Shariram.** While helping others you actually help yourself as others are not different from you, they are simply the extension of your Atma, i.e., Paramatma.

The Mantra for long healthy life as per Ayurveda is as followed: **"Nityam hitaharviharsevi samikshyakari vishayesvasaktah Dàta samah satyaparah kshamawàn aptopsevi cha bhavetyarogah** - The one, who takes limited food, hard working (physical and mental)) labouris, have controlled over sense organ, is involved in charity, remains balanced whether in profit or loss, devoted to truth, believes in forgiveness, help the people in need, becomes healthy and lives for hundred years" (Astang Hraday Su. 4/37). Ayurveda treats body and mind from the holistic perspective rather than treating the body as collection of parts in isolation. Ayurveda says it is not the bits and pieces that make the thing; it is the whole, the interchangeableness of the whole that makes a body. There is unity of all parts of body. Similarly, every entity like planets, moon, air, water, sun, human being and other Jeeva, the environment and so on are inseparable from each other. The glow of Sun, luster of Moon, the greenery and so on is felt by human being and glow of human being is also felt by the Sun, Moon and so on. Similarly, hard work and controlled diets are treated as the key to good health- **Parishram Mitaharao Bhugta Vashwani Sutao** (Harit Samhita). Further, a Shloka says that at the root of good health lies pursuit of Dharma, Arth, Kaam and Mokshya (Purusharth).

In the 15th Chapter of this scripture, the Shath-chakra has been elaborated. Shath-chakra and Yoga Sadhana are also the path to Mokshya. They pave the way by purifying the sense organs, Pran, Chit, heart, thought, feeling and the Atma. The union of healthy body, mind, wisdom and Atma, is called Yoga. The purpose of Yoga is to get the Atma connected to Paramatma from which we got separated. It is due to attachment with the Maya and Ahankar of human beings that the Atma got alienated from its true self, Paramatma. The practice of Shat-chakra is one of the means to re-establish the lost connection.

Aatama-bhav (sense of selfhood) by concentration of mind. The Yogi is released from the bondage of this deep ocean of the world and is empowered with all the powers. The place above the throat is the place of **Shakti** (power). The journey from **Mooladhar** (at the base of spine) to **Sahasraar** (located at the top of head) is called 'the great journey'. Yogis achieve their destination by scaling this path with the process of self realization. The Yoga Sandhana is performed for this purpose and this is also the aim of **Kundalini Jagran**.

The awakening of chakras affects the attributes like nature and capabilities of the practioner. With the awakening, the Yogi feels in him the circulation of a new power, increased stamina and courage. Awakening may also be in the form of raised creativity, increased sensitivities and feeling of exhilaration.

The **Aagya-chakra** is said to be the production centre of Sahasraar. All the chakras are situated in the **Sushumna** (spinal cord) and they impact upon the **Naadi** (nerve) system.

Soham japa, Shakti-chalini mudra, Tra-tak, Naad-yog, Bindu-Shadhna are some of practices done for awakening of Kundalini. Further, **Anulom-vilom, Surya Bedhan and Pranaayam** have to be mastered for the above.

The chakras situated on lower part are connected with the bodily functions and the chakras situated in upper part of body are connected with knowledge and wisdom. By concentrating and stabilizing the Pran at Sahasrar chakra, one can go into Samadhi stage. Chakra is the place of **pure chetna** and **param-anand**. All the nerves, situated on both side of backbone, pass parallel. The left Naadi is called "Ida" and right Naadi is called "Pingla" and the Naadi passing through the central rout is called "Sushumna".

The "Ida" and "Pingla" represent the duality of life which we may call **Purush** and **Prakriti** or simply **Shiv** and **Shakti**. The awakened kundalini crossing the path situated in Sushusmna goes upwards to meet Param-shiv in Sahisraar chakra. Wherever these three Naadis meet, they form the **Shatchakras** which are called **Brahma-randhra**, which are the centers of life elements. The lotus petals are the symbols of chakras. The number of lotus petals depends upon the Naadi's joining there. In meditation, the Yogis pronounce "Om" mantra. The Shath-chakras have been defined in many scriptures and require help of Guru to practice them properly.

Based on the above it is concluded that the modernity should come from antiquity but keep improving the antiquity and become modern (Dr. B.M Hegde).

SNAAN (BATH) AND TARPAN (OBLATION): The **Shuddhi** (purification) is of two types: outer and inner. Water purifies the outer body whereas inner part is purified by the **Atma-chintan** (purification of thought and mind). The outer bath is considered important for purification (13/6-9). "The body having nine holes, discharges refuses day and night. The body is purified by taking daily bath in the morning and this is called **Nitya** (daily) **Snaan**". It is said that people taking morning bath receive ten benefits: cleanliness, beauty, aura, strength, purity, health, greedlesness, and freedom from bad dreams, Tapa and wisdom. After taking bath, one should perform Tarpan to Deities, Rishis and Pitr.

The second is called the **Naimattik snaan** (bath for a particular purpose in mind) to be taken at a particular occasion and purpose. The third is called **Kaamya-snan** taken for the fulfillment of a wish. However, persons who are unwell should avoid bath (Mansamurti-4/129). Those unable to take bath or who reside in cold places should take bath below the neck or should clean the body with a wet cloth. Particularly when taking bath in a holy river, in pilgrim places or in the open place, one should not remain naked. Similarly, keep the bathing place clean so that the next bathing person finds the place cleaner than the one you received. Safety of your body and also of others while taking bath in river or other places should also be kept in mind.

In addition to these main baths, there are some minor baths which can be taken without the use of water (Daksh-2/48).Under the **'Brahmn or Mantra'** bath one may utter **'Aapo Hishtha or Atineel Ghanshyamam'** mantras while sprinkling some drops of water on the body.

In addition, **Aag-ney** (pasting ashes on the body), **Parthiv** (by rubbing soil on body),**Vaayavya** (by cow dust), **Divya** (by sun rays) and **Yogik** (bath by remembering the Hari) are other types of baths for purification.

BRAHMIN, VIPRA, DVIJ: These words have frequently been used in this Puran, however, meaning of words may change according to specific context. The words Dvij denotes a noble person who has gone through **Upanayana Sanskaar** (sacred thread ceremony);**Vipra** denotes the knower of Veda-Shastra, educated or simply a thinker; Brahmin connotes to the one involved in worship of Ishwara, or rituals, professing Purohitai, priest, or one who has attained self realization and so on. These words have been used mainly for those who are devoted to Ishwara. Therefore, there is no provision of Daan to a Brahmin, who is without **Dwijatav** (knowledge of Vedas). In Manusmruti, six tasks have been assigned to the Brahmins – Swadhyay (self study and recitation of Vedas or one's own reading), teaching others, to perform Yagya himself and get it performed by others, to take Daan himself and to give Daan to others. The three tasks- to teach, get Yagya performed and to take Daan, are for livelihood. To study, to perform Yagya and to give Daan-these three tasks are actions on the part of a Brahmin (Manu-1/88). There are strict rules for Brahmins regarding type of food for intake. However, non-Brahmins have been given relaxations regarding intake of food and general discipline in living.

In Purans, the word "Brahmin" has been used for a highly educated person who understands the Vedas, perform Sandhya, carries out daily worship, who is without greed and is principled one and of good character; whose life is controlled by **Yam-Niyam**. These are also the qualities which entitle the Brahmin to receive Daan and perform worship. It is said that the Brahmin having above attributes is sure to achieve Mokshya for himself and also Yajmaan. Due to these characteristics, the Brahmin should be honored and respected.

LIFE MANTRA IN GARUD PURAN: Garud Puran gives the mantra for good life and says that one should lead a controlled life, keep healthy, acquire knowledge, remain alert, keep clean, wear clean cloths, observe fasting on Ekadashi, uphold Dharma, keep Tulsi plant at home, reverence for temples and devotion to Ishwara and Devas, respect for parents, Gurus, Dharmika, Children and women. Various ways have been described in Vedic scriptures to reduce the accumulated Paap which include acceptance of one's guilt for the Paap done, repentance, Japa of Omkar, Pranaayam, Tapa, Homa, Daan, fasting and pilgrimage.

TEERTHATAN (PILGRIMAGE): Teerth are the places which represent purity, calmness, holiness and bring positive change in people. Teerths are holy place in the banks of Ganga, Yamuna, Godavari, Saraswati, Narmada, Sindhu, Kaveri, etc., and the places associated with Bhagwan Shiv, Bhagwan Vishnu (Shri Ram and Krishna) and Bhagwati Durga. The important places are like Haridwar, Kashi, Prayag, Gagansagar, Gaya, Kurukshetra,

Mathura-Vrindavan, Puri-Jagannath, Pandarpur, Padmanabha, Sabarimala, Dakshineswar, Somnath, Ujjain, Dwarika, Kamakhya, Tirupati, Ayodhya, Mansarovar, Vaishno Devi and many other places are listed in various scriptures including Garud Puran. A large number of new temples have come up in various countries and there are also major rivers in those countries each of them are holy to Hindus. (9.27)

Ishwara is kind and merciful to all creatures, He does not harm or punish anyone as He is the ocean of compassion (Karuna-sagar) you must not fear anyone but your deeds, you are the master of your destiny.

DESH-KAAL AND SOCIAL CHANGES: The Sanatan Dharma prescribes that consideration of the traditions of a country, changing times and the situation should be kept in mind while observing the morals and other rules (Manusmriti 7/10 and 7/16). This ensures that every personal law should be in tune with present constitution of that society and environmental laws. Thus, social practices get modified according to time and Sanatan Dharma accepts that. For example, in view of environmental pollution there is a restriction on immersing of dead bodies in the rivers. Similarly, there is a shortage of wood for cremation. The Environmental Pollution Acts, particularly in the western countries, are very strict and the Hindus reside in almost every part of the world today. Fortunately, the Vedic Dharma is open for assimilation of these changes and rather encourages it.

A place for logic and rationality is what makes the Sanatan Dharma a living Dharma which is ever evolving with passing time. **This makes the Sanatan Dharma a most ancient as well as the most modern Dharma.**

EAKAM SAT VIPRA BAHUDHA VADANTI: In Sanatan Dharma, the concept of Ishwara is all-encompassing. It is not polytheistic rather, there are many paths prescribed to reach the one and only Brahmn; The Vedic hymn which says **"Eakam sat vipra bahudha vadanti** - truth is one but the wise speak of it in different ways"- makes Sanatan Dharma the most evolved, most liberal Dharma of all times. Looking superficially, one may find the different manifestation of this Brahmn or Ishwara with various attributes, may find 33 deities, endless mythological stories and so on but deeper one goes, one finds a divine, a matchless and a sublime Darshan layered in such a way that it can take one, step by step, to divinity having answers to all ones' queries. It is not a philosophy but Darshan, meaning what was witnessed by the seers. Brahmn (not Brahmaa-Dev) is an abstract reality but since it is not possible to connect with the abstract, human mind being limited. Thus the need for manifestation in the form of Shiv, Vishnu and Devi. We believe in a Murti Pooja of these manifestations in Murti where Pran-pratistha (consecration) has been done through Mantras. Our Bhagwan are also not someone living in unknown world but stay with us and are like mother, father having family just like us humans. It is because human beings can connect only with what is known to them and not the unknown ones therefore, these manifestations.

The worship of Lord Vishnu in the form of Shaligram and Shiv in the form of Shiv Lingam, as universal micro symbol for concentration, are only the effort to bring down limitless to something that is approachable to human capabilities. At the same time, the faith and devotion of one can bring down Ishwara as Bhagwan incarnated in these Murtis. This is a question of the intensity of devotion by individuals which leads to realization. Sanatan Dharma is a **Saadhanaa Dharma** where Ishwara has to be realized by individuals, something invisible, therefore, the Murti helps. Therefore, it is said; **Jaaki Rahi Bhagwana Jaisi; Prabhu moorat dekhe tin taisee**. It is the only way to reach abstract reality called Brahmn or Ishwara. Thus, Brahmn is the ultimate power and it manifests in the forms known as Bhagwan (Bhagwan Ram and Bhagwan Krishna and Devi Bhagwati). Bhagwan is the manifest form of Brahmn. The Devi-devtas (deities) like Surya, Hanuman, Indra, Varun, Agni are part of the 33 category (not 33 Crores) Deities who are appointed by Ishwara to run His creation. The most important touch of Ishwara is received by us every moment from these very deities in the form of energy and light from sun, in the form of life giving air from Vayu and water from Varuna and so on. Thus, say the Veda **"O Agni! Bring us radiant light to be our mighty aid, for you are our deity"** (Sava-Veda- 1.1.1). The presence of Ishwara is also felt every time and everywhere: it is in the mercy of a mother; it is in the love of a lover; in the affection of father; in the friendship of a friend; in beauty; in the creativity of art and music; in the service of the poor and needy; in every form of ecstasy; in the play of child; in Hanuman in the form of strength; in Shri Krishna having the mastery over 64 type of arts and graces; in the Maryaada of Shri Ram; in the all powerful Shri Devi **(Sarva roop mayi Devi Sarva Devi Mayam jagat)**; in form of meditation of an Yogi or in any of the forms which one can easily recognize. You are free to choose the form of the Brahmn you feel closer to your level of evolved state. It is omnipresent, beyond time and the whole creation belongs to Brahmn. **It is present in the creation and It also has a separate existence**. The Brahmn and universe is derived from Brahmand and the entire Brahmand is within the Brahmn. Thus, the Sanatan Dharma offers the freedom for personalization of Ishwara. In Sanatan Dharma, there is freedom of worship, which is mother of all freedoms. However, where Sanatan Dharma gives one freedom of thought and action it also binds human life with a regularity and discipline so that it does not disintegrate. The **Ashtang Yoga** (Yoga having eighth parts) like Yama, Niyam, etc., put control over human behavior so that one follows the path of Dharma. The Sanatan Dharma is the mother of all faiths and it also offers a complete philosophy because it is based on the

Universal Cosmic Principles. Thus comes the concept of **Vasu-Dhaiv-Kutumbakam** (entire world is a family).

SOME CONTEMPORARY ISSUES: Garud Puran emphasises to keep the place of cremation neat and clean because it is also a form of **Shradhaanjali** (homage) to the departed. Similarly, due respect must be given to the **Paarthiv Sharrir** (dead body) of the departed; it should be cleaned, kept in a neat place, properly covered, decorated with clean clothes and it should be lifted with due care and respect and the rites should also be followed as prescribed. Therefore, the changes in the method of cremation and use of electric crematorium should not be compromised on these aspects.

There had been many changes taking place in the Sanatan Hindu society for the centuries but the changes which have taken place during the last one century have been revolutionary. The old form of Varna system - Brahmin, Kshatriya, Vaish and Shudra— have almost came to an end. Today, all the earlier castes have attained equality in their attributes and functions and nobility in the morals and behavior. Moreover, the Dharma has acquired a global proportion. Therefore, it would not be out of place to treat all adherents of Dharma, whether Asian, American or African and others in one category. Today we are again marching towards the divine casteless society of the Vedic age. Let us remember what our forefathers have directed us: "Civilize the world by destroying the non-liberal and jealous ones (Rig 9.63.5).

In the present times the role of the priestly class has increased manifold. Known by different names; Purohit, Ojha, Bhagat, Guru, Pandit, Baman, Archak, Mahajan, Poojari, etc., they form the nerve centre of Dharma. How to reach out to various sections on society is a challenge before them. Devi-Bhagwat says that the aim of Puran is to reach out to Dvij, woman, out-casts, deprived, illiterate, ignorant, children and all people. Even non-Hindus should be educated about the precepts of Vedic Sanatan Dharma. Efforts may be made to bring them to Vedic fold so that no one remains deprived of the liberating Dharma —"**Alpa-ayusho alpa-buddheensh ch vipraan gyaatvaa kalaavath. Puraanaa-snhitaam punayaam kurute asau yuge-yuge. Straaee-shoodr-dvija-bandhoonaam n veda-shravanam smritam. Teshaam-ev hita-arthaay puraanaani kritaani hi**" (Devibhagwat-1/3/20,21). To bring all human beings into Sanatan Dharma and to enlighten them is the duty of all Sanatani Hindus (Gita-18/66). Dharma is not religion; in fact Dharma tradition is far more encompassing. There is no parallel word in English dictionary (or other non-Indian languages) for Dharma concepts like Atma, Karma, Darshan, Pitr, Dharma, Mokshya, Purusharth and others because they encompass a different paradigm altogether.

Swami Vivekananda (Complete works -3, Page 454-461), Swami Shivanand (Sadhna, 1985) and other Sant have given a call to all to spread the wisdom of Vedas, Puranas and Gita to all human beings without any distinction of caste, creed, religion, gender and age. But we must not convert people as it is a movement and not an organization. Sanatan Dharma is open to all; it does not belong to anyone but a Saadhana for individuals, the oldest heritage of human race.

CALL TO THE YOUTH AND DEPRIVED: In Sanatan Dharma, there is no restriction on women and persons of any caste or tribes, nationality or origin to perform the priestly functions (Hari Bhakat Vilas-1/55,5/,452,2/12), Skand Puran, Padam-Puran, Yajurved-26/2). For centuries, this Vriti has been performed by these classes. It is ordained in Rig-Veda that the women in particular should acquire the knowledge of science, Ayurveda, economics, history, grammar, glossary, astrology, arms, training, music and other discipline along with the Vedas. Rig-Veda also says that such women, who impart the above mentioned knowledge, are a fortune to the entire world and take the humanity ahead (Rig-Veda -1/

164/41). Today, time demands that the participation of deprived sections, in Priestly function, gets increased. Further, the educated class of new generation should take ahead this great heritage and accept this divine Vriti not only for their own elevation but also to fulfill the spiritual expectations of masses. Today, Sanathan Dharma needs many more Rishis, Munis, Sadhus, Sants and Gurus like Ved Vyas, Apala, Gargi, Gautama Buddha, Bhagwan Mahavir, Gyaneswar, Baba Gorakhnath, Valmiki, Tulsidas, Nanak, Adi-Shanka, Kamban, Sri Narayana Guru, Meera Bai, Basava, Kabir, Ravidas, Srila Prabhupad, Aurobindo, Dayanand Sarawasati, Sri Narayan Guru, Ramkrishan Paramhans, Akka Mahadevi, Annamacharya, Surdas, Tulsidas, Gorakhnath, Chaitnya Mahaprabhu, Kripalu Maharaj, Morari Bapu, Mata Amritanandmayi, Dadi Janki, Anandmayi Ma, Dongreji Maharaj, Ramana Maharshi and modern ascetics like Swami Ram Sukh Das, Shri Chinmayanand, Mahesh Yogi, Pramukh Swami, Baba Ramdev, Jeddu Krishnamurti, Sadguru Jaggi, Shri Shri Ravi Shankar, Mahatma Gandhi, Europeans like Schopenhauer, Henry David Thoreau, Lin Yutang the African Hindu Sants, an many others. Most importantly, Swami Vivekananda who converted the Vedic principles into modern context.

Garud Puran tells about righteous way of living and the duties of offsprings towards their ancestors, Devta and Rishis. The substance of the Garud Puran is that by performing our duties through Purusharth, while remaining unattached, we should take the refuge of Ishwara.

The object of human life is to achieve Mokshya. It is hoped that human beings will make their life purposeful by taking benefit from the profound knowledge in this Puran. **The present version is revised one, easy to understand and most authentic edition. It is**

intended not only for the narration by Priests and Purohit but also for the reading by general public.

THE PUROHIT WILL AWAKEN THE NATION: It is seen that the priestly function, which is like the nervous system of Dharma, is getting weakened. The number of persons quitting it is far more than the number of persons adopting the priestly functions. This is a fact, However, the number of followers are increasing in various continents. As a result there is erosion in the knowledge of Dharma. It is in the interest of society that this function gets strengthened, is made inclusive, accessible and the Purohits are supported by society and their capabilities are improved and diversified. On the other side, the Purohits need to develop devotion, purity, affection and Karuna for deprived section in particular and people of various countries and races in general.

Purohit is such a teacher who can help people in purifying their heart and mind and also help them for release from existential problems and strains. Dharam does not permit that someone remains deprived of the spiritual needs. Similarly, it is also necessary that the alienation of people from the Sanskaar makes the Purohit in particular and all the people in general worried. Yajurved (9/23) says **"Vayam Raashtre Jaagriyam Purohita** - we priests will keep this nation of humanity awakened and alive"**. The same should also be the objective of Priest, Purohit, Sant and Mahatmas today.

The author is indeed thankful to Shri VVSN Rao, Shri Nandu Pandey and Shri Ravi Paliya and many other people for their contribution at various stages. The author is thankful to **'Hindu Purohit Sangh'** for giving this opportunity to serve this divine vriti. A book on Garud Puran in Hindi has also been brought out by this author. The tradition of Sanatan Dharma says that the author is always Ved Vyas, therefore, writing the name of author is nothing more than a formality. What is important is to spread the greatest wisdom on earth to one and all.

The Puran is composed in Poetic form with an amazing meter and some of the Sanskrit words used are matchless. Therefore, people memorize and narrate them during their day to day conversation. Thus, neither an accurate translation is possible nor does it serve the purpose as that of Sanskrit version. Still, we need to keep improving the translation. Most of the available versions in Hindi have been referred while compiling the present revised version; however, three of them are worth mentioning: The Garud Puranam by Shivraj Acharya, Kondinnyaanan (Chaukambha, 2004) is one of the finest works on Garud Puran. Similarly, an English translation of Garud Puran carried out by Ernest Wood and S.V Subrahmanyam in 1911 is a great effort in this regard. The third one is published by Gita Press Gorakhpur. However, the current version is different in a number of ways and it is hoped that this will pave the way for proper understanding of Garud Puran.

"Bhadraah kratavah nah vishvatah aayantu- Let noble thoughts come to us from all sides."

"Aa ! Nah bhadraah kratavah vishvatah yantu- Let our noble thoughts spread across the universe."

(Rig-veda 1.89.1)

Hira Ballabh Joshi
C/O Sh.Prakash Joshi
Jagdamba Market, At&P.O.Devidhura
Distt. Champawat (Uttrakhand) PIN-262 580
Mobile:9811756450 Email:-hiraballabh@hotmail.com

──────────**Hari Om Tat-Sat**──────────

ॐ(Om) Vishnave Namah
ॐ(Om) Shri Krishnaay Namah
(Invocation for successful recitation of Garud Puraan)

**Naaraayanam namas-kritya naram chaiv nar-ottamam,
Deveem sarasvateem vyaasam tato jaya-maudeerayet.**

We recite Garud Puraan after paying reverence to Bhagwan Vishnu (Ishwar or God), Devi (Goddess) Saraswati and Ved Vyas, who bestow victory on us. May Ishwara bless us for the successful recitation of this Puraan.

**Annadi-nidhano Devah Shankh Chakra Gadaa-dharah,
Akshayah pundreeka-akash Preta-mokshya-prado-bhav.**

May Bhagwan Vishnu, who is without beginning or end, one who is adorned with **Shankh** (Conch), **Chakra** (disc) **Gadaa** (club) & **Padma** (Lotus), (symbolizing sound, time, energy and beauty). Become giver of Mokhsya to the departed.

1

CHAPTER 1

THE DEEDS LEADING TO SWARGA AND NARAK, OFFERING OF PIND AND FORMATION OF BODY, AN ACCOUNT OF THE TERRI-FYING TORMENTS EXPERIENCED BY THE PAAPI (SINNER) DUR-ING JOURNEY TO YAMA-LOK (REALM OF YAMA) AND NARRATION OF MISERIES OF THE PAAPIS ON THIS EARTH AND IN THE PARLOK (OTHER-WORLD) AND SO ON.

Dharma-dridha-baddha-moolo veda-skandhah Puraanaa-shaakhaadhyah,
Kratu-kusumo moksha-falo madhu-soodana-paadapo jayati(1)
Naimishe-animisha-kshetre rishayah shaunaka-adayah,
Satraam svargaay lokaay sahstra-sama-maasat(2)
Ekadaa munayah sarve praatar-hutahut-aagnayah,
Sat-kritam sootama-aseenam paprachchhuridama-adaraat(3)

The great Rishi (sage) Ved Vyas says that **Bhagwan Vishnu** (a form of the ultimate reality, the Ishwara, i.e., the Brahmn) is like the **Kalp-vriksha** (wish-fulfilling divine tree). The roots of Kalp-Vriksha have been strengthened by the grandeur of Dharma; the four Vedas are like the trunk and the tree is decorated by the branches of Puraanas. **Yagya** offerings, invocation and prayers are like the flowers of this tree and **'Mokshya'** (to become one with Ishwara on Mokshya from the cycle of birth and death called Sansaar) is the fruit of this Kalp-vriksha. We bow at the lotus feet of such a 'Madhu-sudana' (Bhagwan Vishnu).(1) With a view to attain Swarga, Rishi Shaunak and other Rishis performed a Yagya, lasting thousands of years at **Naimi-sharnya** (holy place related to Bhagwan Vishnu). (2) Once, in the morning, having completed the **Havan** (oblations to Ishwara through offerings made on sacrificial fire), the Rishis respectfully asked the revered Rishi Soot, who was adorning the presidential seat; (3)

2

RISHAY OOCHUAH

Kathito bhavataa samyag-deva-maargah sukha-pradah,
Idaaneem shrotum-ichchhaamo yama-maargm bhaya-pradam(4)
Tathaa snsaara-dukhaani tat-klesha-kshaya-saadhanam,
Aihika-amushmikaan kleshaan yathaa-vad vaktumarhasi(5)

SOOT UVAACH

Shrunaudhvm bho! Vivakshyaami yama-maargm su-durgamam,
Sukhadm punaya-sheelaanaam paapinaam dukhadaayakam(6)
Yathaa shreevishnaunaa proktm vainateyaay prichchhate,
Tathaiv kathayishyaami sandeha-ch-chhedanaay vah(7)
Kadaachit sukham-aaseenm vaikunathm shree-harim gurum,
Vinaya-avanato bhootvaa paprachchh vinataa-sutah(8)

GARUD UVAACH

Bhakti-maargo bahu-vidhah kathito bhavataa mam,
Tathaa ch kathitaa dev! Bhaktaanaam gatir-uttamaa(9)
Adhunaa shrotum-ichchhaami yama-maargm bhayankram,
Tvad-bhakti-vimukhaanaam ch tatrauv gamanm shrutam(10)

RISHIS SAID-"O revered Soot! You have deliberated on the path leading to Divinity. We now wish to hear about the fearful **Yama-marg** (Path to Yama-lok). (4) Also, please tell us about the miseries associated with **Sansaar** (cyclical change in the universe through creation, destruction and recreation, i.e., birth, death and rebirth of animate and inanimate), and how to overcome that and also tell about the afflictions in this world and the other. (5) **RISHI SOOT SAID**-Oh Rishies! Listen! The Yama-marg is very arduous to tread; pleasant for the virtuous whereas it is miserable for the Paapi. (6) In fact, the same question was once asked to Bhagwan Vishnu by Garuda, his **Vaahan** (celestial chariot). In order to remove your doubts, I repeat the discourse delivered by Shri Vishnu to that very question. (7) Once, when the supreme Guru Vishnu was sitting at ease in **Vaikunth** (abode of Vishnu), Garuda, the son of Vinta, very politely asked; (8) **GARUD SAID** -"O Bhagwan! You have described to me various paths of devotion and also told me about the supreme attainments of the devotees. (9) Now, I wish to hear about the fearful Yama-marg. I have heard that those who are not devoted to You, go to that Yama-marg. (10)

Sugamam bhagavan-naam jihvaa ch vasha-vartinee,
Tathaapi narakm yaanti dhig dhigastu nara-adhamaan(11)
Ato me bhagavan! Broohi paapinaam yaa gatir-bhavet,
Yama-maargasy dukhaani yathaa te praapnuvanti hi(12)

SHREE BHAGAVAAN-UVAACH

Vaksye-ahm shrunau pakshe-endra yama-maargm ch yen ye,
Narake paapino yaanti shrunavataamapi bheetidam(13)
Ye hi paapa-rataas taarkashya dayaa-dharma-vi-varjitaah,
Dushta-sngaash-ch sach-chhaasatra-sat-sangti-paraan-mukhaah(14)
Aatma-smbhaavitaah stabdhaa dhana-maana-mada-anvitaah,
Aasurm bhaavamaapannaa daivee-sampad-vi-varjitaah(15)
Aneka-chitta-vibhraantaa   moha-jaala-sama-avritaah,
Prasaktaah kaama-bhogeshu patanti narake-ashuchao(16)
Ye naraa gyaana-sheelaash-ch te yaanti paramaam gatim,
Paapa-sheelaa naraa yaanti dukhen yama-yaatanaam(17)
Paapinaam-aihikm dukhm yathaa bhavati tach-chhrinau,
Tat-aste maranam praapy yathaa gachchhanti yaatanaam(18]

Chanting Your Name is very easy and simple and the tongue is also under our control, yet people go to the Narak. Such type of wretched people are ought to be condemned repeatedly. (11) Therefore, O Bhagwan, tell me as to what fate the Paapi meet and also in what way they suffer the miseries on their Yam-marg. (12) **BHAGWAN SAID-** Listen, O king of Birds, the path through which Paapi go to **Yama-loka** (realm of Yama) is terrifying even to the listeners. Now, listen about the Yama-marg. (13) Those who indulge in sinful misdeeds, devoid of Dayaa (compassion) and Dharma, are in bad company and those who are averse to the **'Shastra'** (holy scriptures) and the company of pious people, (14) People, who are full of vanity, intoxicated with the arrogance of wealth and vanity, having demonic attitude and are devoid of divine attributes. (15) With fickle mindedness due to lustful thoughts, enveloped in the web of **Maya** (delusion pronounced as Maya), reveling in the enjoyments of lust, such type of people fall into impure Narak. (16) People who are seekers of wisdom get Mokshya; and those who are Paapi, face the miserable torments of Yama. (17) Listen, how the Paapi encounters the miseries in this world. The type of torments one faces after passing through death, listen to all that also. (18)

Sukritm dushkritm vaa-api bhuktvaa poorvm yathaa-arjitam,
Karma yogaat-tadaa tasy kashchid vyaadhiah prajaayate(19)
Aadhi-vyaadhi-samaayuktm   jeevitaashaasam-utsukam,
Kaalo baleeyaan-ahi vad-agyaatah prati-padyate(20)
Yatra-apyajaata-nir-vedo mriya-maanaah svayam-bhritaiah,
Jarayopaatta-vairoopyo marana-abhi-mukho grihe(21)
Aaste-avamatyopanyastm   griha-paal   ivaaharan,
Aamayaavya-pradeepta-agnir-alpa-ahaaro-alpa-chestitah(22)
Vaayunot-kramatottaarah   kafa-sanruddha-naadaikah,
Kaas-shvaasa-kritaayaasah kanathe ghur-ghuraayate(23)
Shayaanah pari-shocha-adibhiah pari-veetah sva-bandhubhiah,
Vaachyamaano-api n broote kaala-paasha-vashngatah(24)
Evm   kutamba-bharanae   vyaapritaatmaa-ajitendriyah,
Mriyate rudataam svaanaamuruvedanayaastadheeah(25)
Tasmin-ant-kshanae taarkshaya daivee dristiah prajaayate,
Ekee-bhootm jagat-sarvm n kinchid-vktum-eehate(26)

In accordance with good or bad **Karma** (deeds) of human beings during their previous life, they get some disease. (19) Despite being stricken with physical and mental diseases, the desire to live, remains ardent. But the person is unexpectedly poached by the powerful death, like the sudden bite of a serpent. (20) Nearing death and till the last moment - with body deformed due to old age and being cared for by dependents living in his house – one is not tired of life; (21) Diseased, with failing digestion, poor appetite and diminished craving, eating what is ungraciously placed before, dependent like a house-dog and being humiliated in the old age; (22) At the time of death, with death rattling in throat, eyes of the Paapi open up through loss of vitality, throat obstructed by phlegm and exhausted by coughing and difficult breathing; (23) Lying encircled by grieving relatives, being caught in the **'Kaal-pash'** (noose of death) one is unable to speak despite the desire to speak. (24) Mind occupied by the concerns to support the family, with senses unconquered, fainting with intense pain, dies listening to the lamentation of relatives. (25) In these last moments, O Taarkshya, one attains a divine vision by virtue of which the whole world appears to be as one but he is unable to express anything. (26)

Vikal-endriya-snghaate   chaitanye   jadataam   gate,
Prachalanti tatah praanaa yaamyair-nikatavartibhiah(27)
Sva-sthaanaach-chalite shvaase kalpa-akhyo hyaatura-kshanaah,
Shata-vrishchika-danshtrasy yaa peedaa saa-anubhooyate(28)
Fenamudgirate   so-ath   mukhm   laalaakulm   bhavet
Adho-dvaarena gachchhanti paapinaam praanaa-vaayavah(29)
Yama-dootau tadaa praaptau bheemau sarabhase kshanaau,
Paasha-danada-dharau nagnau dantaiah kata-kataayitau(30)
Oordhva-keshau kaaka-krishnaau vakra-tunadau nakha-ayudhau,
Taan drishtvaa trasta-hridayah sakrin-mootram vimuchti[31]
Angustha-maatrah purusho haa haa kurvan kalevaraat,
Tadaiv grihyate dootair-yaamyaiah pashyan svakm graham(32)
Yaatanaa-deham-aavrity paashair-baddhvaa gale balaat,
Nayato deerghama-dhvaanm danadaym raaja-bhataa yathaa(33)
Tasy-aivm neeyamaanasy dootaah santarjayanti ch,
Pravadanti bhaym teevrm narakaanaam punah punah(34)
Sheeghrm prachal dushta-atman yaasy-asi tvm yama-alayam,
Kumbhee-paaka-adi-narakaans-tvaam nayaavo- Ady maa chiram(35)

At the time of death, when all the senses are decayed and with the numbing of the consciousness, the **Yama-doot** (messengers of Yamraj) approach and the life departs. (27) When the breath is fading away, even a moment is felt like an era and pain is felt like the stinging of hundred scorpions. (28) During this time, mouth is filled with saliva and one emits foam. The **Pranvaayu** (vital breath) of the Paapi departs from the lower openings. (29) Then, two terrifying naked Yama-doots appear, grinding their teeth with rage while holding nooses and rods. (30) With hair erect, dark like crows, ugly faces, having nails as their weapons; on seeing them the heart palpitates and the Paapi releases excrements due to fear. (31) Crying loudly, the person is relived of the physical body and acquires new body, the size of a thumb **(Yaatanaa-deh)**. Caught by the Yama-doots he looks at his home with attachment. (32) This **Yatanaa-deh** (thumb sized body) which is formed for torments, is bound by the noose around the neck by the Yama-doots and they forcibly drag it through the long way, like a king's soldiers drag a convict. (33) On this long path, though the Paapi is completely tired, yet the Yama-doots keep on terrorizing Paapi by telling accounts of Narak again and again and say: (34) "Hurry up, you wicked. From here, you shall go to the abode of Yama. Thereafter, we will lead you, without delay, to "Kumbhi-paak" and the other Narak". (35)

6

Evm vaachas-tadaa shrunavan bandhoonaam ruditm tathaa,
Uchchair-haa-heti vilapns-taadayate yama-kinkraiah(36)
Tayor-nirbhinnahridayastarjanairjaatavepathuah,
Pathi shvbhir-bhaksyamaana aarto-aghm sva-manu-smaran(37)
Kshuttritpareeto-arka-daavaanal-aanilaih-santapyamaanah pathi-tapta-baaluke,
Krichchherna pristhe kashayaa ch taadaitshchlatya-shakto-api nir-aashra-modake(38)
Tatraa tatraa patnchhraanto moorchachhatah punar-utthitah,
Yathaa paapeeyasaa neetastamasaa yama-saadanam(39)
Tribhir-muhoortair-dvaabhyaam vaa neeyate tatraa maanavah,
Pradarshayanti dootaastaah ghoraa naraka-yaatanaah(40)
Muhoorta-maatraat tvaritm yamm veeksy bhaym pumaan,
Yama-agyayaa samm dootaiah punaraayaati khecharah(41)
Aagamy vaasanaa-baddho deham-ichchhan yama-anugaiah,
Dhritah paashen rudati kshut-tridabhyaam pari-peedaitah(42)
Bhunkte pindam sutair-dattm daanm chaatura-kaalikam,
Tathaapi naastikas-taarkshyaa tripnit yaati n paatakee(43)

Hearing these words of Yama-doots and the sobbing of relatives, the 'Pret' also starts crying loudly but the Yama-doots rebuke him repeatedly. (36) With failing heart and trembling at their threats, bitten by dogs on the way, the afflicted, recollects his misdeeds. (37) Distressed by hunger and thirst, burning in the sun, harmed by forest-fires and hot winds, flogged on the back, Paapi is feeble but forced to walk on the shelter-less and water-less path of burning sand. (38) On this path, exhausted and thus fainting here and there, Paapi rises again and again. In this way, in a miserable condition he is led through the darkness by Yama-doots to the abode of Yama. (39) Taking the Paapi to the Yama-loka for two to three **Muhurt** (a time scale wherein one Muhurt is equal to 48 minutes), the Yama-doots show him the terrible torments of Narak. (40) Within a Muhurt of seeing the appearance of Yama and the fearful torments, the departed, by command of Yama along with Yam-doots, swiftly comes back to his house through the areal root. (41) Having returned, bound by unfulfilled desires, Paapi wants to enter into the dead body again but being tied with a noose by the Yama-doots and tortured by hunger and thirst, he weeps. (42) The Paapi and the **Nastik** (those who do not accept authority of Vedas, and have no faith in Atma and Paramaatma) are not gratified by eating the Pind (made of cooked rice and barley flour balls mixed with Ghee and black sesame seeds, etc., given by s**ons** (the word 'son' denotes to both daughter and son) and the **Daan** (charity or benevolent alms; virtuous donations) made at the time of the death. (43)

7

Paapinaam nopatisthanti daanm shraaddhm jalaanjliah,
Atah ksud-vyaakulaa yaanti pindadaanabhujo-api te(44]
Bhavanti   preta-roopaaste   pinda-daana-vivarjitaah
Aakalpm nirjan-aaranaye bhramanti bahu-duhkhitaa(45]
Naabhuktm   ksheeyate   karm   kalpa-koti-shatairapi,
Abhuktvaa yaatanaam jantur-maanushym labhate n hi(46)
Ato dadyaat-sutah pindaan dineshu dashasu dvij,
Pratyahm te vibhaajyante chaturbhaagaiah khagottam(47)
Bhaagadvaym tu dehasy pushtidm bhootapanchake,
Triteeym yama-dootaanaam chaturthm sopajeevati(48)
Ahoraatraishch navabhiah pretah pindamvaapnuyaat,
Jantur-nispannadehshcha dashame balmaapnuyaat(49)
Dagdhe   dehe   punar-dehah   pindairutpadyate   khag,
Hastmaatraah pumaan yen pathi bhunkte shubha-ashubham(50)

The Daan offered at the time of death, Shraddh performed
and the **Jalanjali** (offering oblation of water from both
hands), do not reach the Paapi. Therefore, not having
received the Pind-daan, etc., he suffers with never
satisfying torturous hunger. (44) Due to non-receipt of
Pind, one becomes **Pret** (wandering spirit with unfulfilled
desires) and wanders about in great misery, in an
uninhabited forest, until the end of an era. (45) The
consequences of Karma will have to be faced. Past karma,
if not experienced, do not fade away even in thousands
of millions of ages; it is for certain that the one who has
not experienced the consequences of bad deeds of past
in the form of torments, does not obtain human form
through rebirth, this is for certain. (46) The son should
offer Pind for ten days from the date of death. Every day
these are divided into four portions, O Supreme Bird.
(47) Out of these four portions, two parts of Pind give
nourishment to the physical body consisting of Panch-
bhoot (five elements); the third goes to the Yama-doots;
the Pret lives upon the fourth. (48) In this way, after
offering Pind for nine days, the body of Pret is formed.
From the Pind of the tenth day, the body gains strength to
walk. (49) Once the old body is consigned to flames, a new
body of the size of a hand is formed and it is through this
body that the departed experiences the consequences of
good and evil Karma. (50)

8

Prathame-ahani yah pindasten moordhaa prajaayate,
Greevaa-skandhau dviteeyen triteeyaad hridaym bhavet(51)
Chaturthe tu bhavet pristhm panchmaan-naabhirev ch,
Shasthe ch saptame chaiv katir-guhym prajaayate(52)
Oorush-ch-aashtame chaiv jaanvanghree navame tathaa,
Navabhirdehmaasaady dashame-ahain kshudhaa trishaa(53)
Pindajm deham-aashrity ksudhaa-vishtas-trisaarditah,
Ekaadashm dvaadashm ch preto bhunkte din-dvayam(54)
Traayodashe-ahani preto yantriaato yama-kinkraih,
Tasmin maarge vrajaty-eko griheet iv markatah(55)
Shadasheeti-sahstraanai yojanaanaam pramaanatah,
Yama-maargasy vistaaro vinaa vaitaranaeem khag(56)
Ahanyahani vai preto yojanaanaam shatadvayam,
Chatvaarimshat tathaa sapt divaa-raatrena gachchhati(57)
Ateety kramasho maarge puraanaeemaani sodash,
Prayaati dharmaraajasy bhavanm paatakee janah(58)

From the offering of Pind of the first day, the head is-formed; the neck and shoulders by the second day's offerings; heart is formed by the third day's offerings. (51) By the offerings of the fourth day, the back is formed; by the fifth, the navel; by the sixth day, the waist, while the private parts are formed by the seventh day's offerings. (52) Likewise, the knees, by eighth day's offerings; feet, by ninth day's and hunger and thirst are formed from tenth day's Pind offerings. (53) In this way, dwelling in the body which is formed by offering the Pind, very hungry and thirsty, the departed eats on both the eleventh and twelfth days' offerings. (54) On the thirteenth day, the Pret, bound by the Yama-doots, walks alone on the path to Yama, like a captured monkey tied with a rope, goes with its owner. (55) The extent of the path leading to Yama measures eighty-six thousand **Yojan** (unit for measurement of distance) excluding the length of Vaitaranee river, O Bird. (56) The Pret travels two hundred Yojan each day. Walking day and night, he reaches Yamlok in 47 days. (57) Having passed through these sixteen **Puris** (cities) on the way, the Paapi goes to the place of the **Dharam-raaj** (due to his judicious approach Yama-raj is known as Dharam-raaj i.e., upholder of Dharma). (58)

9

Saumym sauripuram Nagendrabhavanm Gandharva-Shailaagamau
Kraunchm Kroorapuram Vichitraa-bhavanm Bahvaapadm Duhkhadam,
Naanaakranda-puram Sutapta-bhavanm Raudrm Payo-varsanam
Sheetaadhym Bahubheeti Dharma-bhavanm Yaamym puram chaagratah(59)
Yaamya-paashair-dhritah paapee haaheti prarudan pathi,
Svagrihm tu parityajy puram yaamya-manu-vrajet(60)

The sixteen cities on the way to the abode of Yama
are- Saumya-pur, Sauri-pur, Nagendra-bhavan,
Gandharv-pur, Shailagam, Kraunch-pur, Karura-pur,
Vichitr-bhavan, Bahwapad-pur, Dukhad-pur,
Nanakrand-pur, Sutapt-bhavan, Raudra-pur,
Payovarshan-pur, Shitadhya-pur, Bahubhiti-pur. After
traversing through these 16 cities, the Pret comes to
the abode of Dharam-raaj. (59) Having left his own
house and held by the noose of Yama, the crying Paapi
reaches the city of Yama. (60)

**Annadi-nidhano Devah Shankh Chakra Gadaa-dharah,
Akshayah pundree-kaakash Preta-mokshya-prado-bhav.**

* * *

10

CHAPTER 2

ENTRY INTO THE SIXTEEN PURIS (CITIES) LEADING TO YAM-LOK, THE AGONIZING VAITARNEE RIVER, TORMENTS OF YAM-LOK, OFFERING OF PIND, ETC.

GARUD UVAACH

Keedrisho yamlokasy panthaa bhavati duhkhadah,
Tatra yaanti yathaa paapaastanme kathay keshav!(1)

SHREE-BHAGAVAANUVAACH

Yama-maargm mahad-duhkhapradm te kathayaamyaham,
Mam bhakto-api tachchhrutvaa tvam bhavisyasi kampitah(2)
Vriksha-chchhaayaa n tatraasti yatra vishramate narah,
Yasmin maarge n chaannaadym yen praanaan samuddharet(3)
N jalm drishyante kvaapi trishito-ateev yah pibet,
Tapyante dvaadash-aadityaah pralayaante yathaa khag(4)
Tasmin gachchhati paapaatmaa sheeta-vaaten peedaitah,
Kanatakair-vidhyate kvaapi kvachit-sarpair-mahaavisaiah(5)
Singhai-vryaaghraiah shvbhir-ghorair-bhaksyate kvaapi paapakrit,
Vrishchikair-dnshyate kva-api kvachid-dahyati vahinnaa(6)

GARUD SAID -O Keshav! Please tell me in what way the **Yam-marg** (path to Yama) is miserable and what befalls upon the Paapi (Paapi)? (1) **BHAGWAN SAID-** The path of Yama is full of harsh misery which I will narrate to you. You will be terrified upon hearing it even though you are my devotee. (2) On that path, there is no shade of trees where one could take shelter from the scorching sun and neither there is foodstuff available to support. (3) On this path, thirst cannot be quenched as water is not even visible anywhere. Twelve suns blaze, O Bird, as though it is **Pralay** (doomsday). (4) On this path, the Paapi's Atma is pierced by cold wind and sometimes torn by thorns while sometimes stung by extremely venomous serpents. (5) While walking on this path, the Paapi is attacked by ferocious lions, tigers and dogs; stung by scorpions and is burnt by fire. (6)

11

Tatah   kvachin-mahaaghora-masipatravanm   mahat,
Yojanaanaam sahstre dve vistaaraayaamatah smritam(7)
Kaak-olooka-vata-gridhra-saraighaa-dnsha-snkulam,
Sadaavaagni ch tat-patraish-chhinna-bhinnah prajaayate(8)
Kvachit pataty-andh-koope vikataat parvataat kvachit,
Gachchhate ksuradhaaraasu shanku-naam-upari kvachit(9)
Skhalatyandhe   tamasyugre   jale   nipatati   kvachit,
Kvachit pankajalaukaadhye kvachit-santapta-kardame(10)
Santapta-baalukaa-keernae dhmaatataamramaye kvachit,
Kvachid-angara-raashau ch mahaadhoomaakule kvachit(11)
Kvachid-anaara-vristishch   shilaa-vristiah   savajrakaa,
Rakta-vristiah shastr-vristiah kvachid-usnaambuvarshanaam(12)
Kshaara-kardama-vristishch mahaa-nimnaani ch kvachit,
Vaprapr-arohanam kvaapi kandareshu praveshanam(13)
Gaadha-andhakaaras-tatra-asti dukha-aroha-shilaah kvachit,
Pooya-shonaita-poornaashch visthaa-poornahndaah kvachit(14)

Walking ahead, the Paapi reaches the terribly dense forest named "**Asipatra Van**" (having trees with sword-like leaves) spread over two thousand Yojan. (7) This forest is infested with crows, owls, hawks, vultures, bees, mosquitoes, etc., and burning wildfires. The Paapi is pierced and torn by sharp leaves. (8) In some places, Paapi falls into the Narak known as '**Andhkoop**' (dark pit) while in other places, falls from a rugged mountain; has to tread on razor-edge and on spear-points from place to place. (9) Occasionally, the Paapi enters into awfully dark Narak where sometimes stumbles into water; sometimes falls in mud abounding in parasites and sometimes falls into a Narak named as '**Santapt Kardum**' (hot slime). (10) On this path, the Paapi, at certain junctures, falls into a Narak full of hot sand; sometimes falls into a spot as hot as smelted copper on the fire; in some place, falls on a mound of embers; somewhere, in a spot full of heavy cloud of smoke. (11) The Paapi have to bear the downpour of charcoal, stones and thunderbolts, rain of blood, weapons, rain of boiling water. (12) On this path, sometimes the Paapi has to face rain of caustic mud; in some places, enters into deep chasm; sometimes, has to climb hills and sometimes, finds himself in mountain caves. (13) There is pitch darkness on the path with huge rocks at places. It is miserable for Paapi to climb over these rocks as there are ponds filled with pus, blood and excrement. (14)

Maarga-madhye vahatyugraa ghoraa vaitaranaee nadee,
Saa drishtvaa dukhadaa kim vaa yasyaa vaartaa bhayaavahaa(15)
Shata-yojana-visteernaa   pooya-shonaita-vaahinee,
Asthi-vrinda-tataa durga maansa-shonaita-kardamaa(16)
Agaadhaa dustaraa paapaiah kesha-shaivaala-durgamaa,
Mahaa-graaha-samaakeernaa ghora-pakshi-shatairvritaa(17)
Aagatm paapinm drishtvaa jvaalaa-dhooma-samaakulaa,
Kvathyate saa nadee taarkshyaa kataahaantarghritm yathaa(18)
Krimibhiah snkulaa ghoraiah soochivaktrauah samantatah,
Vajra-tunadair-mahaa-gridhrair-vaayasaiah parivaaritaa(19)
Shishumaaraishch makarair-jalaukaa-matsya-kachchhapaiah,
Anyair-jalasthair-jeevaishch pooritaa maansa-bhedakaiah(20)
Patitaastat-pravaahe   ch   krandanti   bahupaapinah,
Haa bhraatah haa bhraatah putra! Taateti pralapanti muhurmuhuah(21)
Kshudhitaas-trishitaah paapaah pibanti kil shonaitam,
Saa   sarid-rudhiraa-poorm   vahantee   fenilm   bahu(22)
Mahaa-ghora-ati-garjantee dur-nireekshyaa bhayaavahaa,
Tasyaa darshana-maatren paapaah syurgata-chetanaah(23)
Bahu-vrishchika-snkeernaa   sevitaa   krisnaapannagaiah,
Tanmadhye patitaanaam ch traataa ko-api n vidyate(24)

In the midst of the path flows the dreadfully ferocious Vaitarnee river whose mere sight inflicts misery and even the talk of it arouses fear. (15) It is a stream of pus and blood extending to a hundred Yojan. Heaps of bones, flesh and mud full of blood are on its banks. (16) For the Paapi, the river is awfully unbearable as it is obstructed with hairy moss, infested with huge crocodiles and where hundreds of dreadful birds circle overhead from all directions. (17) On seeing the Paapi approaching, this river overspreads itself with flames and smoke is like butter when poured on a hot frying-pan. (18) The river is infested with throngs of insects having piercing stings, huge predators and crows having sharp beaks. (19) It is filled with porcupines, crocodiles, leeches, fishes and turtles and other flesh-eating water based creatures. (20) The Paapi, fall into the river and keep on crying. "Oh Brother, Oh Son! Oh Father!" and keeps on wailing again and again. (21) Due to hunger and thirst, the Paapi drink the bloody stream in which muck, foam and filth flow. (22) Due to its dreadful roar, the Paapi faint away at the very sight of this river. (23) Flooded with scorpions and black snakes, there is no one who can rescue those Paapi who have fallen into river. (24)

Aavarta-shata-saahastraih paataale yaanti paapinah,
Kshanam tisthanti paataale kshanaadu-parivartinah(25)
Paapinaam patanaayaiv nirmitaa saa nadee khag,
N paarm drishyate tasyaa dustaraa bahu-duhkhadaa(26)
Evm bahu-vidha-kleshe yama-maarge-ati-duhkhade,
N paarm kroshantshch rudantshch duhkhitaa yaanti paapinah(27)
Paashen yantriaataah kechit krishyamaanaastatha-angkushai,
Shastra-agraiah pristhatah protairneeyamaanaashch paapinah(28)
Naasa-agra-paasha-krishtaashch karnaa-paashaistathaapare,
Kaala-paashaiah krishya-maanaaah kaakaiah-krisyaastathaapare(29)
Greevaa-baahushu paadeshu baddhaah pristhe ch shrinkhalaiah,
Ayobhaarachaym kechid-vahantah pathi yaanti te(30)
Yama-dootair-mahaa-ghoraistaadayamaanaashch mudgraiah,
Vamanto rudhirm vaktraat tadevaashnanti te punah(31)
Shochantah svaani karmaanai glaanin gachchhanti jantavah,
Ateev dukha-sampannaah prayaanti yama-mandiram(32)
Yathaa dhenusahsteshu vatso vindati maataram,
Tathaa poorva-kritm karm kartaaram-anugachchhati(33)

Hundreds of thousands of whirlpools draw the Paapi to its very depths. The Paapi stay for a moment in the deep and ascend soon after. (25) O Bird, that river has been carved out only for the Paapi to fall into. It is difficult to cross it as the very river gives utter misery. (26) In this Yam-marg, there are many kinds of discomforts causing extreme misery. The Paapi, in miserable condition, keeps on moving while crying and weeping loudly. (27) The Paapi are hauled up on this path while bound by the noose, dragged by hooks and pierced on the back with pointed weapons. (28) The Yam-doots drag some Paapi by loop running through the end of their nose or through the ears, while some are bound by Kaal-paash (noose of death). While on the path, crows attack them with their beaks. (29) On the Yam-marg, the neck, arms, feet and back of Paapi are bound with chains while some are bearing loads of iron on their head. (30) The Paapi are beaten with hammers by the formidable Yam-doots. They vomit blood and are forced to drink the same vomited blood again. (31) The Paapi are extremely repentant upon recollecting their misdeeds of the past life. Thus, deeply pained, they go to the mansion of Yama. (32) O Garud! As a calf can trace out its mother from the herd of thousands of cows, likewise, the karma of the past life follow their doers. (33)

Mahataa punayayogen maanushm janm labhyate,
Tat-praapy n kritaa dharmah keedrishm hi mayaa kritam(34)
Mayaa n dattm n hutm hutaashane tapo n taptm tridasho n poojitaah,
N teertha-sevaa vihitaa vidhaanato dehin kvachinnistar yat tvayaa kritam(35)
N poojitaah vipra-ganaaah suraapagaa n chaashritaah sat-purushaa n sevitaah,
Paropakaaraa n kritah kadaachan dehin kvachinnistar yat tvayaa kritam(36)
jalaashayo naiv krito hi nirjale manushya-hetoah pashu-pakshi-hetave,
Go-vipra-vrittyarthama-kaari naanavapi dehin kvachinnistar yat tvayaa kritam(37)
N nitya-daann n gavaahinkm kritm n veda-shaastra-artha-vachah pramaanaitam,
Shrutm puraanam n ch poojito gyo dehin kvachinnistar yat tvayaa kritam(38)
N gyaanamaargo n ch yogamaargo n karmmamaargo n ch bhaktimaargah,
N saadhusngat kimapi shrutm mayaa shareer he nistar yat tvayaa kritam(39)

The Paapi thinks, "by great accumulation of **Punya** (meritorious deeds), I achieved birth as human. Having obtained that, I did not perform my Dharma. What a blunder I have committed!" and he repents. (34) Neither I did charity and **Daan** (donations) nor did I perform Havan (offering to Ishwara through fire). I neither performed Tapa (penances) nor worshiped the deities. I did not perform service in **Teerth** (place of pilgrimage) as prescribed; O **Dehee** (dweller of the body), you have done condemnable deeds. Now undergo the sufferings for whatever you have done. (35) I failed to honor the wise; did not inhale the holy water of river Ganga; did not render service to the seekers of truth; never performed any benevolent acts; O Dehee, now undergo the sufferings for whatever you have done. (36) Alas, I did not construct reservoirs in parched places for the benefit of human beings, animals and birds; did not spend even a little for the support of cows and the benefit of "**Brahm- gyanies**" (knower of Brahmn); O Dehee, now undergo the sufferings for whatever you have done". (37) In this way, while weeping, the Pret says, "I gave no daily alms and did not give daily feed to the cows; nor did I study the Vedas and **Shastra** (holy scriptures); did not listen to the preaching of Puranas, nor honored the wise; O Dehee, now undergo the sufferings for whatever you have done. (38) Neither I followed the **Gyan Marg** (path of knowledge) nor **Yog Marg**; neither **Karm Marg** (path of action and duty) nor **Bhakti Marg** (path of devotion) for achieving Mokshya neither I joined the company of **Sadhus** to listen the divine ways. O Dehee, now undergo the sufferings for whatever you have done. (39)

15

Maanushym labhyate kasmaaditi boorate prasarpati,
Mahataa punaya-yogen maanushm janm labhyate,
N tat praapy pradattm hi yaachakebhyah svakm dhanam,
Paraadheenm tadabhavaditi broote sagadgadah(40)
Sukhasy dukhasy n kopi daataa paro dadaateeti kubuddhiresaa,
Puraa kritm karm sadaiv bhujyate dehin kvachin nistar yat tvayaa kritam(41)
Evm vilapy bahusho snsmaran poorva-daihikam,
Maanushatvm mam kut iti kroshan prasarpati(42)
Dasha-sapta-dina-anyeko vaayu-vegen gachchhati,
Astaa-dashe dine taarkshyaa pretah saumyapuram vrajet(43)
Tasmin puravare ramye pretaanaam ch ganao mahaan,
Pushpa-bhadraa nadee tatraa nyagrodhah priya-darshanah(44)
Pure tatraa s vishraamm praapyate yamakinkraiah,
Daara-putra-adikm saukhym smarate tatraa dukhitah(45)
Dhanaani bhritya-pautraanai sarvm shochati vai yadaa,
Tadaa pretaastu tatraatyaah kinkaraashchedama-bruvan(46)

By which deeds the human birth is obtained?" Paapi
murmurs and keeps on moving. "Consequent upon the
substantial accumulation of good deeds, I obtained human
birth. But after obtaining that, I did not share my surplus
wealth with the needy. Now that wealth has passed on to
someone else" he grumbles. (40) "No one other is the cause
of your pleasure or pain. To think that someone else is the
reason of your happiness or misery, is foolish. Therefore,
O Dehee, face the consequences accordingly." (41) While
remembering the deeds of previous births, the Paapi cries
and laments "when would I attain this human form once
again?" and moves on. (42) For seventeen days, the Pret
goes on alone at the speed of the wind. O Taarkshya, the
Pret reaches "Saumyapur" (city of Saumya), on the
eighteenth day. (43) A large number of Prets have abode in
that beautiful city. The river Pushpbhadra flows over there
and a delightful Banyan tree named "Priyadarshan" is also
there. (44) In that city, Yam-doots allow the departed to take
rest. Then, the Paapi recollects the good time spent with
spouse, son and others and is grief stricken. (45) When the
Paapi ponders over separation from family, wealth, etc., then
the other Prets and the Yam-doots present there, say: (46)

16

Kv dhanm? Kv suto jaayaa? Kv suhrit? Kv ch baandhavaah?,
Svakarmo-paarjitm bhoktaa moodh! Yaahi chirm pathi(47)
Jaanaasi smbalabalm balamadhva-gaanaam no smbalaay yatase paraloka-paanth,
Gantavyam-asti tav nishchtamev ten maargena yatraa n bhavatah kraya-vikrayau n(48)
Aabaalakhyaata-maargo-aym naiv martye shrutastvayaa,
Puraanaa-sambhavm vaakym kim dvijebhyo-api n shrutam(49)
Evamuktastato dootaistaadayamaanshch mudgraiah,
Nipatannutpatan dhaavan paashairaa-krishyate balaat(50)
Atraa dattm sutaiah pautrauah snehaadvaa kripayaa-athavaa,
Maasikm pindaamashnaati tatah sauripuram vrajet(51)
Tatraa naamana-asti raajaa vai jangmah kaala-roopa-dhrik,
Tad dristvaa bhayabheeto-asau vishraame kurute matim(52)
Udakm ch-aanna-snyuktm bhunkte tatraa pure gatah,
Trau-paakshike vai yad-dattm s tat-puram-ati-kramet(53)
Tato nagendra-bhavanm preto yaati tvaraanvitah,
Vanaani tatraa raudraanai dristvaa krandati dukhitah(54)

"Where is your wealth now? Where are your children and where have gone your life companion? Where are your well-wishers and siblings now? You have to suffer the outcome of your Karma. Therefore, Oh fool! Go alone on this path. (47) O Traveler to **Parlok** (other realm), you do not know the power of Yama and his Doots. You know that provisions are the strength of a traveler. Yet, you do not strive to escape punishment. On this path, the good deeds are neither purchased nor sold. Therefore, you keep on moving on that path. (48) Have you not heard of this path, which is familiar even to the children on the earth? Have you not heard of it from the learned, while they were narrating the Puranas?" (49) Saying so, the Yam-doots beat the Paapi with hammers. Then, the Pret falls down and gets up again and again and the Yam-doots forcibly drag him by binding him with the noose. (50) Here he eats the monthly Pind offered by offspring either due to affection or compassion and thereafter goes to "Sauri-pur." (51) In Sauri-pur, there is a king named Jangam who has the appearance of Yam-raj. Having seen him, the Paapi is shaken with fear and wants to take rest. (52) In Sauri-pur, Pret eats the Pind offered by the kin at the end of three fortnights and then departs from that city. (53) Soon after, the Pret reaches Nagendra-bhavan and, having seen the fearsome forests over there, cries grief- stricken. (54)

Nir-ghrinaaiah krishyamaanaastu rudate ch punah punah,
Maasa-dvaya-avasaane tu tatpuram vyathito vrajet(55)
Bhuktvaa pindam jalm vstram dattm yad baandhavairih,
Krishya-maanaah punah-paashair-neeyate-agre ch kinkraiah(56)
Maase triteeye sampraapte praapy gandharva-pattanam,
Triteeya-maasikm pindam tatraa bhuktvaa prasarpati(57)
Shailaagamm chaturthe ch maasi praapnoti vai puram,
Paashaanaas-tatraa varshanti pretasy-opari bhoorishah(58)
Chaturtha-maasikm pindam bhuktvaa kinchit-sukhee bhavet,
Tato yaati puram pretah krauncham maase-ath panchame(59)
Hasta-dattm tadaa bhunkte pretah kraunchapure sthitah,
Yat-pancha-maasikm pindam bhuktvaa kroorapuram vrajet(60)
Saardhakaiah pancha-bhir-maasair-nyoonashaanamaasikm vrajet,
Tatraa datten pindaen ghatenaapyaayitah sthitah(61)
Muhoortaardhm tu vishramy kampamaanah sudukhitah,
Tatpuram tu parityajy tarjito yama-kinkraiah(62)
Prayaati chitraa-bhavanm vichitro naam paarthivah,
Yamasyaiva-anujo bhraataa yatraa raajym prashaasti hi(63)

Being dragged mercilessly by the Yam-doots, Pret cries again and again. At the end of two months, the afflicted leaves that city. (55) There, having consumed the Pind, water and cloths offered by the siblings for the second month, the Paapi is tied-up once again and dragged onwards by the Yam-doots. (56) In the third month, he arrives at "Gandharv-pur" and there, after eating the Pind of third month, moves on. (57) In the fourth month, the Pret reaches "Shailagam-pur." There the Pret faces rain of stones. (58) There, having consumed the Pind of fourth month, the Pret feels some relief. In the fifth month, the Pret reaches "Kraunch-pur." (59) In "Kraunch-pur," the Pret eats the Pind, offered by hand. Thereafter, eating the Pind offered in the fifth month, he goes to "Kroor-pur." (60) On completion of five and a half months, **Nyunshan-mashik** (rite before the six-month) is performed. He becomes some-what satisfied with the Pind and earthen pots given there. (61) The Pret feels very miserable and shaken within few minutes of stay there. Threatened by the Yam-doots, leaves that city for Chitra-bhawan. (62) Chitra-bhawan is a kingdom which is ruled by a king named Vichitra, the younger brother of Yama. (63)

18

Tm viloky mahaakaaym yadaa bheetah palaayate,
Tadaa snmukham-aagaty kaivartaa idama-bruvan(64)
Vaym te tartukaamaay mahaa-vaitaranaeem nadeem,
Naavamaadaay sampraaptaa yadi te punayamee-drisham(65)
Daanm vitaranam proktm munibhis-tattva-darshibhiah,
Iym saa teeryate yasmaat-tasmaad-vaitaranaee smritaa(66)
Yadi tvayaa pradattaa gaustadaa naurupasarpati,
Naa-anyatheti vachasteshaam shrutvaa haa daiv bhaashate(67)
Tn drishtvaa kvathate saa tu taam drishtvaa so-ati-krandate,
Adatta-daanah paapa-atmaa tasyaam-ev nimajjati(68)
Tanmukhe kanatakm dattvaa dootair-aakaasha-snsthitaiah,
Badaishen yathaa matsyas-tathaa paarm pranaeeyate(69)
Shaana-maasikm ch yat-pindam tatraa bhuktvaa prasarpati,
Maarge s vilapan yaati bubhukshaa-peedaito hyalam(70)
Saptame maasi sampraapte puram bahvaapadm vrajet,
Tatraa bhunkte pradattm tat saptame maasi putraakaiah(71)
Tat-puram tu vyatikramy dukhadm puram-richchhati,
Mahad dukhamavaapnoti khe gachchhan khechar-eshvar(72)

Seeing the horrible appearance of the king, he runs away in fear. Then some boatmen come to him and say: (64) 'We have come to you along with the boat to cross the Vaitarnee. Now, if you have any Punya (merits), tell us. We will get you across the mighty Vaitarnee river. (65) The Munis (sages) and Tatvadarshis (knowers of truth), have defined the **Daan** (virtuous donations) as **Vitaran** (distribution). Therefore, it is called **Vaitarnee** because it is crossed over by virtues earned as a result of Daan. (66) If you have given a Daan of cow (and other valuables), then the boat will come to you, otherwise it never goes to anyone.' Having heard their words, the departed Atma repents 'Oh Ishwara! Why I did not make daan.' (67) Seeing the terrible Vaitarnee, the Pret cries loudly with fear. The Paapi who have not performed the Daan are certain to drown in that Vaitarnee. (68) Hooked through lips, the Doots-floating in the sky- carry the Paapi across like a fish in the hook of a fisherman. (69) After consuming the Pind of the sixth month, he moves on. On the way, the Pret afflicted with hunger, laments. (70) On the arrival of the seventh month, the Pret reaches Bahwaapad-pur. There he eats the Pind offered by his sons in the seventh month. (71) After passing beyond that city, the Pret arrives at Duhkhad-pur. He undergoes deep misery, like a helpless bird in the sky, O Ruler of Birds. (72)

19

Maasya-shtame pradattm yat-pindam bhuktvaa prasarpati,
Navame maasi sampoornae naanaa-kranda-puram vrajet(73)
Naanaa-kranda-ganaan drishtvaa krandamaanaan sudaarunaan,
Svaym ch shoonya-hridayah samaa-krandati dukhitah(74)
Vihaay   tat-puram   pretas-tarjito   yama-kinkraih,
Sutapta-bhavanm gachchhed-dashame maasi krichchhratah(75)
Pind-daanm jalm tatraa bhuktvaa-api n sukhee bhavet,
Maasi ch-aikaadashe poornae puram raudrm s gachchhati(76)
Dash-aika-maasikm tatraa bhunkte dattm suta-adibhiah,
Saardhe ch-aikaadashe maasi payo-varsanaam-richchhati(77)
Meghaas-tatraa pravarsanti pretaanaam dukha-daayakaah,
Nyoon-aabdikm ch yachchhraaddhm tatraa bhunkte s dukhitah(78)
Sampoornae tu tato varshe sheetaadhya-nagarm vrajet,
Him-aachchhata-gunam tatraa mahaa-sheetm tapatyapi(79)
Sheet-aartah kshudhitah so-api veekshate hi disho dash,
Tisthate baandhavah ko-api yo me dukhm vyapohati(80)
Kinkraaste vadantyatraa kv te punaym hi taadrisham,
Bhuktvaa ch vaarshikm pindam dhairyam-aalambate punah(81)

After consuming the Pind, offered in the eighth month, the Pret moves on. Then, at the end of the ninth month, reaches Naanaakrand-pur. (73) In that city, various individuals are seen crying in agony. Hearing that, Pret starts weeping himself in deep misery, being in a faint-hearted condition. (74) In the tenth month, threatened by the roars of Yaam-doots, the Pret leaves Naanaakrand-pur and goes to Sutapt-bhavan. (75) Having eaten the Pind of the tenth month, the Pret still remains unsatisfied. On completion of the eleventh month, goes to Raudra-pur. (76) On reaching there, eats Pind offered by son and others in the eleventh month. After eleven and half months, proceeds for the city known as Payovarshan-pur. (77) There, a miserable heavy downpour takes place over the Pret. The Pret, while crying miserably, eats the Pind offered in the Shraddh,. (78) On completion of the year, goes to Sheetaadhya-pur, which is hundred times colder than snow. (79) On reaching there, afflicted by severe cold and hunger, Pret looks all around and ponders, 'there might be some relative who would get me relieved from this misery.' (80) Then the Doots say, 'You are not fortunate enough to be relieved from these miseries by anyone.' Having eaten the annual Pind, gets some endurance. (81)

Tatah smvatsarasya-ante pratyaasanne yamaalaye,
Bahu-bheeti-pure gatvaa hasta-maatraam sam-utsrijet(82)
Angustha-maatro vaayushch karma-bhogaay khechar,
Yaatanaa-dehamaasaady sah yaamyaiah prayaati ch(83)
Audhrvadaihika-daanaani yairn dattaani kaashyap,
Ati-kashten te yaanti griheetaa dridha-bandhanaiah(84)
Dharmaraajapure santi chatur-dvaaraanai khechar,
Yatraaym dakshina-dvaara-maargaste parikeertitah(85)
Asmin pathi mahaa-ghore kshut-trishaa-shrama-peedaitaah,
Yathaa yaanti tathaa proktm kim bhooyah shrotum-ichchhasi(86)

On completion of a year, having reached near the Yam-lok in Bahubheeti-pur, the Pret casts off his hand-sized body. (82) Getting a body of the size of thumb, for experiencing torments, the Paapi sets out through the aerial route along with Yam-doots. (83) Those who do not offer Daan intended for Parlok during their life-time, O Kaashayap, thus go to Yam-lok, painfully bound in tight bonds. (84) In the city of the Dharm-raaj there are four gateways, O Bird, I have narrated only the Path of the southern Gate to you. (85) How the Paapi afflicted with hunger, thirst and exhaustion, go on this most dreadful path I have narrated. What else do you wish to hear now? (86)

Annadi-nidhano Devah Shankh Chakra Gadaa-dharah,
Akshayah pundree-kaakash Preta-mokshya-prado-bhav.

***

21

CHAPTER 3

AN ACCOUNT OF TORMENTS OF YAMA, BRIEFING TO YAMA BY CHITRAGUPTA AND FEEDBACK FROM SHRAVANA, DHARM-RAAJ DELIVERS THE JUDGMENT.

GARUD UVAACH

Yama-maargam-ati-kramy gatvaa paapee yamaalaye,
Keedrisheem yaatanaam bhunkte tanme kathay keshav!(1)

SHREEBHAGAVAANUVAACH

Aady-antm ch pravakshyaami shrinausv vinata-atmaj,
Kathyamaane-api narake tvm bhavishyasi kampitah(2)
Chat-vaarim-shad-yojanaani chatur-yuktaani kaashyap,
Bahu-bheeti-puraad-agre dharma-raaja-puram mahat(3)
Haahaa-kaara-samaa-yuktm drishtvaa krandati paatakee,
Tat-krandanm samaa-karnay yamasy pura-chaarinaah(4)
Gatvaa ch tatraa te sarve pratee-haarm vadanti hi,
Dharma-dhvajah pratee-haaras-tatraa tisthati sarvadaa(5)

GARUD SAID-O Keshav! Please tell me what are the torments suffered by the Paapi (Paapi) on reaching the abode of Yama, after passing the **Yam-marg** (path to Yama)? (1) **BHAGWAN SAID**-Listen, O son of Vintaa, I will narrate the torments of Narak from the beginning to the end. You will tremble even upon hearing the account of it. (2) O Kaashayap, forty four Yojanas beyond Bahubheeti-pur, lies Dharamraaj-pur (the city of dispenser of Justice). (3) This place is full of numerous wails of 'Oh, Oh.' The Paapi cry seeing all that. Having heard their cries, the Yam-doots intimate to the gatekeeper of having brought another Paapi to Yam-lok.(4) They bow before the gate-keeper, reaching there. Dharma-dhwaja is the door keeper who is always present at the door. (5)

22

S gatvaa chitraa-guptaay broote tasy shubha-ashubham,
Tatastm chitraa-gupto-api dharma-raajm nivedayet(6)
Naastikaa ye naraas-taarkshay mahaa-paapa-rataah sadaa,
Taamshcha sarvaan yathaa-yogym samyag jaanaati dharmaraat(7)
Tathaapi chitraa-guptaay teshaam paapm s prichchhati,
Chitraa-gupto-api sarvagyah shravanaan pari-prichchhati(8)
Shravanaa brahmanaah putraah srav-bhoo-paataala-chaarinaah,
Doora-shravanaa-vigyaanaa doora-darshana-chakshushah(9)
Teshaam patnyas-tathaa-bhootaah shravanayah pritha-gaahvayaah,
Stree-naam vicheshtitm sarvm taa vijaananti tattvatah(10)
Naraih prachchhannm pratyaksm yat-proktm ch kritm ch yat,
Sarva-maavedayantyev chitraa-guptaay te ch taah(11)
Chaaraaste dharma-raajasy manushyaanaam shubha-ashubham,
Manovaakkaayajm karm sarvm jaananti tattvatah(12)
Evm teshaam shaktirasti matrya-amatrya-adhikaarinaam,
Kathayanti nrinaam karm shravanaaah satya-vaadinah(13)

Then, Dharma-dhwaja reports the good and evil deeds of the Paapi to Chitragupt. Then Chitragupt, who has divine vision, tells it to the Dharmraaj (due to his judicious nature Yamraj is also known as Dharamraj, the dispenser of Justice). (6) Those who are Deniers and always indulge in sinful deeds; these all are well-known to the Dharamraaj, O Taarkshya. (7) Yet, Dharam-raaj enquires from Chitragupt about their sins. Chitragupt, though all knowing, further enquires from the Shravans. (8) The Shravans wander in Swarga, on earth and in the Paataal (nether regions). They are the sons of Brahma. They have the ability to hear and understand from a distance and can see from far off. (9) The wives of Shravans possess similar powers and are called Shravani. They accurately know all the thought processes and acts done by women. (10) They report to Chitragupt every wrong or right which is done by men and women; whether overtly and secretly. (11) They are the emissaries of the Dharam-raaj and know the essence of all the virtues and vices of the mankind and the Karma (action) born of mind, speech and body. (12) The Sharvans have the authority over mortals and immortals. Thus, these truth-speaking Shravans convey the good or bad actions of people to Chitragupt. (13)

23

Vratair-daanaishcha satyoktyaa yastoshayati taannarah,
Bhavanti tasy te saumyaah svarga-moksha-pradaayinah(14)
Paapinaam paapa-karmaanai gyaatvaa te satyavaadinah,
Dharma-raaja-purah proktaa jaayante dukha-daayinah(15)
Aaditya-chandraa-v-anilo-analshcha dyaur-bhoomi-raapo hridaym yamshcha,
Ahshcha raatrishcha ubhe ch sandhye dharmshcha jaanaati narasy vrittam(16)
Dharma-raajsh-chitraaguptah shravanaa bhaaskar-aadayah,
Kaayasthm tatraa pashyanti paapm punaym ch sarvashah(17)
Evm sunishchaym kritvaa paapinaam paatakm yamah,
Aahooy taannijm roopm darshayatyati bheeshanaam(18)
Paapisthaaste prapashyanti yamaroopm bhayankaram,
Danadaa-hastm mahaa-kaaym mahisho-pari-snsthitam(19)
Pralaya-ambuda-nirghoshaka-jjalaachalasannibham,
Vidyut prabhaa-yudhair-bheemm dvaa-trimshabhuaja-snyutam(20)
Yojana-traaya-vistaarm   vaapee-tulya-vilochanam,
Dnshtraa-karaala-vadanm raktaakshm deergha-naasikam(21)
Mrityu-jvara-adibhir-yuktaash-chitraagupto-api bheeshanaah,
Sarve dootaashcha garjanti yama-tulyaastadantike(22)

The acts of austerity, charity and truthful speech please them and they become benevolent, granting Swarga and Mokshya to those human beings. (14) Knowing the wicked actions of the Paapi, these truthful Shravans bring the facts before the Dharam-raaj and become dispensers of misery to the Paapi according to their deeds. (15) The sun, moon, fire, wind, sky, earth, water, the inner-soul, day, night, the two twilights and Dharma- these all know the character of humans and they become witness to the acts of good and evil actions. (16) Dharam-raaj, Chitragupt, Shravans, the Sun and others know fully all the Paap and virtues of the embodied being. (17) The Yama, having judged the sinful deeds of the Paapi, summons them and shows them his very terrible form. (18) The Paapi behold the terrifying appearance of Yam-huge body, rod in hand, seated on a buffalo. (19) Roaring like a thunderstorm at the time of Pralaya (holocaust), with pitch-dark body, terrible appearance with weapons gleaming like lightning, possessing thirty-two arms. (20) Whose body extends to three Yojan, with eyes look like wells, with mouth gaping with formidable fangs, with red blood in eyes and a long nose. (21) Even Chitragupt, attended by Death, Fever and others, makes his appearance terrible. Coming near to the Paapi, all the Doots, resembling Yama, start thundering. (22)

Tam drishtvaa bhaya-bheetastu haa heti vadate khalah,
Adatta-daanah paapa-atmaa kampate krandate punah(23)
Tato vadati taansarvaan krandamaanaamshcha paapinah,
Shochantah svaani karmaanai chitraagupto yama-agyayaa(24)
Bho bhoah paapaa duraa-chaaraa ahankaara-pradooshitaah,
Kim-artham-arjitm paapm yushmaabhiravivekibhiah?(25)
Kaama-krodhaady-utpannn sangmen ch paapinaam,
Tat-paapm dukhadam moodhaah kim-arthm charitm janaah(26)
Kritavantah puraa yooym paapaany-atyanta-harsitaah,
Tathaiv yaatanaa bhogyaah kimi-daaneem paraan-mukhaah(27)
Kritaani yaani paapaani yushmaabhiah subahoonyapi,
Taani paapaani dukhasy kaaranam ch n vaym janaah(28)
Moorkhe-api panadaite vaapi daridre vaa shriya-anvite,
Sabale nirbale vaapi sama-vartee yamah smritah(29)
Chitraa-guptasy-eti vaakym shrutvaa te paapinastadaa,
Shochantah svaani karmaanai tooshnaeem tishthanti nishchalaah(30)

Seeing them, the wretch become fearful and cry 'Oh, Oh'. The Paapi, who made no Daan tremble and cry again. (23) The Paapi repent on their past Karma. Then, by command of Yam, Chitragupt relates the deeds of Paapi. (24) You, O Paapi! Evil-doers, full of ego, why ever did you lose your Viveka (power to discriminate) and commit sin? Why you indulged in misdeeds and why you committed injustice? (25) In the bad company of Paapi, 'O, you people, why ever did you commit those misery-giving sins which are born of lust and anger. (26) In the past life you have committed Paap with great delight and thereby you are now destined for torment. It is no use now turning your face away. (27) So many sinful deeds committed by you, are actually the cause of your unavoidable misery and not we. (28) Yama does justice with impartiality, be he a Pandit or a fool, poor or wealthy, the strong or the weak. (29) Hearing these words of Chitragupt, the Paapi then grieve over their karmas and remain silent and motionless. (30)

25

GARUD PURAAN

Dharma-raajo-api taan drishtvaa choravan-nishchalaan-sthitaan,
Aagyaa-payati paapaanaam shaasti chaiv yatho-chitam(31)
Tataste nirdayaa dootaas-taadaayitvaa vadanti ch,
Gachchh paapin mahaa-ghoraan-narakaan-ati-bheeshanaan(32)
Yama-agyaa-kaarinao dootaah prachanadaa-chanadaaka-adayah,
Eka-paashen taan baddhvaa nayanti narakaan prati(33)
Tatra vriksho mahaan-eko jvalad-agni-sama-prabhah,
Pancha-yojana-visteernaah eka-yojanam-uchchhritah(34)
Tad-vrikshe shrinkhalair-baddhvaa-adho-mukhm taadaayanti te,
Rudanti jvalitaas-tatraa teshaam traataa n vidyate(35)
Tasminnev shaalmalee-vrikshe lambante-aneka-paapinah,
Kshut-pipaasaa-pari-shraantaa yama-dootaishcha taadaitaah(36)
Kshamadhvm bho-aparaadhm me krit-aanjali-putaa iti,
Vigyaapayanti taan dootaan paapisthaaste nir-aashrayaah(37)
Punah punshch te dootair-hanyante lauhayastibhiah,
Mudgrais-tomaraiah kuntair-gadaabhir-musalair-bhrisham(38)
Taadaanaa-chchaiv nishchestaa moochrchhitaashcha bhavanti te,
Tathaa nishchestitaan drishtvaa kinkraaste vadanti hi(39)

Dharm-raj, seeing them standing motionless like thieves,
orders to give the befitting punishment to the Paapi in
accordance with their Paap. (31) Then, the cruel Yam-
doots present there, rebuke the Paapi and say, 'Go along,
you Paapi, to the very dreadful terrifying Narak.' (32)
Prachand , Chand and other dutiful Yam-doots, having
bound all of them with one noose, lead them towards the
Narak. (33) There exists a big tree named "Shalmali",
blazing like fire. It is spread in five Yojans and is one
Yojan in height. (34) Having tied them on the Shalmali
tree with chains, head downwards and feet upward, Yam-
doots beat them up mercilessly. They cry while burning
in the fire but there is no one to save them. (35) Many
Paapi are hung on that Shalmali tree exhausted by
hunger and thirst and beaten by the Yam-doots. (36) 'Oh,
forgive our crime,' those helpless grave Paapi implore the
Yam-doots with folded hands. (37) Again and again, they
are forcibly hit by the doots with metal rods, hammers,
iron clubs, spears, maces and big pestles.(38) Due to
this hard hitting, they faint and become motionless. Then,
seeing them motionless, the doots address them and
say: (39)

26

Bho bhoah paapaah duraa-chaaraah kim-arthm dushtacheshtitam,
Sulabhaani n dattaani jalaanyannaany-api kvachit(40)
Graasa-arddham-api no dattm n shva-vaayasayor-balim,
Namaskritaa na-atithayo n kritm pitri-tarpanaam(41)
Yamasy chitraa-guptasy n kritm dhyaanam-uttamam,
N japtshcha tayor-mantro n bhaved-yen yaatanaa(42)
Na-api kinchit-kiritm teerthm poojitaa naiv devataah,
Griha-ashrama-sthite-na-api hantakaaro-api n-oddhritah(43)
Shushrooshitaashcha no santo bhunksv paapa-falm svayam,
Yata-stvm dharma-heeno-asi tatah santa-adayase bhrisham(44)
Kshama-aparaadhm kurute bhagavaan harire-eshvarah,
Vaym tu saaparaadhaanaam danadaadaa hi tad-aagyayaa(45)
Evam-uktvaa ch te dootaa nirdaym taadaayanti taan,
Jvalad-angaara-sadrishaah patitaas-taadaanaadadhah(46)
Patanaat-tasy patraushcha gaatraach-chhedo bhavet-tatah,
Taanadhah patitaan-shvaaano bhaksayanti rudanti te(47)
N chaishaam jeevita-bhrnsho jaayate pakshisattam,
Chhinnaani teshaam shatashah khanadaany-aikym vrajanti hi(48)

'O, Paapi, evil doers, why did you commit such wicked deeds?
You did not offer even the easily available water and food,
etc., to needy. (40) You did not offer even a half bite of food,
nor you fed the dog or the crow. You did not respect your
Atithi (guests), nor made the offerings to your ancestors.
(41) You did not contemplate about the Yama and Chitragupt,
nor repeated their mantra which eliminate the torment of
Yama. (42) Neither you visited any Teerth (place of pilgrimage),
nor worshipped the Ishwar. Though living as a householder
you did not even offer food to Saadhus and Sants. (43) You
did not render any service to Sants. Now, suffer the miseries
of your own Paap! Since you are devoid of Dharma, you
deserve to be beaten up. (44) No one other than Ishwara, can
forgive one's offence. We only execute orders of Yama. (45)
Having said so, the Doots beat the Paapi mercilessly; and as
a result of the beating they fall down like burning charcoal.
(46) The leaves of Shalmali tree fall over them. Their limbs
are cut by the sharp leaves falling down and they cry, the
pieces of their body parts are eaten by dogs. (47) O Greatest
of Bird! The life of the Paapi is not yet over despite being cut
like this, as the hundreds of their separated pieces join
together once again. (48)

Evm varsh-sahastraanai bhraamyante paapa-karminaah,
Taa-vad yaa-vada-shesm ch tat-paapm sankhsaym gatam(49)
Ardhm khaatvaa-avate kechid-bhidyante moordhin saayakaiah,
Apare yantraa-madhyasthaah peedayante chekshu-danadvat(50)
Kechit prajvalamaanaistu saanaaraiah parito bhrisham,
Ulmukairvestayitvaa ch dhmaayante lohapindaavat(51)
Kechid-ghritamaye paake taila-paake tathaa-apare,
Kataahe kshipta-vata-vat-prakshipyante yatastatah(52)
Kechin-matta-gajendraanaam kshipyante puratah pathi,
Baddhvaa hastau ch paadau ch kriyante ke-apy-adho-mukhaah(53)
Kshipyante ke-api koopeshu paatyante ke-api parvataat,
Nimagnaah krimi-kunadaeshu tudyante krimibhiah pare(54)
Vajra-tunadaair-mahaa-kaakair-gridhrair-aamisha-gridhnubhiah,
Nishkrishyante shirodeshe netre vaasye ch chanchubhih(55)
Rrinam vai praarthayantyanye dehi dehi dhanm mam,
Yamaloke mayaa drishto dhanm me bhakshitm tvayaa(56)
Evm vivadamaanaanaam paapinaam narakaalaye,
Chhittvaa sndnshakair-dootaa maansa-khanadaan dadanti ch(57)

Thus, till all the Paap of the Paapi are not washed out, they are dragged like this for the thousands of years. (49) Some, with their bodies half-buried in a pit, are pierced in the head with arrows by Doots. Others, fixed in the middle of a juicer machine, are squeezed like sugar-cane. (50) Some are enveloped with blazing woods and smelted like a lump of iron ore. (51) Some are plunged into boiling Ghee, and others into boiling oil, and like a cake thrown into the frying-pan, they are tossed and turned around. (52) Some are thrown in front of big mad elephants, and some with hands and feet tied up, are thrown with head downwards. (53) Some are thrown into wells; some are thrown from hills; others plunged into pits full of worms, are made to be eaten away by them. (54) Hit by the pointed beaks of crows and huge flesh-eating vultures, they are pecked in the head, eyes and faces, like thunderstorm. (55) These birds say, 'Return my wealth which you borrowed and failed to return. Now I have seen you in the world of Yama. Now return that wealth.' (56) Seeing quarrel between the Paapi in the Narak, Yam-doots take one piece of flesh from body of Paapi and give it to the demanding bird. (57)

Evm sntaaday taan dootaah snkrishy yamashaasanaat,
Taamistraadisu ghoreshu kshipyante narakeshu ch(58)
Narakaa dukha-bahulaas-tatra vriksha-sameepatah,
Teshv-asti yan-mahad-dukhm tad-vaachaamapyagocharam(59)
Chaturaa-sheeti-lakshaanai narakaah santi khechar,
Teshaam madhye ghoratamaa dhaureyaastveka-vinshatiah(60)
Taamistro loha-shnkushcha mahaa-raurava-shaalmalee,
Rauravah kudamalah kaala-sootraakah pooti-mrittikah(61)
Snghaato lohitodshcha savishah snprataapanah,
Mahaa-nirayakaakolau sanjeevana-mahaa-pathau(62)
Aveechi-randhataa-mistrah kumbhee-paakas-tathaiv ch,
Sam-prataapana-naama-ekastapanastveka-vinshatiah(63)
Naanaa-peedaa-mayaah sarve naanaa-bhedaih prakalpitaah,
Naanaa-paapa-vipaakaashcha kinkraughairadhisthitaah(64)
Etesu patitaa moodhaah paapishthaa dharma-varjitaah,
Yatraa bhunjanti kalpa-antah taastaa naraka-yaatanaah(65)
Yaastaa-mistra-andhataa-mistra-raurava-adyaash-cha yaatanaah,
Bhunkte naro vaa naaree vaa mithah sngen nirmitaah(66)

Beating the Paapi like this, they are held up by the Doots and with the orders of Yama, are thrown into 'Tamistra' and other dreadful Narak. (58) There are Narak full of extreme miseries near Shalmali tree which cannot be described in words. (59) There are eighty-four lakhs of Narak, of which twenty-one are the most dreadful, O Bird. (60) Names of these wenty one Narak are- Taamistra, Loh-shanku, Mahaaraurava, Shalmali, Raurav, K u d m a l, K a a l s u t r a, P o o t i m r i t t i k a, (61) Sanghat, Lohitod, Savish, Mahaaniray, Kaak, Ulu, Sanjeevan, Mahaa-path,(62) A v e e c h i, A n d h a t a a m i s r a, K u m b h i - p a a k, Samprataapan, and Tapan. (63) All have been formed for various afflictions and diseases of different classes, for facing the consequences of various Paap and are inhabited by multitudes of Yam-doots. (64) Those Paapi like fools, devoid of Dharma, fall into these and go through various torments of these Narak until the end of the era. (65) Men and women who are into excessive indulgence suffer the torments of Taamistra, Andhataa-mistra, Raurava, etc. (66)

29

Evm kutumbm bibhraana udarambhar ev vaa,
Visrijyeho-bhaym pretya-bhunkte tat-falamee-drisham(67)
Ekah prapadyate dhvaantm hitvedm sva-kalevaram,
Kushaletara-paatheyo bhoota-drohena yad-bhritam(68)
Daivenaasaaditm tasy shamale niraye pumaan,
Bhunkte kutumba-poshasy hrita-dravy ivaaturah(69)
Kevalen hyadharmena kutumba-bharanao-otsukah,
Yaati jeevo-andhataa-mistraam charamm tamasah padam(70)
Adhastaan-nara-lokasy yaavateeryaatanaadayah,
Kramah samanu-kramy punaratraa vrajechchhuchiah(71)

One who is concerned only to gratify own belly or family alone, suffers miseries in the Narak. (67) The one who nourishes own body at the cost of other creatures, goes alone to Narak, provisioned with those bad deeds which bring misery. (68) A person who abandons Ishwara and feeds own family by immoral means, feels like the one who has been robbed of his wealth and the support of his family, in the Narak, (69) The one, who supports his family by Adharm means alone, after suffering miseries in all the Narak, goes to 'Andhataa-mistra', which is the place of uttermost darkness. (70) Having suffered the consequences of bad deeds, once the Paap are washed off, one is purified and reborn. (71)

**Annadi-nidhano Devah Shankh Chakra Gadaa-dharah,
Akshayah pundree-kaakash Preta-mokshya-prado-bhav.**

CHAPTER 4

*HOW PAAPI (SINNER) FALL INTO VAITARNEE RIVER, FOUR
GATEWAYS LEADING TO THE CITY OF DHARM-RAAJ, TRUTH
SEEKERS AND THEIR COMPANY, CONSEQUENCES OF GOOD AND
BAD DEEDS.*

GARUD UVAACH

Kair-gachchhanti mahaa-maarge vaitaranayaam patanti kaiah?,
Kaiah paapair-narake yaanti tanme kathay keshav(1)

SHREEBHAGAVAANUVAACH

Sadaiva-akarma-nirataah shubha-karma-paraan-mukhaah,
Narakaan-narakm yaanti dukhaad dukhm bhayaad bhayam(2)
Dharma-raaja-pure yaanti tri-bhi-dvaarair-astu dhaarmikaah,
Paapaastu dakshinaa-dvaara-maargenaaiv vrajanti hi(3)
Asminnev mahaa-dukhe maarge vaitaranaee nadee,
Tatraa ye paapino yaanti taanahm kathayaami te(4)

GARUD SAID -O Keshav! tell me what makes one tread
on Yam-marg (way to Yam)? Why they fall into the
Vaitarnee? What are the Paap leading to Narak? (1)
BHAGWAN SAID- Who always indulge in Paap (sinful
deeds), who turn away from virtuous deeds, these Paapi
go from Narak to Narak, undergo from one misery to
another. (2) (There are four gates leading to Dharamraaj-
pur, the city of the dispenser of Justice). The Dharmik
go to Dharmraaj-pur from the first three Gateways i.e.
eastern, western and northern. The Paapi enter it only
from the southern Gate. (3) The Vaitarnee river also
falls on this miserable (southern) way. I will tell you
about the Paapi who go through this way. (4)

31

Brahma-ghnaashcha suraa-paashcha go-ghnaa vaa baala-ghaatakaah,
Stree-ghaatee garbha-paatee ch ye ch prachchhanna-paapinah(5)
Ye haranti guror-dravym deva-dravym dvijasy vaa,
Stree-dravya-haarinao ye ch baala-dravya-haraash-cha ye(6)
Ye rinam n prayachchhanti ye vai nyaasa-apahaarakaah,
Vishvaaasa-ghaatakaa ye ch savishaannen maarakaah(7)
Dosha-graahee guna-ashlaaghee gunaavatsu samatsaraah,
Neecha-anuraaginao moodhaah satsúngti-paraanmukhaah(8)
Teertha-sajjana-satkarma-gurudeva-vinindakaah,
Puraanaa-veda-meemaansaa-nyaaya-vedaanta-dooshakaah(9)
Harshitaa dukhitm drishtvaa harshite dukha-daayakaah,
Dushta-vaakyasy vaktaaro dushta-chittaashcha ye sadaa(10)
N shrinavanti hitm vaakym shaastra-vaartaam kadaapi n
Aatma-sambhaavitaah stabdhaa moodhaah panadaita-maaninah(11)

One who murders human being; intoxicated by Suraa; slays cows, kills children and women; kills fetus and those who secretly commit Paap; (5) Who steal the wealth of their Guru; the wealth of the Devas (deities) or of the Dvij (who follow the Sanskaar); those who take away the possessions of women and the children; (6) Who do not repay their debts; those who misappropriate inheritance; those who breach the trust and those who kill by giving poisonous food; (7) Who embrace the vices of others but denounce their merits, who are jealous of meritorious people, who are associated with the wicked and are alienated from the company of Sat-sanga (company of truthful); (8) Those who vilify the Teerth (places of pilgrimage), noble people, noble deeds, Gurus, deities; those who denigrate Puraans, Vedas, Meemaansa, Nyaay and Vedaant (Upanishad); (9) Those who get sadistic pleasure in seeing the others in misery, who cause pain to happily living people, who use harsh language and who always are evil-minded; (10) Those who do not listen to benevolent advice, never heed to the words of the Shastra, who are full of vanity, the foolish who consider themselves learned; (11)

Ete cha-anye ch bahavah paapisthaa dharma-varjitaah,
Gachchhanti yama-maarge hi rodamaanaa divaa-nisham(12)
Vishvaaasa-prati-pannaanaam svaami-mitraa-tapasvinaam,
Stree-baala-vikalaa-deenaam vadhm kritvaa patanti hi,
Pachyante tatraa madhye tu krandamaanaastu paapinah(13)
Maatarm ye-avamanyante pitarm gurumev ch,
Aachaarym cha-api poojym ch tasyaam majjanti te naraah(14)
Pati-vrataam saadhu-sheelaam kuleenaam vinaya-anvitaam,
Striym tyajanti ye dveshaad vaitaranayaam patanti te(15)
Sataam gunaa-sahstreshu doshaana-aropayanti ye,
Teshv-avagyaam ch kurvanti vaitaranayaam patanti te(16)
Braahmanaay prati-shruty yathaarthm n dadaati yah
Aahooy naasti yo boorayaat-tayor-vaasshcha santatam(17)
Svaym dattaa-apahatrtaa ch daanm dattvaa-anutaapakah,
Para-vritti-harsh-chaiv daane datte nivaarakah(18)
Yagya-vidhvnsaksh-chaiv kathaa-bhangkarsh-cha yah,
Kshetraa-seemaa-harsh-chaiv yshcha gochara-karsakah(19)

These and others who have committed many Paap (sins) and those who are devoid of Dharma, certainly go through Yam-Marg while weeping day and night. (12) Deceitful to the master, to friend, to Tapasvi (ascetic), to woman, to child, to specially abled people and poor, fall in Vaitarnee. In the middle of the river, those Paapi are roasted while they cry. (13) The people who humiliate their mother, father, Acharya, Guru and the reverend ones, are drowned in Vaitarnee. (14) Those who wickedly abandon their wives, who are faithful, of gentle disposition, modest and well mannered; such Paapi fall into Vaitarnee. (15) Those who malign the gentle people possessing thousands of qualities and treat them disrespectfully, fall into Vaitarnee. (16) Who do not fulfill the promises made to Purohit (priests) of Daan (donations), and who, having invited priest for Daan, refuse the same, they stay in Vaitarnee. (17) Who steal the donations made by themselves; who repent after giving Daan; who snatches the livelihood of others; who prohibits others from making donations; (18) Who creates obstacles in Yagya (offerings to Ishwar through sacred fire); who hinders recitation of Hari-katha (devotional saga); who snatches property of others; who ploughs up pastoral land, fall into Vaitarnee River; (19)

Braahmanao rasa-vikretaa yadi syaad vrishalee-patiah,
Vedokta-yagyaad-anyatraa svaatma-arthm pashu-maarakah(20)
Brahma-karma-paribhrashto maansa-bhoktaa ch madyapah,
Uchchhrinkhala-svabhaavo yah shaastra-adhyayana-varjitah(21)
Vedaan-abhyasate naiv kulaachaarm n sevate,
Aalasyaat karmanaam tyaago nisiddhe-apyaadarah sadaa(22)
Raaja-bhaaryaa-abhilaashee ch para-daara-apahaarakah,
Kanyaayaam kaamuksh-chaiv sateenaam dooshaksh-cha yah(23)
Ete chaa-anye ch bahavo nishiddha-acharana-otsukaah,
Vihita-tyaagino moodhaa vaitaranayaam patanti te(24)
Sarvm maargam-atikramy yaanti paapaa yamaalaye,
Punar-yamaagyayaa-a-agaty dootaastasyaam ksipanti taan(25)
Yaa vai dhurandharaa sarva-dhaureyaanaam khaga-adhip,
Atastasyaam praksipanti vaitaranayaam ch paapinah(26)
Krishnaa gauryadi no dattaa nodhrvadehakriyaa kritaah,
Tasyaam bhuktvaa mahad dukhm yaanti vrikshm tatodbhavam(27)
Koota-saakshya-pradaataarah koota-dharma-paraayanaaah,
Chhalena-arjan-snsaktaash-chaurya-vrittyaa ch jeevinah(28)

The Brahmin (priest and Purohit) who sells intoxicants, indulges in prostitution; molests the minor, who kills animals for own gratification not for the sacrifices prescribed in Vedas; (20) The priest who has put aside priestly duties; who eats flesh and consumes liquor; who is nasty; the priests and Brahmins who are devoid of the knowledge of Shastra (scriptures); (21) Those who do not practice Ved, do not follow the great traditions of family; who lack Purusharth (self effort or human endeavor) due to laziness, who tread the forbidden path; (22) Those who covet the King's wife; who abduct others' wives, who are lustful towards virgins and who slander virtuous women; (23) All these and many other fools, fond of treading forbidden paths and abandoning prescribed duties, fall into Vaitarnee. (24) After crossing all such paths, the Paapi reach the abode of Yam, and having reached, the Doots hurl them into that river again under the command of Yama. (25) O Khageshwar, Vaitarnee is most dreadful among all the Narak. Therefore, the Yam-doots throw the Paapi into that river. (26) Who did not make Daan of black cow, nor performed the Aurdhv-dehic rites; having suffered great misery, go under Shalmali tree, standing on the bank of the river. (27) Those who testify false witness; who indulge in Paap; who make money by cheating and who earn livelihood by theft; (28)

34

Chhedayantyati-vriksaanshch vana-araama-vibhnjakaah,
Vratm teerthm parityajy vidhavaa-sheela-naashakaaha(29)
Bhartaarm dooshayen-naaree parm manasi dhaarayet,
Ityaadyaah shaalmalee-vrikshe bhujante bahu-taadaanam(30)
Rodhe goghno bhooranaahaa ch agni-daataa narah patet,
Sookare brahmahaa majjet suraapah svarnaa-taskarah(31)
Naastikaa bhinna-maryaadaah kadaryaa vishayaatmakaah,
Daambhikaash-cha kritaghnaash-cha te vai naraka-gaaminah(32)
Koopaanaam ch tadaagaanaam vaapeenaam devasarninaam,
Prajaa grihaanaam bhettaaraste vai naraka-gaaminah(33)
Visrijyaashnanti ye daaraanichhashoon bhrityaamstathaa guroon,
Utsrijy pitri-devejyaam te vai naraka-gaaminah(34)
Shnkubhiah setubhiah kaasthaiah paasaanaaiah kanatakaistathaa,
Ye maargam-uparundhanti te vai naraka-gaaminah(35)
Shivm shivaam harim soorym ganaeshm sadgurum budham,
N poojayanti ye mandaaste vai naraka-gaaminah(36)

Those who cut down big trees; who destroy the gardens and forests; break the promises; who pollute the Teerth (holy, pilgrim and places), who outrage the modesty of widow and neglect her; (29) The life-partner who despises the spouse and who have crush for another, they all experience much miseries under Shalmali tree. (30) The people who slaughter the holy cow, destroy the embryo, burn down houses of others, fall in the Narak known as "Rodh." The killers of human, who drink Suras and the thieves of gold, they all fall into a Narak known as "Sooker". (31) Naastik (deniers), those who break the tenet of morality, giving pains to others, those who are attached to physical pleasure, hypocrites, the ungrateful, they all go to Narak. (32) Those who destroy wells, tanks, ponds, shrines or the people's houses, they all go to Narak. (33) Those who take meal neglecting their wives, infants, helpers, teachers and eat without prior offerings to the Pitr (ancestors) and the Devas (deities), they go to Narak. (34) Those who obstruct the footpaths and roads with nails, mounds, woods, stones or thorns- they all go to Narak. (35) Those who do not worship Shiva, Durga, Vishnu (Shri Ram and Shri Krishna), Sun, Ganesa, Sadguru and Buddha, they go to Narak. (36)

Asi-patraa-vane-ashauchee krodhanash ch pated-api,
Agni-jvaalm mriga-vyaadho bhojyate yatraa vaayasaiah(37)
Yah kukkutaan nibadhnaati maarjaaraan sookaraansh ch taan,
Pakshinaash ch mrigaansh chhaagaan soapyevm narakm vrajet(38)
Aaraameshv-agni-daataa   ch   ete   yaanti   vishnjane,
Asat-pratigrahee   yas   tu   tathaivaa-ayaajyayaajakah,
Nakshatraur jeevate yastu naro gachchhed-adho-mukham(39)
Ananya-sharana-streenaam   ritu-kaala-vyati-kramam,
Ye prakur-vanti vidvesaatte vai naraka-gaaminah(40)
Ye-api gachchhanti kamaandha nara nareem rajaswalam,
Parvswapsu diva sharadhe tw v narakgameen 41)
Ye shaareerm malm vahanau prakshi-panti jale-api ch,
Aaraame pathi goshthe vaa te vai naraka-gaaminah(42)
Shastraanaam ye ch kartaarah sharaanaam dhanushaam tathaa,
Vikretaarsh-cha ye teshaam te vai naraka-gaaminah(43)

Who do not perform the ritual of purification after Sutak (death and birth related impurity) and the person full of anger, falls in the Narak called 'Asipatra Van'. One who kills birds with arrows falls into Narak named as 'Agnijwal' where he would be fed to crows by the Yam-doots. (37) The one who keeps in bondage the cocks, cats, pigs, birds, deer and antelope, fall in Narak. (38) Who destroy green belt, fall in the Narak called 'Vishanjan'; those taking donations from wrong persons, of wrong commodity, performing Yagya for a person who is ineligible to perform Yagya; earning livelihood from the practice of astrology, fall in 'Adho-mukh' Narak. (39) Those who, commit transgression through deceit, at the time of conception, with women who have no other refuge- they go to Narak. (40) Who due to excessive sex appeal make relations with a woman in menstruation period, in festive dates, in water, in Shraddh day, they all go to Narak. (41) Those who throw their bodily refuse into fire, water, in garden, on pathways, or in a cow pen, they go to Narak. (42) Those who manufacture swords, bow-arrows and other weapons (for the purpose of killing the innocents) and those who sell them, they also go to Narak. (43)

Charma-vikrayinao vaishyaah kesha-vikreyakaah striyah,
Vedo vikreeyate yaishcha vedm dooshayate tu yah,
Visha-vikrayinaah sarve te vai naraka-gaaminah(44)
Anaathm naa-anu-kampanti ye sataam dvesha-kaarakaah,
Vinaa-aparaadhm danadaanti te vai naraka-gaaminah(45)
Upavishtm tveka-panktyaam vishamm bhojayanti ye,
Patanti niraye ghore vidabhuje naatra snshayah(46)
Sarva-bhooteshvavishvastaastathaa teshu vinirdayaah,
Sarva-bhooteshu jivhmaa ye te vai naraka-gaaminah(47)
Niyamaansam-upaadaay ye pshchaada-jitendriyaah,
Viglaapayanti taan bhooyaste vai naraka-gaaminah(48)
Adhyaatma-vidyaataarm naiv manyanti ye gurum,
Tathaa puraanaa-vaktaarm te vai naraka-gaaminah(49)
Mitraa-droha-karaa ye ch preeti-chchheda-karaash-cha ye,
Aashaa-chchheda-karaa ye ch te vai naraka-gaaminah(50)
Vivaahn deva-yaatraam ch teertha-saarthaan vilumpati,
Svasen-narake ghore tasmaan-naa-vartanm punah(51)
Agnim dadyaan-mahaa-paapee grihe graame tathaa vane,
S neeto yama-dootaish-cha vahin-kunadaeshu pachyate(52)

The tradesmen who trade in hide; women who indulge in flesh trade; those who sell the Vedic knowledge; those who denigrate the holy Vedas, those who sell poison; all of them go to Narak. (44) Those who are uncompassionate to the destitute, who are jealous of the noble people, who punish the innocents; they go to Narak. (45) While serving food, those who differentiate between the people sitting in the same row, fall in the 'Vidbhuj' Narak. There is no doubt about it. (46) Those who are suspicious of all the beings and who are cruel to all the creatures, those who deceive all, go to Narak. (47) The persons lacking self control, perform Vrit (observances) and afterwards, due to greed, discard Vrit go to Narak. (48) Those who do not respect the Guru imparting spiritual knowledge and the narrator of Puraan, go to Narak. (49) Those who betray their friends and break-up friendship and those who shatter the hopes, they go to Narak. (50) Those disrupting the marriage ceremonies, (procession of deities), dispossessing the Teerth-yaatris (pilgrims); dwell in a dreadful Narak from which there is no return. (51) The one who sets on fire someone's house, village or a forest, is captured by the Yam-doots and baked in pits of fire. (52)

Agninaa dagdha-gaatro-asau yadaa chhaayaam prayaachate,
Neeyate ch tadaa dootair-asi-patraa-vana-antare(53)
Khadaga-teekshnaaish-cha tat-patraur-gaatraa-chchhedo yadaa bhavet,
Tad-ochuah sheetala-chchhaaye sukha-nidraam kurushv bho(54)
Paaneeym paatum-ichchhanvai trishaarto yadi yaachate,
Paana-arthm tailam-aty-ushnam tadaa dootaiah pradeeyate(55)
Peeyataam bhujyataam paanamannamoochus-tadeti te,
Peetamaatrona tenaiv dagdha-antraa nipatanti te(56)
Kathanchit-punarutthaay pralapanti sudeena-vat,
Vivashaa uchchhvasantsh-cha te vaktum-api naashakan(57)
Ityevm bahushas-taarkshya yaatanaah paapinaam smritaah,
Kimetair-vistaraat-proktaiah sarva-shaastreshu bhaashitaiah(58)
Evm vai klishyamaana-aste naraah naaryah sahastrshah,
Pachyante narake ghore yaa-vadaa-bhoota-samplavam(59)
Tasyaa-kshaym falm bhuktvaa tatrauvotpadyate punah,
Yama-agyayaa maheem praapy bhavanti sthaavaraadayah(60)

When the organs are burnt with this fire, he begs for the shade. And then, the Yam-doots take him to thorny forest named "Asipatra Van." (53) In that forest, when the body of Paapi is cut with the sword- like-sharp leaves of the trees, then the Yam-doots say, "Now, sleep comfortably in this cool shade." (54) When, Paapi begs for water to drink due to extreme thirst, then the Doots give him boiling oil to drink. (55) Then the Yam-doots say, 'Drink this water and eat this food.' As soon as he drinks it, his abdomen is burnt and he collapses. (56) The Paapi tries to get up with difficulty, wails piteously. Helpless, he tries to take breath to speak but unable to do so. (57) O Taarkshya, there are various torments met out to Paapi. They are deliberated in all the Shastra, therefore, no need for further deliberations? (58) Thus, thousands of men and women are tortured and baked in the dreadful Narak until the coming of the Maha-pralaya. (59) Having experienced the unending consequences of Paap, the Paapi are born again in Narak at the time of re-creation of the universe. By order of Yam, they return to the earth and get birth in Sathavar form. (60)

Vriksha-gulma-lataa-valleegiraysh-cha trinaani ch,
Sthaavaraa iti vikhyaataa mahaa-moha-tama-avritaah(61)
Keetaash-cha pashavsh-chaiv pakshinash-cha jalecharaah,
Chatura-sheeti-laksheshu kathitaa deva-yonayah(62)
Etaah sarvaah pari-bhramy tato yaanti manushyataam,
Maanushe-api shvapaakesu jaayante narakaa-gataah,
Tatra-api paapa-chinaiste bhavanti bahu-dukhitaah(63)
Trishnaayaa chaabhibhootas tu narakm prati-padyate,
Trishnaamuktaas tu ye kechit svarga-vaasm labhanti te(64)

Trees, bushes, plants, creepers, rocks and grasses, are called as Sathavar birth. These all are enveloped in great delusion. (Maha-moh) (61) Insects, animals, birds and aquatic lives; it is said that the Paapi have to experience births into eighty-four lakhs species. (62) The Paapi, after traversing through all these fates, get the human form, even then they get the Narak-like miserable life and by the stains of Paap, suffer pain on earth. (63) The people with Trishna (lust, desires and longings) go to Narak and those who are free from all these, go to Swarga. (64)

Annadi-nidhano Devah Shankh Chakra Gadaa-dharah,
Akshayah pundree-kaakash Preta-mokshya-prado-bhav.

***

39

CHAPTER 5

VARIOUS BIRTHS ACCORDING TO KARMA OF INDIVIDUALS; DESCRIPTION OF DIFFERENT DISEASES AND SO ON.

GARUD UVAACH

Yen yen ch paapen yad-yach-chihanm prajaayate,
Yaam yaam yonim ch gachchhanti tanme kathay keshav(1)

SHREEBHAGAVAANUVAACH

Yaiah paapair-yaanti yaam yonim paapino narakaa-gataah,
Yen paapen yach-chihanm jaayate mam tach-chhrinau(2)
Yathaa-yathaa kritm karm taantaam yonin vrajen narah,
Tat tathaiv ch bhunjaano vicharet sarva-lokagah(3)
Maanushatvm pashutvm ch pakshitvaady-ati-dukhadam,
Karmanaam taaratamyen bhavateeh khag-eshvar(4)
Ashaashvatm parigyaay sarva-lokottarm sukham,
Yadaa bhavati maanushym tadaa dharmm samaacharet(5)
Parasyaa-a-ananasnsthm yo graasm harati mandadheeah,
Dharma-patneem tyajna chhabda-vedhee praanaee bhavet kshitau(6)

GARUD SAID-O Keshav, what signs are manifested by which Paap (sin), and to what sorts of birth those Paap lead to, please tell me? (1) **BHAGWAN SAID**-The Paapi (Paapi) returning from Narak (hell) go to particular births on account of Paap, and what signs are manifested by specific Paap, hear all that from me. (2) All human beings will get their next birth depending on their past **Karma** (deeds), and will dwell on all realms experiencing the consequences of Karma. (3) O Lords of Birds, the happy and divine birth as **Devata** (deity) and the painful birth as human, animal and bird, is the result of Karma only. (4) When getting a human birth, one should treat all earthly comforts as transitory and, therefore, follow path of Dharma. (5) The person who snatches the food of others will be born as fool. The one who abandons lawfully married spouse shall be born on this earth as howling animal like dog, etc. (6)

Evm vichitraur nija-karma-bhir nrinaam sukhasy dukhasy ch janma-naam-api,
Vaichitraya-muktm shubha-karmatah shubhm tathaa-ashubhaach chaa-ashumeerayanti(7)
Bhogaante narakasyaitat sarvam-ityavadhaaray,
Dravya-prakaaraa hi yathaa tathaiv praanai-jaatayah(8)
Yatastato-ashnan maarjaaro khadyoto vana-daahakah,
Krimiah paryushitaadah syaan matsaree bhramaro bhavet(9)
Pravrajyaa-a-agamanaad raajan bhavet maru-pishaachakah,
Jala-prasravanam yastu bhindyaat matsyo bhaven-narah(10)
Striyo-apyanen maargena hritvaa doshama-vaapnuyuah,
Eteshaam-ev jantoonaam bhaaryaatvam-upajaayate(11)
Anna-hartaa bhaveda-akhuah shalabho dhaanya-haarakah,
Chaatako jala-hartaa syaad-visha-hartaa ch vrishchik(12)
Shaakm patraam shikhee hritvaa gandhaansh-chhuchchhundaree shubhaan,
Madhu-dnshah palm gridhro lavanam ch pipeelikaa(13)
Taamboola-fala-pushpa-adi-hartaa syaad-vaanaro vane,
Upaana-ttrinaa-kaarpaasa-hartaa syaan-mesha-yonishu(14)

The inequality of happiness and pains among humans as well as the birth in the form of different creatures, is the result of difference in their past karma. According to holy scriptures, virtuous karma lead to better existence and evil Karma lead to unworthy existence. (7) The signs, of time spent in the Narak, are visible in the next birth, in the form of various types of creature, they are born. (8) One who eats food of anyone and anywhere is re-born as tomcat; arsonist putting forests on fire, becomes glow-worm; who eats stale food, becomes insect; the one who is jealous of other's progress, becomes bee. (9) One who withdraws from Sanyaas is born as devil of desert. The one who destroys water pond becomes fish. (10) The woman will have to bear the same consequences as in the case of men. The husband of the evil doer woman will also bear the consequences of the Paap, being her husband. (11) The one who steals food, becomes a rat; who steals grain becomes a locust; who steals water, becomes a hawk cuckoo and who steals poison, a scorpion. (12) The one who steals vegetables and leaves becomes a peacock; who steals perfumes, a musk-rat; who steals honey, a dragon -fly; who steals flesh, a vulture and who steals salt, an ant. (13) The one who steals betel, fruits and flowers, becomes a monkey in the forest; who steal shoes, grass, wood and cotton, is born as sheep. (14)

Yshch raudr-opajeevee ch maarge saarthaan vilumpati,
Mrigyaa-vyasaneeyastu chhaagah syaad-vadhike grihe(15)
Yo mrito visha-paanen krishnaa-sarpo bhaved girau,
Nirnkusha-svabhaavah syaat kunjro nirjane vane(16)
Vaishva-devama-kartaarah sarva-bhakshaash-cha ye dvijaah,
Apareekshita-bhoktaaro vyaaghraah syur-nirjane vane(17)
Gaayatraaeem n smared-yastu yo n sandhyaam-upaasate,
Antar-dushto bahiah saadhuah s bhaved braahmanao bakah(18)
Ayaajya-yaajako viprah s bhaved graama-sookarah,
Kharo vai bahuyaajitvaatkaako-nnimantraah bhojanaat(19)
Paatre vidyaam-adaataa ch baleevardo bhaved dvijah,
Guru-sevaam-akartaa ch shisyah syaad gokharah pashuah(20)
Gurum hunkrity tnukrity vipram nirjity vaadatah,
Aranaye nirjale deshe jaayate brahma-raaksasah(21)
Prati-shrutm dvije daanamadattvaa jambuko bhavet,
Sataama-satkaara-karah fetkaaro-agnimukho bhavet (22)

The one who earns his livelihood by violent means, who robs caravans and who kills the animals by hunting, certainly becomes a goat in a slaughter house. (15) The one who dies by taking poison, becomes a black snake on a mountain; who is tyrannical, becomes an elephant in a desolate forest. (16) The Dvija, who does not make offerings to the deities prior to having food, and who eat all types of food without consideration, becomes tiger in a desolate forest. (17) The **Brahmin** (priest, Purohit) who does not recite the Gayatri Mantra and does not perform **Sandhyaa** (prayer in the morning and twilights), who is wicked at heart, though disguised outwardly as pious, becomes a crane. (18) The Purohit who, out of greed, presides over sacrificial offerings and spiritual rites for undeserving one, becomes a village hog, and who, out of greed, presides over too many sacrifices, becomes an ass; one who joins the banquet uninvited, becomes a crow. (19) The Dvija who does not impart learning to the deserving, becomes bull; the pupil who does not render services to Guru, becomes an animal, an ass or a cow. (20) The one who challenges his Guru or bullies a learned and wise, is born as a **Brahm-rakshyas** (monster) in a waterless wilderness. (21) The one who does not make Daan to Dvija as per the commitment, becomes a jackal; who is not respectful to the good people, becomes a howling Fire-face. (22)

Mitraa-dhrug-giri-gridhrah syaad-ulookah kraya-vanchanaat,
Varna-ashrama-pareevaadaatkapoto jaayate vane(23)
Aashaa-chchhedakaro yastu sneha-chchheda-karastu yah,
Yo dveshaat stree-parityaagee chakra-vaakshchirm bhavet(24)
Maatri-pitri-guru-dveshee bhaginee-bhraatri-vairakrit,
Garbhe yonau vinashtah syaad-yaavadyoni-sahstrashah(25)
Shvashro-apashabdadaa naaree nitym kalaha-kaarinaee,
Saa jalaukaa ch yookaa syaad bhartaarm bhartsate ch yaa(26)
Sva-patim ch parityajy para-punsaanu-vartinee,
Valgunee griha-godhaa syaad dvi-mukhee vaa-ath sarpinaee(27)
Yah sva-gotropa-ghaatee ch sva-gotraa-stree-nishevanaat,
Taraksah shallako bhootvaa rikshayonishu jaayate(28)
Taapasee-gamanaat kaamee bhaven-maru-pishaachakah,
Apraaptaya-uvana-sngaad bhaved-ajagaro vane(29)
Guru-daara-abhilaashee ch krikalaaso bhaven-narah,
Raagyeem gatvaa bhaved-ushto mitraa-patneem ch gardabhah(30)

The one who betrays a friend becomes a mountain-vulture; who cheats in business, an owl; who challenges the established social order, is born as pigeon in a forest.(23) The one who shatters the hopes; who destroys affectionate relations and who, due to jealousy, abandons his wife, becomes a **Chakava** (a type of duck often mentioned in love stories) and remains there for a long time. (24) One who shows bitterness towards mother, father and Guru, who develops animosity towards sister and brother, dies as an embryo in the womb for a thousand births. (25) The woman who abuses her in-laws and causes constant fights; becomes a leech; and she who denounces her husband, becomes a louse. (26) The woman abandoning her own husband and runs after husband of someone else, becomes a bat, a house-lizard or a double headed female snake. (27) He, who cuts off his Gotra lineage by embracing a woman of his Gotra, having become a hyena and a porcupine, is born as a tree. (28) The lustful that, consorts with a Taapaswini female ascetic, becomes a desert devil; that consorts with a minor, becomes python in a jungle. (29) Who covets his Guru's wife, becomes a chameleon; who cohabits with the king's wife, becomes camel; and with his friend's wife, a donkey. (30)

Gudago vidavaraahah syaad vrisah syaad vrishalee-patiah,
Mahaa-kaamee bhaved yastu syaad-ashvah kaama-lampatah(31)
Mritasy-aikaadashaahm tu bhunaanah shvaa vijaayate,
Labhed-devalako vipro yonim kukkuta-sngyakaam(32)
Dravya-arthm devataa-poojaam yah karoti dvija-adhamah,
S vai devalako naam havyakavyeshu garhitah(33)
Mahaa-paatakajaan ghoraan-narakaan praapy daarunaan,
Karma-kshaye prajaayante mahaa-paatakinastvih(34)
Khar-oshtra-mahisheenaam hi brahmahaa yonimrichchhati,
Vrik-shvaana-shrigalaanaam suraapaa yaanti yonishu(35)
Krimi-keeta-patngtvm svarnaasteyee samaapnuyaat,
Trinaa-gulma-lataatvm ch kramasho gurutalpagah(36)
Parasy yoshitm hritvaa nyaasa-apaharanaen ch,
Brahmasva-haranaach-chaiv jaayate brahma-raakshasah(37)
Brahmasvm pranaayaad bhuktm dahatyaa-saptamm kulam,
Balaat-kaarena chairyena dahatyaa-chandra-taarakam(38)

The homosexual becomes a village pig; who consorts with a characterless, becomes bull; that is lustful, becomes a horse. (31) Who takes meals in the house of departed before the **Ekaadas** (eleventh-day), is born as dog. The Devlak who plunders the property belonging to a temple, is born from the womb of a hen. (32) The wretched among Dvija who worships the Devtas in return of wealth, is called a Devlak and is unfit to offer **Havya** (oblations) to the Devtas and Pitr (ancestors). (33) Those who commit Mahaa-paap (grave sins), having passed through terrible Narak, are born here again upon the exhaustion of their evil karma. (34) The killer of a human being, after suffering the miseries of Narak, goes into the womb of an ass, a camel and a she-buffalo; the one who takes Sura, enters the wombs of a wolf, a dog, a jackal, etc. (35) The thief of gold, takes birth on this earth as a worm, an insect and a bird. Who cohabits with his Guru's wife, takes the condition of grass, bushes and plants, etc. (36) Who abducts another's wife, who misappropriates the heritage articles, who robs a noble Atma, is born as a Brahmn-Raakshyash (monster) after suffering the miseries of Narak. (37) The possessions of pious Brahmin (knower, priest, purohit, sant) acquired by deception, enjoyed even in friendship, afflict the family for seven generations, and who forcibly or secretly, enjoys the wealth of a priest, his family is destroyed so long as the moon and stars exist. (38)

Lauha-choornaashma-choornae ch vism ch jarayen-narah,
Brahmasvm trishu lokeshu kah pumaan-jrayishyati(39)
Brahmasvarasa-pushtaani   vaahanaani   balaani   ch,
Yuddha-kaale visheeryante saikataah setavo yathaa(40)
Deva-dravyopabhogen   brahma-sva-haranaen   ch,
Kulaanyakoolataam yaanti braahmana-ati-kramena ch(41)
Svama-ashritm   parityajy   vedashaa   str-paraayanaam,
Anyebhyo deeyate daanm kathy-ateyam-atikramah(42)
Poorva-janma-kritaat punayaad yallabdhm bahu chaa-alpakam,
N   dattm   dvija-mukhyebhyah   paropakritaye   tathaa,
Raarateeti dhanm tasy ko me bhartaa bhavishyati(43)
Yadanastamite soorye n dattm dhanam-arthinaam,
N jaane tasy tad vittm praatah kasy bhavisyati(44)
Tadee-drisham parigyaay dharma-arthe deeyate dhanam,
Dhanen dhaaryate dharmah shraddhaa-pooten chetasaa(45)
Svayamev   ch   yo   dattvaa   svayameva-apakarshati,
S paapee narakm yaati yaa-vadaabhootasamplavam(46)

One may even digest powdered iron, powdered stone, and poison; but where is the person in **Trilok** (three realms) who can digest a pious Brahmin's wealth? (39) Chariots and troops of king supported by the seized wealth of a pious priest, crumble away in battle like artificial river-culverts made of sand. (40) By appropriating Dev-dravya (property of temples), by taking a Brahmin's possessions and by disrespecting Brahmin's families, the person's coming generations become broken up. (41) The one who, instead of making a Daan to dependent Brahmin well versed in Vedas and **Shastra** (Holy Scriptures), gives it to some other Brahmin, it is called encroachment. (42) In case, the more or less wealth earned by virtue of good karma of the previous births is not donated to the Dharmik and noble people and is not utilized for charity, then that wealth cries, "who will be my owner, who will be my owner" (after your death). (43) I do not know that what would be the fate of the **Dhana** (purse) tomorrow, not donated to the needy before twilight of your life. (44) Daan may be made knowing this fact (that the property does not belong to anyone). Dharma is acquired only by that Daan of purse, which is given with deep faith and pious heart. (45) The Paapi, who forcibly takes back, the Daan made by him in the past, goes into Narak until the coming of the **Pralaya** (deluge). (46)

45

Shraddhaa-virahito dharmo nehaa-amutraa ch tatfalam,
Dharmaach ch jaayate hyartho dharmaat kaamo-api jaayate(47)
Dharm evaa-apavargaay tasmaad dharmm samaacharet,
Shraddhayaa saadhyate dharmo bahubhiah na-artha-raashibhiah(48)
Akinchinaa hi munayah shraddhaavanto divm gataah,
Ashraddhayaa hutm dattm tapas taptm kritm ch yat,
Asadityuchyate paksin prety cheh n tatfalam(49)
Evm duskarma-kartaaro bhuktvaa niraya-yaatanaam,
Jaayante paapashesena proktaasvetaasu yonishu(50)
Tato janma-sahstreshu praapy tiryak-shareera-taam,
Dukhaani bhaara-vahano-bhavaadeeni labhanti te(51)
Pakshi-dukhm tato bhuktvaa vrishti-sheeta-atapod-bhavam,
Maanushm labhate pashchaat samee-bhoote shubhaa-ashubhe(52)
Stree-punso-astu prasangen bhootvaa garbhe kramaadasau,
Garbha-adi-maranaantm ch praapy dukhm priyet-punah(53)

Dharma bereft of faith is meaningless in this world and the other world. Dharma alone is the source of wealth and Dharma alone is the source of **Kaam** (happiness). (47) Dharma is also for Mokshya. Therefore, one should follow the path of Dharma. Dharma is acquired by faith and not by huge wealth. (48) The **Munis**, who had no wealth, went to **Swarga** (paradise) due to deep faith. Daan, Tapa (penances), Homa sacrifices and all that, is fruitless if they are not supported by faith. (49) The Paapi suffering the miseries of bad deeds and having experienced the tortures of Narak, are born with the residues of their Paap, in lower forms like worms, animals and birds. (50) Then, obtaining thousands of births in the bodies of birds and similar creatures suffer miseries by taking birth as beasts of burden like camel and ass. (51) The bird, having experienced the miseries of cold, rain and heat, reaches the human form, when the good and evil karma are balanced. (52) With the cohabitation of man and woman, it becomes an embryo in due course. Having suffered the miseries from conception to death, dies again. (53)

Sam-utpattir-vinaashsh-cha   jaayate   sarva-dehinaam,
Evm pravartitm chakrm bhoota-graame chatur-vidhe(54)
Ghatee-yantraam yathaa martyaa bhramanti mam maayayaa,
Bhoomau kadaachin-narake karma-paasha-samaa-vritaah(55)
Adatta-daanaachcha bhaved daridro daridrabhaavaachch karoti paapam,
Paapa-prabhaavaan-narake prayaati punar-daridrah punar-ev paapee(56)
Avashyamev bhoktavym kritm karm shubhaa-ashubham,
Naa-bhuktm ksheeyate karm kalpa-koti-shatair-api(57)

The birth in the form of **Swedaj** (those born out of sweat)
Udbhij (from earth), **Andaj** (from egg), **Jarayuj** (from
embryo) are the four types of origins of living beings and
the Paapi keep on revolving by the painful cycle of birth
and death. (54) As the needle of clock turns, so mortals
revolve by **Maya** (illusion). They shuttle between earth
and Narak, held fast by the noose of karma. (55) There is
a vicious circle, the one who does not offer Daan, becomes
poverty stricken and due to poverty, commits Paap; by
the force of Paap, goes to Narak, and is again born in
poverty and again becomes Paapi. (56) The consequences
of the **Karma**, whether good or bad, are certainly to be
faced. Without suffering, the Karma do not fade away
even in tens of millions of ages. (57)

**Annadi-nidhano Devah Shankh Chakra Gadaa-dharah,
Akshayah pundree-kaakash Preta-mokshya-prado-bhav.**

47

CHAPTER 6

FORMATION OF EMBRYO, EVOLUTION OF JEEV (CREATURE),
SUFFERINGS IN THE WOMB, THE BAD KARMA OF HUMAN
BEINGS AND THEIR CONSEQUENCES.

GARUD UVAACH

Katham-utpadyate   maatur-jathare   naraka-agatah,
Garbha-adi-dukhm yad bhunkte tanme kathay keshav(1)

VISHNAURUVAACH

Stree-punsostu   prasngen   niruddhe   shukra-shonaite,
Yathaa-aym jaayate martyastathaa vakshyaamyahm tav(2)
Svargaachch narakaat tyaktah streenaam garbhe bhavaty-api,
Naabhi-bhootsh-cha tasyaiv yaati beeja-dvaym hi tat(3)
Evm gatvaa hyasankhyaataa yoneestaah karma-bhoor-api,
Maanushym durlabhm labdhvaa kadaachid daiva-yogatah(4)

GARUDA SAID-Tell me, O Keshav! How the one who
returns from Narak, is born in the womb of the mother?
And what miseries he suffers while in the state of embryo?
(1) **BHAGWAN SAID-** How the union of woman and man,
leads to the birth of a mortal, I will explain to you. (2)
When the consequences of virtues and Paap have been
experienced in the Swarga and Narak, the formation of
embryo takes place in the womb by putting together seeds
of male and female. (3) After going through the numerous
births in different **Yonis** (creatures), it is with a rare
fortune that the birth as human being is acquired -rare
as only this is the **Karamyoni** (action life), rest all are
Bhog Yonis (experiencing the consequences of Karma). It is
here with the divine blessings; one can acquire the knowledge
of Hari (Ishwara) and get liberated (merge with Ishwara). (4)

48

Maanushym yah samaasaady svarga-moksha-ieka-saadhakam,
Tayor n saadhayed-ekm tenaa-a-atmaa vanchito dhuravam(5)
Kalalm tv-eka-raatrena pancha-raatrena budbudam,
Dashaahen tu karkandhooah peshyanadam vaa tatah param(6)
Maasen tu shiro dvaabhyaam baahva-angaady-anga-vigrahah,
Nakha-loma-asthi-charmaanai linga-ch-chhidrobhavstribhiah(7)
Chatur-bhir-dhaatavah sapt panchabhiah kshuttrida-udbhavah,
Shada-bhir-jaraayunaa veetah kukshau bhraamyati dakshinae(8)
Maatur-jagdhaannapaanaadyairedhaddhaaturasammate,
Shete vina-mootraayor-garte s jantur-jantu-sambhave(9)
Krimibhiah kshata-sarvaangah saukumaaryaat prati-kshanaam,
Moorchchhaamaapnotyuru-kleshastatraatyaiah kshudhitairmuhuah(10)
Katu-teekshna-oshnaa-lavanaa-rooksha-amlaadi-bhir-ulbanaaiah,
Maatri-bhuktairupaspristah sarva-angotthita-vedanah,
Ulben snvritastasminnantraushcha bahira-avritah(11)
Aaste kritvaa shirah kukshau bhagna-pristha-shiro-dharah,
Akalpah svaanga-cheshtaayaam shakunt iv pnjare(12)

The person, who having obtained the human birth, which is the only mean to gain Swarga and Mokshya, does not strive either for Swarga or for Mokshya, certainly deprives self of a rare opportunity. (5) In this embryo, the fetus becomes a lump in the first night; by the fifth night, blastula; by the tenth day, like the fruit of the berry; and after that, an egg of flesh. (6) Head is formed by the first month; the arms and other parts of the body are formed by the second month; by the third occurs the formation of nails, hair, bones, skin, private parts and other cavities of ten openings. (7) The seven bodily fluids are formed by the fourth month; by the fifth, hunger and thirst arise; by the sixth, enveloped by the membrane, it moves to the left of the womb. (8) The body is formed from the food and liquid intake of the mother. The creature, at the time of birth, is in slumbers and is in the midst of disgusting microbe and urine. (9) Being bitten constantly by worms, the limbs are hurt. The tender body of the creature often faints due to extreme pain. (10) It is pained by the mother eating many types of food- pungent, bitter, hot, salty, sour and acidic. It feels caged in the womb and bound outside by the tissues. (11) With its head arched towards its belly and its back and neck in curved shape, it is unable to move its limbs, like a parrot in a cage. (12)

Tatra labdha-smritir-daivaat karm janmashat-odbhavam,
Smaran deergha-man-uchchhvaasam sharm kim naam vindate(13)
Naathamaan rishir-bheetah sapta-vadhriah kritaanjaliah,
Stuveet tm viklavayaa vaachaa yen-odare-arpitah(14)
Aarabhy saptamaanmaasaallabdha-bodho-api vepitah,
Naikatraaste sooti-vaatair-vishthaa-bhooriv sahodarah(15)
JEEV UVAACH
Shree-patim jagata-adhaaram-ashubha-kshaya-kaarakam,
Vrajaami sharanam vishnaum sharana-agata-vatsalam(16)
Tvan-maayaa-mohito dehe tathaa putraa-kalatraake,
Ahm mam-aabhi-maanen gato-ahm naath snsritim(17)
Kritm pari-janasya-arthe mayaa karm shubha-ashubham,
Ekaakee ten dagdho-ahm gataaste fala-bhaaginah(18)
Yadi yonyaah pramuchye-ahm tat smarishye padm tav,
Tam-upaaym karishyaami yen muktim vrajaamyaham(19)
Vina-mootraa-koope patito dagdho-ahm jathara-agninaa,
ichchhannito vivasitum kadaa niryaasyate bahiah(20)

There, by divine power, it recollects the Karma generated in hundreds of previous births, and, feeling quite unhappy, sobs for a long time. (13) Getting this insight, bound in seven membranes and frightened; the embryo adores, with folded hands, in plaintive tones to the Ishwara who placed it in the womb. (14) From the seventh month of pregnancy, though gains consciousness, but trembles knowing that it is getting reborn and moves about because of the parturition winds, like a uterine worm. (15) The creature says, "I seek refuge in Vishnu; the consort of mother Lakshami, the one who sustains the universe, the one who destroys evil, the one who is Sharanaangat-vatsal (compassionate to those who come for shelter). (16) O Nath! I am captivated by your **Maya**, attached only to the thoughts of 'me' and 'mine'. Such as my body, my children and my wife; misled by my ego, I am trapped in the cycle of birth and death. (17) I did righteous and wrongful actions for my dependents, but I alone am getting tormented, while they, who enjoyed the fruits, have escaped. (18) O Nath, if I am released from this womb, I will take refuge in you and I will make all out efforts for Mokshya. (19) Fallen into the well of feces and urine, I am burnt by hunger, and anxious to escape from the womb. When shall I get out? (20)

Yene-drishm me vigyaanm dattm deena-dayaalunaa,
Tamev sharanam yaami punarme maa-astu snsritiah(21)
N ch nirgantum-ichchhaami bahir-garbhaat-kadaachan,
Yatraa yaatasy me paapa-karmanaa durgatir-bhavet(22)
Tasmaadatra mahad dukhe sthito-api vigata-klamah,
Uddharishyaami snsaaraadaatmaann te pada-ashrayah(23)

SHREEBHAGAVAANUVAACH

Evm kritamatir-garbhe dasha-maasyah stuvannrisiah,
Sadyah kshipatyavaacheenm prasootyai sooti-maarutah(24)
Tenaavasristah sahasaa kritvaa-avaakshir aaturah,
Viniskraamati krichchhrena niruchchhvaaso hata-smritiah(25)
Patito bhuvi vina-mootro vishthaa-bhooriv chestate,
Rorooyati gate gyaane vipareetaam gatim gatah(26)
Garbhe vyaadhau shma-shaane ch puraanae yaa matir-bhavet,
Saa yadi sthirataam yaati ko n muchyet bandhanaat(27)
Yadaa garbhaad bahir-yaati karma-bhogaad-anantaram,
Tadaiv vaishnaavee maayaa mohayatyev poorusham(28)

I have got this wisdom due to the mercy of the One. I seek refuge in Him. May He release me from transmigration? (21) (He re-thinks) I should not wish to come out of the womb, I may get drawn to Paap karma (sinful) acts leading to **Durgati.** (22) I would rather like to remain in this miserable state and take refuge in your feet and pray for my Mokshya". (23) **BHAGWAN SAID**-Endowed with insight and involved in praying, it is cast out suddenly after ten months; head downwards, into birth by the winds of delivery. (24) Cast out suddenly, bending down head, is anxious and breathless and in the state of destroyed memory. (25) Having fallen on the ground, the Jeeva moves like a worm in excrement. The Jeeva is in changed condition now and cries continuously, deprived of knowledge. (26) Had the state of mind, which crops up while in the womb, during illness, on the cremation ground, while listening the Puraans, been permanent then-who would not be liberated from bondage! (27) After experiencing karma, when the Jeeva comes out of the womb, he is delusional by Maya of Vishnu. (28)

S tadaa maayayaa sprishto n kinchid-vidate-avashah,
Shaishava-adi-bhavm dukhm paraadheenatayaa-ashnute(29)
Para-chchhandm n vidushaa pushya-maanao janen sah,
An-abhi-pretamaapannah pratyaakhyaa tu maneeshvarah(30)
Shaayito-ashuchi-parynke jantu-svedaja-dooshite,
Neshah kanadaooyane-angaanaamaasanotthaanachestane(31)
Tudantyaamatvachm dnshaa mashakaa matkunaadayah,
Rudantm vigatagyaanm krimayah krimikm yathaa(32)
Ityevm shaishavm bhuktvaa dukhm pauganadaamev ch,
Tato yauvanamaasaady yaati sampadamaasureem(33)
Tadaa dur-vyasana-asakto neecha-sango-paraayanaah,
Shaastra-satpurushaanaam ch dveshtaa syaat-kaamalampatah(34)
Drishtvaa striaaym deva-maayaam tadabhaavaira-jitendriyah,
Pralobhitah pataty-andhe tamasy-agnau patangvat(35)
Kurnga-maatnga-patnga-bhrnga-meenaa hataah panchbhirev pancha,
Ekah pramaadee s kathm n hanyate yah sevate panchabhirev panch(36)

Then, when touched by the Maya, he feels helpless and is unable to speak. He experiences the miseries of infancy and childhood arising from dependence. (29) He is nourished by parents without understanding his wishes; He is unable to escape from what is thrust upon him against his will. (30) He is laid on an unclean bed which is smeared with sweat, helpless and unable to scratch his limbs or move. (31) Flies, Mosquitoes, fleas, bedbugs and other insects bite him, but he cannot understand and cries in pain. (32) Having experienced the miseries of infancy and of childhood, he reaches at youth and the evil tendencies crop up. (33) Then he gets into addictions and falls in the company of the wicked; develops dislike for the scriptures and for the company of good people, and becomes lustful. (34) Illusioned by Maya, his senses get destructed seeing a seductive woman, he falls into great darkness, like a moth into a flame. (35) The deer, elephant, bird, bee and the fish: these five are led to death by only one of the senses they have; then, how shall the human being, who is attached to five senses, would escape destruction? (36)

Alabdhaabheepsito-agyaana-adiddhamanyuah shuchaarpitah,
Sah   dehen   maanen   varddhamaanen   manyunaa(37)
Karoti vigrahm kaamee kaamishvantaay chaatmanah,
Bala-adhikaiah   s   hanyet   gajair-anyair-gajo   yathaa(38)
Evm   yo   vishaya-asaktyaa   naratvam-ati-durlabham,
Vrithaa naashayate moodhastasmaat paapataro hi kah?(39)
Jaateeshateshu labhate bhuvi maanushatvm tatra-api durlabha-tarm khalu bho dvijatvam,
Yastann paalayati laalayateendriyaanai tasya-amritm ksharati hastagatm pramaadaat(40)
Tatastaam   vriddhataam   praapy   mahaa-vyaadhi-samaakulah,
Mrityum   praapy   mahad   dukham   narakm   yaati   poorva-vat(41)
Evm gataa-agataiah karma-paashair-baddhaash-cha paapinah,
Kadaapi   n   virajyante   mam   maayaa-vimohitaah(42)
Chakra-dharo-api suratvm surabhaave sakala-sura-patir bhavitum,
Sura-patir-oordhva-gatittvm tathaapi n nivartate trishnaa(43)

Longing for the unachievable, brings anger and sorrow due to ignorance, and his pride and anger increases with the growth of body. (37) The lusty quarrels with another lusty for selfish gains, this is to his own peril and is destroyed by those stronger to him, as an elephant by another stronger one. (38) Who can be more Paapi than the one who, due to attachment to sense objects, spends in vain the human birth which is very rare to obtain. (39) One obtains human birth on earth only after hundreds of lives; and even more difficult is to obtain Dvija status, and even then who only works for satisfaction of senses; lets the nectar to slip from his hand due to foolishness. (40) In the old age, he is troubled with chronic diseases; and dies after lot of miseries; he once again goes to the **Narak** (the vicious circle continues). (41) The Paapi, tied by the noose of karma, come and go (from birth to death in various Yonis and from Narak to Mrityu-loka), never released from the delusion of Maya. (42) The greatest ruler is also not content, he wants to become Devta. Becoming Devta does not satisfy him, thus aspires to become Indra, the ruler of Devlok. Still there is longing, he remains unsatisfied. (43)

Aatma-adheenah pumaanl-loke sukhee bhavati nishchitam,
Shabdah sparshsh-cha roopm ch raso gandhsh-cha tadgunaaah,
Tathaa ch visaya-adheeno dukhee bhavati nishchitam(44)
Pitri-maatri-mayo baalye yauvane dayitaamayah,
Putraa-pautraayamsh-cha ante moodho naa-attmamayah kvachit(45)
Sarveshaam pashyataamev mritah sarvm parityajet,
Ekah prajaayate janturek ev praleeyate(46)

The one, under the control of his Atma, is always satisfied. Sound, touch, vision, taste and smell are the attributes of elements. These are also the subjects of sense organs. As the liberated is always happy; similarly the one attached to sense organs is always unhappy. (44) Attached to parents in childhood, deeply involved with loved one in adulthood, always thinks about children in old age. The fools have no time for introspection. (45) The dying person leaves behind everything within a moment. All the creatures are born with separate destiny; they are born alone and they die alone. (46)

**Annadi-nidhano Devah Shankh Chakra Gadaa-dharah,
Akshayah pundree-kaakash Preta-mokshya-prado-bhav.**

***

CHAPTER 7

WAYS TO ESCAPE NARAK, IMPORTANCE OF DESCENDENTS
FOR PROPER TRANSMIGRATION; AURDHVA-DEHIK KRIYA
(HIGHER BODILY RITE) PERFORMED BY A KING AND
EMANCIPATION OF PRET.

SOOT UVAACH

Iti shrutvaa tu garudah kampito-ashvattha-patraa-vat,
Janaanaam-upakaara-arthm punah paprachchh keshavam(1)

GARUD UVAACH

Kritvaa paapaani manujaah pramaadaad buddhito-api vaa,
N yaanti yaatanaa yaamyaah ken-opaayen kathyataam(2)
Snsaaraarnaavamagnaanaam naraanaam deenachetasaam,
Paapopahata-buddheenaam   vishayopahataatmanaam(3)
Uddhaara-arthm vad svaamin puraan-arthm vinishchyam,
Upaaym yen manujaah sadgatim yaanti maadhav(4)

SOOT SAID-O Saunak! Hearing these accounts, Garuda
started trembling like a leaf of Peepal tree but despite
this, he again asked questions to Keshav, for the benefit
of mankind. (1) **GARUD SAID**-Tell me O Swami! By what
means the people who have committed Paap knowingly or
unknowingly, would escape from the torments of Yam. (2)
The people who are immersed in the ocean of Sansara
(transmigration), of poor wisdom, whose reason is clouded
by their Paap, their self dimmed by attachment to
gratification of sense-objects. (3) For their rescue, tell
me O Swami! The ways as prescribed by Puranas; and
the means by which people may attain **Sad-gati** (Speedy
elevation to truth), O Madhava. (4)

55

Kathm kurvanti te pretaah ken roopena kasy kim,
Gyaayate ken vidhinaa jalpanti n vadanti vaa (4.1)

SHREEBHAGAVAANUVAACH

Saadhu prishtm tvayaa taarkshya maanushaanaam hitaay vai,
Shrinaushvaavahito bhootvaa sarvm te kathayaamyaham(5)
Durgatiah kathitaa poorvama-putraanaam ch paapinaam,
Putrinaam dhaarmikaanaam tu n kadaachit-khageshvar(6)
Putraa-janma-nirodhah syaad-yadi kena-api karmanaa,
Tadaa kshchid-uupaayen putr-otpattim prasaadhayet(7)
Harivnsha-kathaam shrutvaa shata-chanadaee-vidhaanatah,
Bhaktyaa shree-shivam-aaraadhy putraam-utpaadayet-sudheeah(8)
Pun-naamno narakaadyasmaat-pitarm traayate sutah,
Tasmaat putraa iti proktah svayamev svayambhuvaa(9)
Eko-api putro dharmaatmaa sarvm taarayate kulam,
Putrona lokaanjayati shrutireshaa sanaatanee(10)

In which form, what and how the Pret (the temporary conditions of departed before getting a new body and the spirit of departed) work? How to know about the function of Pret, do they speak or not? (4.1) **BHAGWAN SAID**-O Taarkshya (Garud), you have posed a pious question for the benefit of human beings. Now, listen attentively, and I will tell you everything. (5) As already said, **Dur-gati** (speed to untruth) is in the store for the Paapi and those without son (**the word "son" used in Puranas, implies to both daughter as well as son. The use of the word "son" is mainly due to limitations of the diction**). But never so, O Khageshwar, to those who have son and who follow Dharma. (6) In case, due to Karma, the birth of offspring has been denied, then efforts should be made to beget one. (7) Listening Hari-vansha (Vishnu Katha) or recital of Shat-chandi (Shri Durga Sapt-Sati) with due procedure, or worship of the Shri (glorious) Shiva with devotion, the wise should beget an offspring. (8) The son saves his father (**father implies to mother as well**) from the Narak called "Put"; therefore, he was named as "putra" by the "Svayam-bhu" (Self-existent). (9) Even lone Dharam-atma son can ferry the whole of the clan. Thus, comes the eternal saying that by son one conquers the worlds. (10)

Iti vedair-api proktm putraa-maahaatmyam-uttamam,
Tasmaat-putraa-mukhm drishtvaa muchyate paitrikaad-rinaat(11)
Pautraasy sparshanaan-matryo muchyate ch rinaa-traayaat,
Lokaanatyeddivah praaptiah putraa-pautraa-prapautraakaiah(12)
N bhavech ch yadaa gotraaee paro-api vidhima-acharet,
Straaee vaa-api purushah kshchit tushtaye kurute kriyaam(13)
Vrish-otsarga-adi-luptaash-cha lupta-maasika-pindaakaah,
Antarikshe mritaa ye ch vishnau-smaranaa-varjitaah,
Vishvaasa-ghaatee krooras tu s preto jaayate dhruvam(13.1)
Maatarm bhagineem bhaaryaam snushaam duhitarm tathaa,
Adrishta-doshaam tyajati s preto jaayate dhuravam(13.2)
Vaapee-koopa-tadaagaansh ch aaraamm sura-mandiram,
Prapaam sadan suvrikshaansh ch tathaa bhojana-shaalikaah,
Pitri-paitaamahm dharmm vikreenaati s paapabhaak,
Mritah pretatva-maapnoti yaa-vadaa-bhootasamplavam(13.3)
Kalau pretatva-maapnoti taarkshya-ashuddha-kriyaaparah(13.4)
Dushta-mrityu-vashaad vaapi adagdhavapushastathaa,
Pretatvm Jaayate taarkshya peedayante yen jantavah(13.5)

The great importance of the son is also proclaimed by Vedas. One is released from the debt of the forefathers, by seeing the face of son. (11) The departed is released from the three-fold debt (the debt of ancestors, Rishis and deities) by the touch of his grandson. With the help of sons, grandsons, and great-grandsons, one obtains Swarga. (12) When son is not available to perform the rites of the departed one may take the help of other Gotra (clan). Any man or woman can perform rites for the departed. (13) Departed for whom the Varsho-utsarg and monthly rites were not performed, who died by falling from height, who did not remember Bhagwan Vishnu, those who break the faith and are cruel, certainly become Pret. (13.1) Those who ignore and do not care for their innocent mother, sister, wife, daughter-in-law and the daughter, certainly become Pret. (13.2) Those who sell the reservoirs, wells, ponds, temples, homes, rest houses, grown up trees, parks, play-grounds, banquets and other charitable works created by their forefathers, they are Paapi and remain in Pret-yoni till "Maha-pralaya" (deluge). (13.3) O Garud! In the present age, a person who does not follow the Shastra and who indulges into impure actions gets Pret-yoni. (13.4) In case of unnatural death or where the last rites were not performed with prescribed procedure, the departed is led to that Pret-yoni where it suffers a lot. (13.5)

**Sarva-kriyaa-pari-bhrashto naastiko dharma-nindakah,
Asatya-vaada-nirato narah pretaiah s peedayate(13.6)
Naastikym vritti-lopash ch mahaa-lobhas tathaiv ch,
Syaad dhant kalaho nitym saa peedaa preta-sambhavaa(13.7)
Yatra lobhas-tathaa krodho nidraa shoko bhaym madah,
Aalasym kalaho nitym pretaa bhunjanti tatrau vai(13.8)
Preta-doshah kule yasy sukhm tasy n vidyate,**
Matiah preetir-ratir-buddhir-laksmeeah pancha-vinaashanam(13.9)
**Sva-kulm peedaayet pretah para-chchhidrena peedaayet,
Jeevan s drishyate snehee mrito dushtatvamaapnuyaat(13.10)
Yathaa taaraa-ganaaah sarvechchhaadyante ravi-rashmibhiah,
Evm prachchhaadyate sarvm n preto bhavati kvachit(14)
Shraaddhen putraa-datten svaryaateeti kimuchyate,
Preto-api para-datten gatah svargamatho shrinau(15)
Atrauvodaaharisye-aham-itihaasm puraatanam,
Audhrva-daihikadaanasy parm maahaatmya-soochakam(16)**

Those who do not have faith in Vedas, Puranas and are devoid of all actions; who denounce the Dharma and are not truthful, they all are troubled by Pret. (13.6) Turning Nastik, losing the means of livelihood, rise in greediness, daily quarrel in life, etc. are the incidents which do arise due to affliction of Pret. (13.7) Prets stay in those families where anger, greed, lethargy, anguish, fear, drunkenness, laziness, and quarrel are everyday affairs. (13.8) The happiness is snatched away from the family afflicted by Pret. The Pret destroys five things - capacity to think, to understand, to love, to have carnal desire, and the prosperity. (13.9) Prets torture their family members, but only after finding the loop-holes. A person who was very loving during lifetime, become cruel after death and starts harassing his relatives. (13.10) The Aurdhva-dehik rites eliminate all the Pretatva in a similar way as the stars disappear by the rays of sun. (14) One attains Swarga by the Shraddh performed by a son. But the departed can attain Swarga even though the rites performed by someone other than the son. Now listen a saga. (15) Relating to it, I will tell you, an incident from ancient history, which shows how important is the Aurdhva-dehik for the departed Atma and about the efficacy of Daan for the higher body. (16)

Puraa tretaa-yuge taarkshya raajaa-a-aseed babhru-vaahanah,
Mahodaye pure ramye dharma-nishtho mahaabalah(17)
Yajvaa daana-patiah shree-maan brahmanayah saadhu-vatsalah,
Sheela-achaara-gunaopeto dayaa-daaksinaya-snyutah(18)
Paalayaamaas dharmena prajaah putraanivaurasaan,
Kshatraa-dharma-rato nitym s danadayaan danadaayan-nripah(19)
S kadaachin-mahaa-baahuah sa-sainyo mrigayaam gatah,
Vanm vivesh gahanm naanaa-vriksha-samanvitam(20)
Naanaa-mriga-ganaa-keernam naanaa-pakshi-ninaaditam,
Vana-madhye tadaa raajaa mrigm dooraada-pashyat(21)
Ten viddho mrigo-ateev baanaen sudridhen ch,
Baanaa-maadaay s tasy vane-adarshanameyivaan(22)
Kakshena rudhira-adrena s raajaa-anujagaam tam,
Tato mriga-prasngen vanam-anyad-vivesh sah(23)
Kshut-kshaama-kanatho nripatiah shrama-santaapa-moorchaichhatah,
Jalaashaym samaasaady sa-ashva ev vyagaahat(24)
Papau tad-udakm sheetm padam-gandha-adi-vaasitam,
Tato-avateery salila-ad-vishramo babhru-vaahanah(25)

Formerly, in the Tretaa-yug, over the delightful city of Mahodaya, there reigned a king named Babhru-vaahan, who was very mighty and **Dharm-nisht** (committed to Dharma). (17) The king used to perform Yagya, donate generously, he was prosperous, respectful to the wise, he used to value the pious and good people, was modest, ethical, compassionate, and gave alms. (18) Supporting his subjects with Dharma as though they were his own children, always delighting in Raaj-dharma (moral duties of a ruler) and punishing the guilty. (19) Once, that mighty king went along with his army for hunting. He entered into a thick forest, full of various kinds of trees. (20) The king saw a deer from a distance in the midst of forest, resounding with the clamor of various birds and herd. (21) The deer, wounded by the sharp arrow shot by king, disappeared, running away into the deep forest carrying the arrow along. (22) Then, the king chased the deer following the blood-stains on the grass and entered into another forest. (23) Hungry and with parched throat, fainting with the heat and fatigue, the king reached near a pond and took a bath in it, along with his horse. (24) He drank the cool water of that pond endowed with the fragrance of lotus, and Babhru-vahana felt refreshed. (25)

Dadarsh nyagrodha-tarum sheeta-chchhaaym manoharam,
Mahaa-vitapa-visteernam   pakshi-sngha-ninaaditam(26)
Vanasy   tasy   sarvasy   mahaaketum-iv   sthitam,
Moolm   tasy   samaasaady   nishasad   mahee-patiah(27)
Ath pretm dadarshaasau kshut-tridabhyaam vyaakul-endriyam,
Utkachm malinm kubjm nirmaansm bheema-darshanam(28)
Tm drishtvaa vikritm ghorm vismito babhru-vaahanah,
Preto-api drishtvaa tm ghoraamataveema-agatm nripam(29)
Sam-utsuka-manaa   bhootvaa   tasyaantikamupaagatah,
Abraveet s tadaa taarkshya preta-raajo nripm vachah(30)
Preta-bhaavo mayaa tyaktah praapto-asmi paramaam gatim,
Tvat-snyogaan-mahaa-baaho jaato dhanyataro-asmyaham(31)
Krishnaa-varna karaalaasy pretatvm ghora-darshanam,
Ken   karma-vipaaken   praaptm   te   bahv-amanlam(32)
Pretatva-kaaranam   taat   broohi   sarvama-sheshatah,
Ko-asi tvm ken daanen pretatvm te vinashyati?(33)
Kathayaami   nripa-shresth!   Sarvame-vaaditastav,
Pretatva-kaaranam shrutvaa dayaam kartum tvamarhasi(34)

He saw a delightful Banyan tree giving cool shade with
its thick branches, full of the squeal of various birds.
(26) That tree was standing like a giant flag over the
whole forest. The king approached and sat at its bottom.
(27) At this point, he saw a Pret of terrible appearance,
humpbacked and fleshless, with hair erect, dirty, and
with sense organs distorted due to hunger and thirst.
(28) Babbru-vahana was surprised seeing the deformed
and dreadful Pret. The Pret was also startled seeing
the king who had come to that dreadful forest. (29) And
filled with curiosity, the Pret came near to the king.
Then, spoke to the king, O Taarkshya: (30) "I have been
freed from the Pret-yoni and got Param-gati by just seeing
you, O King having powerful-arms, I am highly blessed."
(31) The king said, "O dark and dreadful Pret! By what
bad deeds did you reach to this condition of the Pret-
yoni, so dreadful to see and highly inauspicious? (32) O
Dear, tell me in detail, the cause of your condition.
Who are you, and by what Daan you can overcome from
your present Pret-yoni?" (33) **PRET SAID** "I will tell you
everything about myself from the beginning, O noble king.
You will certainly have compassion upon hearing the
cause of my Pret-yoni," the Pret replied. (34)

PRET UVAACH

Vaidisham naam nagarm sarva-sampat-samanvitam,
Naanaa-janapada-akeernam naanaa-ratna-samaakulam (35)
Harmya-praasaada-shobhaadhym naanaa-dharma-samanvitam,
Tatraa-ahm nyavasm taat deva-archana-ratah sadaa(36)
Vaishyo jaatyaa sudevo-ahm naamnaa viditam-astu te,
Havyen tarpitaa devaah kavyen pitarastathaa(37)
Vividhair-daana-yogaish-cha vipraah sant-arpitaa mayaa,
Deena-andha-kripanaebhysh-cha dattam-annam-anekadhaa(38)
Tat-sarvm nishfalm raajan mam daivaad-upaagatam,
Yathaa me nishfalm jaatm sukritm tad vadaami te(39)
Mamaiv santatir-na-asti n suhrinn ch baandhavah,
N ch mitraam hi me taadrig yah kuryaad-aurdhvadaihikam(40)
Yasy n syaan-mahaaraaj shraaddhm maasika-shodaasham,
Pretatvm susthirm tasy dattaiah shraaddha-shatair-api(41)
Tvam-aurdhvadaihikm kritvaa maam-uddhar mahee-pate,
Varnaanaam chaiv sarveshaam raajaa bandhurihochyate(42)

PRET SAID-"There was a city named as Vaidish which was possessed of all prosperity with having many districts and abounding in gem stones of various kinds. (35) The city was full of beautiful temples, palaces and mansions, and in which many acts were used to be performed. O respectful king, I dwelt there engaged continuously in worship of Deva. (36) O king! You may like to know that I was a Vaishya (trader) by name Sudeva. I offered Havya (food to duties) and Kavya (food to the Atma of departed ancestors). (37) I pleased the saintly and wise people by offering various type of Daan. I gave food of various kinds to the helpless, poor, the visually impaired and the wretched. (38) O King, due to my bad luck, all this had proved to be fruitless. How my good deeds had gone in vain, I will speak to you. (39) I have no offspring, no well wisher, no siblings and no friend like you who could perform my Aurdhva-dehik rites. (40) O Maharaj, if the sixteen monthly Shraadhs are not performed, the condition as Pret becomes firmly fixed even if hundreds of annual Shradhas are performed. (41) Liberate me then, O Lord of Earth, by performing the Auradhva-dehik rites for my Mokshya. It is said that in this world, the king is the brother of all the Varnas. (42)

61

Tanmaam taaray raajendr manai-ratnm dadaami te,
Yathaa me sad-gatir-bhooyaat-preta-yonish-ch gachchhati(43)
Yathaa kaarym tvayaa veer mam ched-ichchhasi priyam,
Kshudhaa-trisha-adi-bhir-dukhaiah pretatvm dusahm mam(44)
Svaad-oodakm falm cha-asti vane-asmin-chheetalm shivam,
N praapnomi kshudhaarto-ahm trishaarto n jalm kvachit(45)
Yadi me hi bhaved-raajan vidhir-naaraayanao mahaan,
Tad-agre veda-mantraushch kriyaa sarv-aurdhva-daihikee(46)
Tadaa nashyati me noonm pretatvm naa-atraa snshayah,
Veda-mantraastapo-daanm dayaa sarvatraa jantushu(47)
Sach-chhaastra-sharvanam vishnaoah poojaa sajjana-sngatiah,
Preta-yoni-vinaashaay bhavanteeti mayaa shrutam,
Ato vakshyaami te vishnau-poojaam pretatva-naashineem(48)
Suvarnaadvaya-maaneey suvarnam nyaaya-snchitam,
Tasy naaraayanaasy-aikaam pratimaam bhoop kalpayet(49)
Peeta-vastraa-yugachchhannaam sarvaa-bharanaa-bhooshitaam,
Snaapitaam vividhais-toyair-adhivaasy yajettatah(50)

Therefore, O Rajendra, help me for Sad-gati, and I will give you a most precious jewel, so that my Pret-yoni is vanished and Sad-gati achieved. (43) Please do that, O brave king, if you wish my welfare. I am suffering from the misery of hunger and thirst; I cannot endure this Pret condition anymore. (44) In this forest various types of sweet fruits and cool potable water is available but I am not able to relish them at all, despite being afflicted with hunger and thirst. (45) If you perform the great "Narayan-bali" rite for me, O King, along with all the Aurdhva-dehik rites with Vedic mantras; (46) Then my Pret-yoni will surely get vanished. Vedic mantras, devotion (Jap-tap), austerity, Daan and Dayaa (compassion) to all beings, (47) Listening the Holy Scriptures with devotion; worship of Vishnu; company of noble people; these, I have heard, decimate the Pretyoni. Now, I will tell you the procedure of worship of Vishnu, the destroyer of the Pretyoni. (48) Bring, honestly gained, two pieces of gold and make one Pratima (image) of Narayana from them, O King. (49) Adorn the Pratima with a pair of yellow cloths, grace it with various ornaments, bath it with water of many sacred rivers; and placing it on pedestal you should worship thus. (50)

Poorve tu shree-dharm tasy dakshinae madhu-soodanam,
Pshchime vaamanm devam-uttare ch gadaa-dharam(51)
Madhye pitaamahm chaiv tathaa devm maheshvaram,
Poojayechch vidhaanen gandha-pushpa-adi-bhiah prithak(52)
Tatah pradakshinaee-krity vahnau santarpy devataah,
Ghriten dadhnaa ksheerena vishvae-devaansh-ch tarpayet(53)
Tatah snaato vineeta-atmaa yajamaanah samaahitah,
Naaraayana-agre vidhi-vatsvaam kriyaam-aurdhva-daihikeem(54)
Aarabhet yathaa-shaastram krodha-lobha-vivarjitah,
Kuryaach-chhraaddhaani sarvaanai vrishasy-otsarjanm tathaa(55)
Tatah padaani viprebhyo dadyaachchaiv traayodash,
Shayyaa-daanm pradattvaa ch ghatm pretasy nirvapet(56)

RAAJOVAACH

Kathm preta-ghatm kuryaad dadyaat ken vidhaanatah,
Boorahi sarvaanu-kampa-arthm ghatm preta-vimuktidam(57)

PRETOVAACH

Saadhu pristn mahaaraaj kathayaami nibodh te,
Pretatvm n bhaved-yen daanen sudridhen ch (58)

Place Sri-dhara to the east of it, Madhu-sudana to the south, to the west Vamana-deva, to the north Gada-dhara (these all are different manifestation of Bhagwan Vishnu); (51) Place Pitamaha (Brahma) and Maheswara (Shiva) in the middle. Worship them, turn-by-turn, with incense and flowers, etc. as per rituals. (52) Thereafter, take Pradakshina (circumambulation) of the images; make offerings in the fire to these deities; make offerings to the universal deities with Ghee (clarified butter), curds and milk. (53) Afterwards, having bathed, Yajman (patron) should perform, with concentration and devotion, the Aurdhva-dehik rites for the Pret, in front of Narayana. (54) Giving up anger and greed, he should perform all the rites as prescribed and the Varsho-utsarg (bull release) rite. (55) Thereafter, he should donate thirteen utensils and donate a bed (Shaiya-daan) to Purohit, consecrate a Ghat (pot) of water for the sake of the departed (Pret). (56) **KING SAID** How is the Ghat (pot) for the departed prepared? With what procedure it is to be given? Please describe for the benefit of all, about the Ghat, which releases the departed. (57) **PRET SAID** O Great King, you have made a right query. I will describe that Daan by which the Pret-yoni cannot exist. (58)

Daanm preta-ghatm naam sarvaa-ashubha-vinaashakam,
Durlabhm sarva lokaanaam durgati-kshaya-kaarakam(59)
Santapta-haataka-maym tu ghatm vidhaay brahmesha-keshava-yutm sah lokapaalaiah,
Ksheeraajya-poornaa-vivarm pranaipaty bhaktyaa vipraay dehi tav daana-shataiah kim-anyaiah?(60)
Brahmaa madhye tathaa vishnauah shankarah shankaro-avyayah,
Praachyaadishu ch tat-kanathe loka-paalaan kramena tu(61)
Sampoojy vidhi-vad raajan dhoopaiah kusuma-chandanaiah,
Tato dugdhaa-a-ajya-sahitm ghatm deym hirana-mayam(62)
Sarva-daana-adhikm chaitan-mahaa-paataka-naashanam,
Kartavym shraddhayaa raajan pretatva-vinivrittaye(63)

SHREEBHAGAVAANUVAACH

Evm snjalpatastasy preten sah kaashyap,
Senaa-a-ajagaama-anu-padm hasty-ashva-ratha-snkulaa(64)
Tato bale samaayaate dattvaa raagye mahaa-manaim,
Namaskrity punah praathry preto-adarshanameyivaan(65)

The offering, which is known as Pret-ghat Daan, is a destroyer of all evils. It is a rare Daan, which is dissipater of Dur-gati. (59) Having prepared a Ghat of refined gold, consecrate it to Brahma, Shiva and Vishnu and all the Lokpala, fill it with ghee and worship with devotion, give it to a Purohit. After making this donation, there is no need of hundred other donations. (60) Place Brahma, Vishnu and Sankara, the eternal giver of happiness, in the middle; place Lokpala in the east and other directions and in the neck of the Ghat, in order. (61) Having duly worshipped with incenses, flowers and sandal-paste O King, one should donate the golden Ghat, full of milk and Ghee (clarified butter). (62) Ghat Daan, O King, is superior to all other donations in removing grievous Paap and it should be made with firm faith, for the release of the departed from Pretatva (Pret condition). (63) **BHAGWAN SAID-** O Kasyap, while the king was in conversation with the departed, the army of king, which was following him, arrived with elephants, horses and chariots. (64) On arrival of the army, the Pret gave the great jewel to the king, again implored and became invisible after offering Namaskar (salutation) to king. (65)

tasmaad vanaad viniskramy raaja-api sva-purm yayau,
Sva-purm ch samaa-saady tat-sarvm preta-bhaashitam(66)
Chakaar vidhi-vat paksinn-aurdhva-daihikajm vidhim,
Tasy punaya-pradaanen preto mukto divm yayau(67)
Shraaddhen para-datten gatah preto-api sad-gatim,
Kim punah putraa-datten pitaa yaateeti adbhutam(68)
Itihaasam-imm punaym shrinaoti shraavayechch yah,
N tau pretvamaayaatah paapaachaara-yutaa-vapi(69)
Shraaddhen para-datten gatah preto-api sad-gatim,
Kim punah putraa-datten pitaa yaateeti adbhutam(68)
Itihaasam-imm punaym shrinaoti shraavayechch yah,
N tau pretvamaayaatah paapaachaara-yutaa-vapi(69)

O Bird! Having come out of the forest, the king arrived in his city, while remembering all that was said by the Pret. (66)He performed the Aurdhva-dehik rites; the Pret attained Swarga as a result of the rites. (67) The Pret is released by the Sraddha performed even by a stranger, then what to wonder in case a parent attains Sad-gati by the offerings of his son or daughter. (68) He who hears, and narrates to others this pious history, never goes to the Pretyoni, though they may be Paapi. (69)

**Annadi-nidhano Devah Shankh Chakra Gadaa-dharah,
Akshayah pundree-kaakash Preta-mokshya-prado-bhav.**

***

CHAPTER 8

DAAN (DONATIONS AND VIRTUOUS GIFTS), PUNYA (MERITORIOUS DEEDS), DHARMA, KARMA, DUTIES OF THE OFFSPRING AND DAAN FOR THE DEPARTED

GARUD UVAACH

Aamusmikeem kriyaam sarvaam vad sukritinaam mam,
Kartavyaa saa yathaa putraustathaa ch kathay prabho!(1)

SHREEBHAGVAANUVAACH

Saadhu prishtm tvayaa taarkshya maanushaanaam hitaay vai,
Dhaarmikaarhm ch yat-kritym tat-sarvm kathayaami te(2)
Sukritee vaardhake drishtvaa shareerm vyaadhi-snyutam,
Prati-koolaan grahaansh-chaiv praanaa-ghoshasy chaashrutim(3)
Tadaa sva-maranam gyaatvaa nirbhayah syaadatandritah,
Agyaat-gyaata-paapaanaam praayshchittm samaacharet(4)
Yadaa syaada-aturah kaalastadaa snaanm samaarabhet,
Poojanm kaarayed-vishnaoah shaalagraama-svaroopinaah(5)

GARUD SAID -Please tell me, O Prabhu! All about the rites to be performed on behalf of Sukriti (do-gooder) for their benefit in Parlok and also about the duties which are to be performed by the sons (the word son denotes both son and daughter) after the death of parent. (1) **BHAGWAN SAID**- O Taarksya, you have asked good question for the benefit of mankind. I will tell you all the acts and deeds to be performed by Dharmik people at their last moments. (2) The Sukriti, finding the body, in its old age, afflicted with diseases, and the unfavorable planetary conditions, and when he finds himself not hearing the beats of life; (3) Thus, realizing his death to be nearing one should become fearless and alert, and should do Prayaschit atone for the Paap committed knowingly or unknowingly. (4) When the death approaches closely, one must perform the ablutions, and worship Bhagwan Vishnu in the form of Saligrama. (5)

66

Archayed gandha-puspaish-cha kum-kumais-tulasee-dalaiah,
Dhoopair-deepaish-cha naivedyair-bahu-bhir-modaka-adi-bhiah(6)
Dattvaa ch dakshinaam vipraan-naivedyaa-dev bhojayet,
Ashta-aksharm japen-mantraam dvaadasha-aksaram-ev ch(7)
Snsmarech-chhrinauyaachchaiv vishnaor-naam shivasy ch,
Harer-naam haret paapm nrinaam shravanaa-gocharam(8)
Roginao-antikamaasaady shochaneeym ch baandhavaiah,
Smaranaeeym pavitraam me naamadheym muhur-muhuah(9)
Matsyah koormo varaahsh-cha naara-sinhsh-cha vaamanah,
Raamo raamsh-cha krishnash-cha buddhah kalkee tathaiv ch(10)
Etaani das naamaani smartavyaani sadaa budhaiah,
Sameepe roginao boorayur-baandhavaaste prakeertitaah(11)
Krishnaeti mangalm naam yasy vaachi pravartate,
Tasy bhasmee bhavantyaashu mahaa-paataka-kotayah(12)
Mriyamaanao harer-naam grinaan putr-opachaaritam,
Ajaamilo-apyagaad-dhaam kim punah shraddhayaa grinaan(13)

One should perform the worship with fragrant substances, flowers, red saffron, leaves of Tulsi (holy basil), incense, Deepak (lamp), offerings of food and many Modak, and other things. (6) Offer **Dakshina** (donations) to the **Purohit** (priest) and should offer them food. He should do the **Japa** (meditative repetition of divine name) of the eight (Om Namo Narayanay) and the twelve syllable mantras (Om Namo Bhagwate Vasudevay). (7) He should remember and listen the names of Vishnu and Shiva. The recitation of the name of Hari, washes off the Paap. (8) When the last moment of the ailing person comes, the relatives should not mourn. They should rather remember, My holy name (Bhagwan Vishnu) and meditate upon it repeatedly. (9) The Matsya, Kurm, Narsingh, Vaaman , Parasurama, Rama, Krishna, Buddha and also Kalki. (10) These ten holy names of Shri Vishnu pertaining to various incarnations should always be meditated upon by the wise. The relatives should recite these near the ailing. (11) Who recite the auspicious name "Krishna" on his own, his tens of millions of grave Paap are quickly reduced to ashes. (12) Even the dying Ajamila (Ajamila was a man of very evil character, who happened to call his son named "Narayana" at the time of death) reached Swarga by just pronouncing the holy name "Narayana" (another name of Krishna or Vishnu). What to talk of the people who recite it with faith! (13)

Harir-harati   paapaani   dushta-chittair-api   smritah,
An-ichchhaya-api snsprishto dahatyev hi paavakah(14)
Harer-naamni ch yaa shaktiah paapanir-haranae dvij!,
Taa-vat-kartum samartho n paatakm paatakee janah(15)
Kinkrebhyo yamah praah nayadhvm naastikm janam,
Naivaanayat bho dootaa! Hari-naama-smarm naram(16)

Achyutm keshavm raama-naaraayanam krishnaa-daamodarm vaasudevm harim,
Shree-dharm maadhavm gopikaa-vallabhm jaanakee-naayakm raama-chandrm bhaje(17)
Kamala-nayan!Vaasu-dev!Vishnao!Dharanai-dharaachyut! Shankha-chakra-paanae!,
Bhav sharanaamiteerayanti ye vai tyaj bhat dooratarena taanapaapaan(18)
Taanaanayadhvamasato vimukhaan-mukunda-paadaaravinda-makaranda-rasaadajstram,
Nish-kinchanaih-parama-hnsa-kulai rasagyair-jushtaad-grihe nirayavatrmani baddha-trisnaan(19)
Jihvaa n vakti bhagavad-gunaa-naama-dheym chetsh-cha n smarati tach-charana-aravindam,
Krisnaay no namati yachchhir ekada-api taanaanayadhvamasato-akrita-vishnau-krityaan(20)

The name 'Hari', meditated upon even by one who has evil thoughts, takes away his Paap in the same way as the fire burns even if touched accidentally. (14) The name Hari has so much power that it can uproot even such Paap which a Paapi is not capable to commit, O Dvija. (15) Even Yam-raj instructed to his Doots, "Bring the Naastiks only, but do not bring the people who meditate on the Hari's name." (16) The prayer: 'Achyutam, Keshavam, Ram, Narayanam, Krishna, Damodaram, Vasudevam, Harim, Sridharam, Madhavam, Gopika-vallabham, Janaki Nayakam, Raamachandram Bhaje',should be recited. (17) 'O lotus-eyed, Vasudeva, Vishnu, the supporter of the earth, and the holder of conch and discus in hand, you are the guardian of the entire universe.' The Yam-doots do not come near to those Nish-paap people who chant this hymn. (18) Once Yama said to his doots, "the Lotus feet of Shri Hari (Vishnu) are worshipped even by the Param-hansa (enlightened), who know the essence of Divinity and are without possession. Therefore, bring those Paapi who are alienated from Shri Hari, who keep the company of wicked and whose desires are bound to household; leading to Naraka." (19) They deserve Narak whose tongue does not pronounce the name and qualities of Bhagwan, whose heads never bow to the lotus feet of Bhagwan Krishna, who do not offer worship to Vishnu. (20)

Tasmaat snkeertanm vishnaor-jagan-mngalam-nhasaam,
Mahataam-api paksheendr! Viddhyai-kaantika-nishkritim(21)
Praayshchittaani cheernaani naaraayanaa-paraan-mukham,
N nishpunanti n durbuddhim suraa-kumbhamivaapagaah(22)
Krishnaa-naamnaa n narakm pashyanti gata-kilbisaah,
Yamm ch tad-bhataansh-chaiv svapne-api n kadaachan(23)
Maansa-asthi-rakta-vat-kaaye vaitaranayaam patenn sah,
Yo-ante dadyaad dvijebhyshcha nanda-nandana-gaamiti(24)
Atah smaren-mahaa-vishnaor-naam paap-augha-naashanam,
Geetaa-sahastra-naamaani pathedvaa shrinauyaad-api(25)
Ekaadashee-vratm geetaa ganga-ambu tulasee-dalam,
Vishnaoah paada-ambu-naamaani maranae mukti-daani ch(26)
Tatah sankalpayed-annm sa-ghritm ch sa-kaanchanam,
Sa-vatsaa dhenavo deyaah shrotriyaay dvijaayate(27)
Ante jano yad-dadaati svalpam vaa yadi vaa bahu,
Tad-aksaym bhavet-taarkshya yat-putraash-cha-anumodate(28)

Therefore, O Indra of Birds, chanting the name of Vishnu is auspicious and blissful on this universe. It is the best destroyer of even grievous Paap. (21) But even the performance of Praayaschit (penances) does not purify the foolish, who are estranged from Narayana; just as the holy rivers cannot purify a liquor-pot. (22) The one, who remembers the name of Krishna, is always saved from Narak and never sees Yama or his Doots even in dreams. (23) If the human being made of flesh, bones and blood; towards the end of life, donates a cow to the priest recitng "Nand-nandanam," never falls into the Vaitaranee. (24) Therefore, one should remember the name of Maha-Vishnu, which effaces multitudes of Paap and should read or listen hymns of Gita and Vishnu Sahastra-naam (thousand names of Bhagwan Vishnu). (25) 'Ekaadashi Vrit' (the fast on the eleventh day of each fortnight); the recitation of Gita; intake of holy water of river Ganga, Tulsi (holy basil), Charana-amrit and recitation of his names at the time of death -all these liberate (Mukti-Daayi) the human beings. (26) Thereafter, grains, ghee, gold, and a cow along with a calf be donated with firm resolution, to Dvija who is well conversant with Vedas. (27) With the consent of the heirs, little or more, whatever a person donates in his last days, it becomes inexhaustible, O Taarkshya. (28)

Anta-kaale tu sat-putraah sarva-daanaani daapayet,
Etad-arthm suto loke praathryate dharmakovidaiah(29)
Bhoomishthm pitarm drishtvaa ardhonmeelita-lochanam,
Putraus-trisnaa n kartavyaa tad-dhane poorva-sanchitie(30)
S tad-dadaati sat-putro yaa-vaj-jeevatyasau chiram,
Ativaahastu tan-maarge dukhm n labhate yatah(31)
Aature choparaage ch dvaym daanm vishishyate,
Ato-avashym pradaatavyam-ashta-daanm tila-adikam(32)
Tilaa lohm hiranaym kaarpaaso lavanam tathaa,
Sapta-dhaanym kshitir-gaavo hyekaikm paavanm smritam(33)
Etad-ashta-mahaa-daanm mahaa-paataka-naashanam,
Anta-kaale pradaatavym shrinau tasy ch sat-falam(34)
Mam svedasam-udbhootaah pavitraas-trividhaas-tilaah,
Asuraa daanavaa daityaas-tripyanti tila-daanatah(35)
Tilaah shvaetaas-tathaa krisnaa daanen kapilaas-tilaah,
Snharanti tridhaa paapm vaanmanah kaayasanchitim(36)
Lauha-daanm ch daatavym bhoomi-yukten paanainaa,
Yama-seemaam n chaapnoti n ichchhet tasy vatrmani(37)
Kuthaaro musalo danadaaha khadagsh-ch chhurikaa tathaa,
Shatraanai yama-haste ch nigrahe paapa-karmanaam(38)

In the last days, an obedient son (heir) should make all the prescribed Daans. For this reason, the wise pray for a righteous offspring in this world. (29) The sons, seeing their parent lying on the ground in death bed with eyes half-closed, should not covet his parent's earned wealth. (30) The Daan made by good son will prolong life of parent, and free him or her from misery on the path, while going to the next world. (31) In disease and in hardship, two Daan are most indispensable- eight Maha-daan including sesamum; and the others. (32) Sesamum, iron, gold, cotton stuff, salt, the seven grains, a plot of land, a cow,—each of these is said to purify. (33) The eight great Daan to be given during the last moments, are the effacers of grave Paap. Now, listen their good rewards: (34) There are three kinds of holy sesamums that have been produced from my sweat. Asuras, Danavas and Daityas are gratified by the Daan of these sesamums. (35) The Daan of white, black and brown sesamum remove the Paap committed by speech, thought and action. (36) The Daan of iron should be made with the hands touching the ground, this will ensure that one neither enters the domain of Yama, nor steps on Yam-marg. (37) To punish the Paapi, Yama holds an axe, a threshing-pestle, a rod, a sword and a dagger in his hands. (38)

Yama-ayudhaanaam santushtyai daanam-etad-udaahritam,
Tasmaad-dadyaal-lohadaanm yama-loke sukhaa-vaham(39)
Uranaah shyaama-sootraash-cha shanada-amarko-apyadumbarah,
Shesambalo mahaa-dootaa loha-daanaat sukha-pradaah(40)
Shrinau taarkshya parm guhym daanaa-naam daanam-uttamam,
Datten ten tushyanti bhoo-bhurvah svarga-vaasinah(41)
Brahma-adyaa rishayo devaa dharmaraaja-sabhaa-sadaah,
Svarnaa-daanen santushtaa bhavanti vara-daayakaah(42)
Tasmaad-deym svarnaa-daanm pret-oddharanaa-hetave,
N yaati yama-lokm s svargatim taat gachchhati(43)
Chirm vaset satya-loke tato raajaa bhavedih,
Roopa-vaan dhaarmiko vaagmee shreemaan-atula-vikramah(44)
Deenaa-naatha-vishistebhyo dadyaach-chhaktyaa ch dakshinaam,
Evm yah kurute taarkshya- putraa-vaana-pya-putraavaan,
S siddhim samavaapnoti yathaa te brahmachaarinaah(45)
Ayo-lavana-kaarpaas-til-kaanchana-daanatah,
Chitraa-gupta-adayas-tushtaa yamasy pura-vaasinah(46)

This Daan is aimed to gratify these weapons of Yama. Therefore, one should donate iron, which gives relief in Yam-lok. (39) The Maha-Doots of Yama—Urana, Syamsutra, ShuGdamarka, Udumbara, Sheshambul bestow relief with the Daan of Iron. (40) Now hear this profound secret, O Taarkshya, about best of the Daans by which, the dwellers in Bhu, Bhuvar and Swar (earth, astral and heaven) worlds are pleased. (41) Brahma and others, the Rishis, Devas and the members of the assembly of Dharam-Raaj grant boon for Daan of gold as they are gratified by it. (42) Therefore, gold should be donated for the Mokshya of the Pret. He does not go to the world of Yam, O child, but reaches Swarga. (43) He dwells in Swarga for a long time and is then reborn here as a king, with pleasant looks, as full of Dharma, eloquent, prosperous, and of velour. (44) One must give **Dakshina** (alms and donations) to poor, orphans, and the especially able. The people who do this achieve fulfillment even if they do not have offspring as the celibates achieve Mokshya without even having an offspring. (45) By donating the iron, salt, cotton-stuff, sesamum and gold; Chitragupta and the other dwellers of Yampur are gratified. (46)

71

Sapta-dhaanya-pradaanen preeto dharma-dhvajo bhavet,
Tushtaa bhavanti ye-anye-api trishu dvaareshv-adhishthitaah(47)
Vreehayo yava-go-dhoomaa mudgaa maashaah priyngavah,
Chanaakaah saptamaa gyeyaah sapta-dhaanya-mudaa-hritam(48)
Pratigrahaa-adhyaapana-yaajaneshu pratigrahm sveshtatamm vadanti,
Pratigrahaachchhudhyati jaapyahomairn yaajanm karm punantiah vedaah(49)
Varsha-vrittim tu yo dadyaad braahmanae dosha-varjite,
Sarvm kulm sam-uddhrity svarga-loke maheeyate(50)
Aasanne maranae kuryaat sannyaasm ched vidhaanata,
Aavartet punarnaasau brahma-bhooyaay kalpate(51)
Tato yenaa-ambu-daanaani kritaanyatraa rasaastathaa,
Tadaa khag tathaa-a-ahlaadamaap-adi prati-padyate(52)
Amritm tu gavaam ksheerm yatah patagasattam,
Tasmaad dadaati yo dhenum-amritattvm s gachchhati(53)
falgu kaarym parityajy satatn dharmavaan bhavet,
Daanm damo dayaa cheti saarametat traaym bhuvi(54)

By Daan of the seven grains, Dharam-dhwaj (the flagbearer of the Dharma) is pleased and Dwarpals (gatekeepers), who stand at the three gates of Yampur, are propitiated. (47) Paddy, barley, wheat, green lentil, black gram, maze and chickpeas are called Sapta-dhanya(seven seeds). (48) Accepting offerings for priestly work, teaching, and Vedic worship is appropriate because the peccancy brought by accepting the donations is washed away by recitation of Vedas, Homa sacrifice, etc. (49) One who offers livelihood to impeccable Brahmin (priest) who is without Paap, who carries out sacraments, keep Shikha (crest), who takes bath, meditates, worships Ishwara everyday and offers oblation), gets his whole family redeemed from Narak and goes to paradise. (50) In his last days, who becomes Sanyaasi (ascetic who abstains from worldly indulgence) as per the procedure laid down in the Shastra, obtains divinity and is never born again. (51) O Garuda, who gives water and sweet beverages to the thirsty, feels happy even if goes through the Yam-marg. (52) The cow milk is like Amrut (nectar), O best of the Birds. Therefore, by donating a cow, one gets Mokshya. (53) Giving up meaningless, a person should continuously follow the Dharma. Daan (Charity), Dam (restraint on sense-organs) and Daya (compassion) - the sum of these three, is at the core of virtues on this earth. (54)

Daanm saadhor-daridrasy shoonya-lingasy poojanam,
Anaatha-preta-snskaarah koti-yagya-fala-pradah(55)
Varnaash-cha chatvaar ih prashastaa varnaeshu dharmistha-naraah prashastaah,
Dharmena saukhym samupaiti sarvm gyaanm samaapnoti mahaa-pathe sthitah(56)
Dadyaad-vaitaranaeem dhenum vishesha-vidhinaa khag,
Taarayanti narn gaavs-tri-vidhaach-chaiv paatakaat(57)
Baalatve yachch kaumaare yat-paapm yauvane kritam,
Vayah parinaatau yachch yachch janma-antareshv-api(58)
Yan-nishaayaam tathaa praataryan-madhyaahna-aparaahnyoah,
Sandhyayor-yat-kritm paapm kaayen manasaa giraa(59)
Dattvaa dhenum sakridva-api kapilaam ksheera-snyutaam,
S-opaskaraam sa-vatsaam ch tapo-vritta-samanvite(60)
Braahmanae veda-vidushe sarva-paapaiah pramuchyate,
Uddhared-anta-kaale saa daataarm paapa-sanchiyaat(61)
Ekaa gauah svastha-chittasy hyaaturasy ch goah shatam,
Sahstram mriya-maanaasy dattm chitta-vi-varjitam(62)

The Daan given to Sadhu, poor people, the prayer performed at the "Shoonya-Lingam" (subtle nothingness), and the performance of funeral rites of destitutes and orphans, are as much rewarding as performing crores of Yagyas. (55) In the land of Bharat, the four Varnas - Brahmin, Kshtriya, Vaishya, and Shudra are the chosen ones. Of the people of these Varnas, the person dedicated to Dharma is the noblest. By following the Dharma one becomes happy. Wisdom is obtained only by the one who follows this great path of Dharma (Dharm-marg). (56) Daan of Vaitarnee cow with special rites, O Bird, releases one from three types of Paap. (57) The Paap committed in childhood, in youth, in adulthood, in old age and during previous births; (58) The Paap committed by action, speech and thought; in the night, in the morning, in the forenoon, in the afternoon and in the twilight, (59) Daan of a milk giving tawny cow with the calf and other required material, to ascetic; (60) Austere; knower of Vedas, removes all Paap. Absolves from all the Paap during the last moments of the donor. (61) The Daan of only one cow while one is in full alertness of mind, the Daan of a hundred cows when one is suffering from diseases, Daan of a thousand cows when one is in dying condition and bereft of mental faculties; (62)

73

Mritasyaitat-punar-lakshm vidhi-pootm ch tat-samam,
Teertha-paatraa-samopetm daanam-ekm ch laksadhaa(63)
Paatre dattm ch yad-daanm tal-laksha-gunaitm bhavet,
Daatuah falam-anantm syaann paatraasy prati-grahah(64)
Svaadhyaaya-homa-snyuktah   para-paaka-vi-varjitah,
Ratna-poornaam-api maheem prati-grihy n lipyate(65)
Visha-sheetaapahau mantra-vahnee kim dosha-bhaaginau,
Apaatre saa ch gaur-dattaa daataarm narakm nayet(66)
Aakara-pravartane paapm gosahasravadhais samam,
Vritti-chchhede tathaa vritteah karanam laksha-dhenukam(67)
Ekaa hyekasy daatavyaa bahoonaam n kadaachan,
Saa vikreetaa vibhaktaa vaa dahatyaa-saptamm kulam(68)
Kathitaa yaa mayaa poorvm tav vaitaranaee nadee,
Tasyaa hyuddharana-opaaym godaanm kathayaami te(69)
Krishnaam vaa paatalaam vaa-api dhennum kuryaada-lada-kritaam,
Svarnaa-shringeem raupya-khureem kaansya-paatropa-dohineem(70)

And the Daan of hundred thousand cows after the death, all these have equal value in terms of rewards. Even a single Daan made to a deserving person and the Daan made at a Teerth (holy place), is equal to lakhs of Daan. (63) The Daan given to a deserving person multiplies a hundred-thousand-fold. It brings unending rewards to the donor and does not harm the recipient. (64) The one who is into Swaathyay (reading of scriptures) offers Havan (offerings to Ishwar through fire) and who does not eat food cooked by others, does not suffer from guilt of receiving Daan even of the earth filled with jewels. (65) The Mantras remove poison and the fire removes cold, but do not themselves acquire these evil characteristics. But the Daan of cow to an undeserving person leads the donor to Narak. (66) Mining of gold, iron-ore, etc., brings Paap equal to killing of thousand cows. Snatching away the livelihood of someone is equally Paapi. Similarly, providing livelihood to someone is equal to donation of hundred thousand milch cows. (67) One cow should be donated to one person only, and never to many. In case, it is either shared or the recipient sells it, it destroys the coming seven generations of the person. (68) I already have told you about Vaitarnee River. Now, I will tell you about "Godaan" (donation of cow) as a means to cross that river. (69) A (prosperous) person should decorate a black or reddish cow; tip its horns with gold, its feet with silver and a bronze vessel to milk that cow; (70)

Krishnaa-vstr-yugaa-ch-chhannaam kanatha-ghanataa-samanvitaam,
Kaarpaas-opari snsthaapy taamra-paatraam sachailakam(71)
Yamm hemm nyaset tatraa lauha-danadaa-samanvitam,
Kaansya-paatre ghritm kritvaa sarvm tasy-opari nyaset(72)
Naavam-ikshu-mayeem kritvaa patta-sootrona veshtayet,
Gartm vidhaay sajalm kritvaa tasmin-kshipettareem(73)
Tasy-opari sthitaam kritvaa soorya-deha-sam-udbhavaam,
Dhenum sankalpayet tatra yathaa-shaastra-vidhaanatah(74)
Sa-alnkaaraanai vastraanai braahmanaay prakalpayet,
Poojaam kuryaad-vidhaanen gandha-pushpa-akshata-adi-bhih(75)
Puchchhm sngrihy dhenostu naavam-aashrity paadatah,
Puraskrity tato vipram-imm mantraa-mudeerayet(76)
Bhava-saagara-magnaanaam shoka-taapormi-dukhinaam,
Traataa tvm hi jagan-naath sharanaa-gata-vatsal(77)
Vishnau-roop dvija-shresth maam-uddhar mahee-sur,
Sa-dakshinaam mayaa dattaam tubhym vaitaranaeem namah(78)
Yama-maarge mahaa-ghore taam nadeem shata-yojanaam,
Tartu-kaamo dadaamyetaam tubhym vaitaranaeem namah(79)
Dhenuke maam prateekshasv yama-dvaare mahaa-pathe,
Uttaarana-arthm deveshi vaitaranayai namo-astu te(80)

Now cover the cow with a pair of black cloths, hang a bell round its neck, and place the covered bronze vessel upon some cotton-stuff, (71) Place there a golden image of Yam holding an iron rod; and place all these on a bronze vessel filled with Ghee. (72) Make a boat of sugarcanes, fasten it with silk threads; make a pit, fill it with water, and float the boat in it. (73) On it, place the material born from the body of the sun, make a resolve for Godaan there in accordance with the Shastra. (74) Donate the cloths along with the ornaments to the priest; worship with fragrances, flowers and Akshat (whole rice) as per procedure. (75) Hold the tail of the cow, place a foot in the boat, and, having honored a Priest, recite this mantra- (76) "O Lord of the Universe, compassionate to those who take your refuge, You are the savior of those who are immersed in the ocean of existence, made miserable by the waves of sorrow and remorse. (77) O Best of the Dvija, the very form of Vishnu upon earth; uplift me. I have presented this Daan to you along with Dakshina; Namah (salutation) to Vaitarnee! (78) I have presented this to you, being desirous of crossing that river, which is a hundred Yojanas in extent, and lies on the very dreadful Yam-marg. Namah to Vaitarnee. (79)O Cow, Please wait for me at the gateway of Yam to get me through the Vaitarnee of the Yam-marg. Namo to you, O Devesi. (80)

Gaavo me agratah santu gaavo me santu pristhatah,
Gaavo me hridaye santu gavaam madhye vasaamyaham(81)
Yaa laksmeeah sarva-bhootaanaam yaa ch deve pratisthitaa,
Dhenu-roopena saa devee mam paapm vyapohatu(82)
Iti mantraush-cha sam-praathry sa-anjalir-dhenukaam yamam,
Sarvm pradakshinaee-krity braahmanaay nivedayet(83)
Evm dadyaad-vidhaanen yo gaam vaitaranaeem khag,
S yaati dharma-maargena dharma-raaja-sabha-antare(84)
Svastha-avastha-shareere tu vaitaranayaam vratm charet,
Devaa ch vidusaa dhenustaam nadeem tartum-ichchhataa(85)
Saa naayaati mahaa-maarge godaanen nadee khag,
Tasmaad-avashym daatavym punaya-kaaleshu sarvadaa(86)
Ganga-adi-sarva-teertheshu braahmana-avasatheshu ch,
Chandra-sooryo-paraageshu snkraantau darsha-vaasare(87)
Ayane vishuve chaiv vyatee-paate yuga-adi-shu,
Anyeshu punaya-kaaleshu dadyaad go-daanam-uttamam(88)

(Here the cow represents Devi) May cows be in front of me; may cows be behind me; may cows be in my heart; and may I dwell in the midst of cows. (81) The Lakshmi (manifestation of Shakti in the form of prosperity), who is present in all the creatures and among the deities, that Devi, in the form of cow, may remove my Paap." (82) With folded hands, should pray to the cow and Yam with these mantras, and having taken Pradakshina round all these things, give them to the Priest. (83) O Bird, one who, with these rites, donates the Vaitarnee cow, goes by a path of Dharma into the assembly of the Dharmraaj. (84) Whether the body is healthy or unwell, one should perform the observances pertaining to Vaitarnee. The wise person, desiring to cross that river, should make the Daan of Cow.(85) O Bird! the Vaitarnee, does not confront in the Great Path if the Godaan (donation of a cow) is performed. Therefore, it is necessary to donate a cow, always during the Punya-Kaal (auspicious time for performance of meritorious deeds). (86) At Ganga and all other holy pilgrimage-places, at the dwelling-places of Priests; during the eclipses of the sun and moon, on Sankranti and Amaawasya; (87) During the equinoctial and solstitial; at Vyatipaata, on the beginning and ending day of Yuga and at other Punyakaal; the Godaan, which is the best of all Daans, should be made. (88)

Yadaiv jaayate shraddhaa paatraan smpraapyate yadaa,
S ev punaya-kaalah syaad-yatah sampattira-sthiraa(89)
Asthiraanai shareeraanai vibhavo naiv shaashvatah,
Nitym sannihito mrityuah kartavyo dharma-snchayah(90)
Aatma-vitta-anusaarena tatraa daanam-anantakam,
Deym Vipraay vidushe sva-atmanah shrey ichchhataa(91)
Alpena-api hi vitten sva-hasten-aatmane kritam,
Tad-akshayym bhaved-daanm tat-kaalm ch-opatisthati (92)
Griheeta-daana-paatheyah sukhm yaati mahaa-dhvani,
Anyathaa klishyate jantuah paatheya-rahitah pathi(93)
Yaani yaani ch daanaani dattaani bhuvi maanavaiah,
Yamaloka-pathe taani hyupa-tishthanti cha-agratah(94)
Mahaa-punaya-prabhaavena maanusm janm labhyate,
Yastat-praapy chared-dharmm s yaati paramaam gatim(95)
Gaayaanti devaah kil geetakaani dhanyaastu ye bhaarata-bhoomi-bhaage,
Svarga-apavargasy fala-arjanaay bhavanti bhooyah purushaah suratvaat(95.1)
Jeevitm maranam chaiv dvaym shikshet panadaitah,
Jeevitm daana-bhogaabhyaam maranam ranaa-teerthayoah(95.2)

Punyakaal is that time whenever you are in a devotional frame of mind and a deserving person is available to receive Daan because the wealth is unstable. (89) Body is transitory; splendor is not eternal; only the death is always approaching. Therefore, one should accumulate Dharma. (90) The one who desires well-being should make unending Daan to a learned person or priest, depending on the availability of wealth. (91) Daan of even a little money, donated with one's own hand, becomes everlasting, and rewards instantly. (92) Daan is like provision for a traveler. One, who has made Daan, goes happily on the Great Path. Otherwise, suffers miseries on the path, which has no provision. (93) All the Daan made by human beings in this world clear the way for them, the path to Yam-lok. (94) As a result of great good karma, birth of human being is obtained. One who, having gained human birth, follows Dharma, gets Paramgati (speed to supreme, i.e., Mokshya). (95) The resident of Swarga also sing the song in which they say that those born in Bharat are more blessed ones then even them because the land of Bharat is most suitable for Saadhana to obtain Swarga and get emancipation. (95.2)

yo dharma-sheelo jita-maana-rosho vidyaa-vineeto n paropa-taapee,
Sva-daara-tushtah para-daara-doorass vai naro no bhuvi vandaneeyah(95.3)
Avigyaay naro dharmm duahkhamaayaati yaati ch,
Manushya-janma-saafalym kevalm dharma-sevanam(96)
Dhan-putraa-kalatra-adi shareeram-api baandhavaah,
Anitym sarvamevedm tasmaad-ddharmm samaacharet(97)
Taavad bandhuah pitaa taa-vad-yaavajjeevati maanavah,
Mritaa-naam-antarm gyaatvaa kshanaat sneho nivartate(98)
Ati-kleshen labdhasy prakrityaa chnchalasy ch,
Gatir-ekaiv vittasy daanamanyaa vipattayah(98.1)
Aatmaiv hyaatmano bandhuriti vidyaanmuhurmuhuah,
Jeevannapeeti sanchinty mritaanaam kah pradaasyati(99)
Evm jaanann-idm sarvm sva-hasten-aiv deeyataam,
Anitym jeevitm yasmaat-pshchaat-ko api n daasyati(100)

The wise must learn the art of living and the art of dying. Learn to live while generously donating and prudently using the resources and learn to die in the Teerth of battle field for the establishment of Dharma. (95.3) The one who is devoted to Dharma, who has triumphed over the arrogance and anger, who is blessed to do pious deeds due to right knowledge, who does not give pain to others, who is satisfied with spouse and keeps a distance from other's spouse; has control over desires, is worth salutation on this earth. (95.4) The one who neglects Dharma due to ignorance, suffers miseries repeatedly. The success of human birth depends upon the endevour of Dharma alone. (96) The wealth, offspring, wife-husband and human body, siblings all are transitory. Therefore, Dharma alone should be perused. (97) The relationship of father (it denotes to both father and mother) and siblings, etc., is there so long as a person is alive, but when they have known him to be dead, their affection is soon faded away. (98) The Daan of the wealth, which has a very fickle nature earned with very hard work, is the best course, rest all are adversities only. (98.1) One should constantly remember that he or she only is the true well-wisher of self. If Daan is not made during lifetime, than how someone else will give it for departed? (99) Knowing all this, one should donate on his own. Life is temporary; and who can give afterwards? (100)

Mritm shareeram-utsrijy kaastha-loshta-samm kshitau,
Vimukhaa baandhavaa yaanti dharmastamanu-gachchhati(101)
Grihaad-arthaa nivartante shmashaanaat-sarva-baandhavaah,
Shubha-ashubhm kritm karm gachchhantamanu-gachchhati(102)
Shareerm vahinaa dagdhm kritm karm saha-sthitam,
Punaym vaa yadi vaa paapm bhunkte sarvatraa maanavah(103)
N ko-api kasya-chid-bandhuah snsaare duahkha-saagare,
Aayaati karma-sambandhaad-yaati karma-kshaye punah(104)
Maatri-pitri-suta-bhraatri-bandhu-daara-adi-sngamah,
Prapaayaamiv jantoonaam nadyaam kaasthaughava-chchhalah(105)
Vaapee-koop-tadaagaa-naama-araama-sura-sadninaam,
Jeerna-oddhaarm prakur-vaanaah poorva-kartuah falm labhet,
Jeerna-oddhaarena vaa teshaam tat-punaym dvi-gunam bhavet(106)
Dharmasya-arthasy kaamasy falamaahurmaneesinaah,
Tadaaga-sukritm deshe kshetraam-ekm maha-ashrayam(106.1)
Ateetaana-agate chobhe pitri-vnshm ch bhaarat,
Taarayed vriksha-ropee ch tasmaad vrikshaansh-cha ropayet,
Pushpitaah fala-vantsh-cha tarpayanteeh maanavaan,
Vrikshadm putraa-vat vrikshaas-taarayanti paratraa tu(106.2)

The relatives turn away leaving the dead body on the ground, like a piece of wood or stone, but Dharma alone accompanies one. (101) The wealth of a person falls apart from the house and the relatives from the cremation-ground. The virtuous or evil karma, alone accompany. (102) The body is reduced to ashes by fire but only one's karma accompany. Virtuous or evil Karma, the human being will have to experience them everywhere. (103) This universe is an ocean of sorrow, no one is relative of others. One is born as a result of past Karma, and returns back upon exhaustion of Karma. (104) The relation between human beings, i.e., mother, father, son, brother, kinsmen, wife and the others, is incidental and temporary just like the creatures in a water-pond, and like the contact between floating woods coming together in a river. (105) Renovation of water reservoir, well, pond, park, gardens and temple brings Punya (virtuous reward) to the extent of double the reward which one gets from the new construction of these facilities. (106) The wise say that construction of a pond in a country or village side brings the rewards of Artha, Dharma and Kama, all the three put together. The place graced by ponds becomes a great shelter for all the creatures. (106.1) The person by planting trees and conserving environment liberates all ancestors and descendents. Therefore, one must plant trees. The trees laden with fruits and flowers gratify human beings. Those who make gift of plants or trees, are redeemed in Parlok by the same plants just like (the rites done by) a son. (106.2)

Aatmaa-yattm dhanm yaavat taavad-viprm samarpayet,
Para-adheene dhane jaate n kinchid-viktum-utsahet(107)
Poorva-janma-kritaad-daanaa-datraa labdhm dhanm bahu,
Tasmaad-evm parigyaay dharma-arthm deeyataam dhanam(108)
Dharmaat prajaayate-arthsh-cha dharmaat-kaamo-abhi-jaayate,
Dharm eva-apavargaay tasmaad-dharmm samaacharet(109)
Shraddhayaa dhaaryate dharmom bahu-bhir-na-artha-raashi-bhiah,
Nish-kinchnaa hi munayah shraddhaa-vantoah divngataah(110)
Patraam pushpm falm toym yo me bhaktyaa prayachchhati,
Tadahg bhakty-upahritama-shnaami priyama-atmanah(111)
Tasmaad-avashym daatavym tadaa daanm vidhaanatah,
Alpm vaa bahu veteemaam ganaanaam naiv kaarayet(112)
Dharmaatmaa ch s putro vai daivatair-api poojyate,
Daapayedyastu daanaani pitarm hyaaturm bhuvi(113)
pitror-nimittm yad-vittm putrauah paatroah samarpitam,
Aatmaa-api paavitasten putraa-pautraa-prapautraakaiah(114)

Till the wealth is in your control, donate it to Vipara (person of wisdom). Once it becomes other's possession, one can't even dare to tell others to do that. (107) By virtue of Daan of a former birth, sufficient wealth has been acquired in this life. Hence, realizing this, one should donate for Dharma. (108) Wealth is acquired by pursuing Dharma; desire is conquered by Dharma and Mokshya is also achieved by Dharma. Therefore, practice of Dharma should be imbibed. (109) Dharma is upheld by faith, not by large piles of wealth. The wise, though in poverty, but due to faith, had gone to Swarga (Divangata). (110) One who offers Me, even a leaf, a flower, a fruit or water with pure heart and devotion; I accept the offerings with love to that person etc. (111) Therefore, give Daan, as prescribed. Whether small or great, I do not count that. (112) A heir who makes Daan for parents when they are near to death, is called Dharmatma and is praised even by the Devtas (deities). (113) If the wealth earned by the fore-fathers (inherited wealth) is donated to the deserving people by the offspring, then, by that Daan, the Atma of his (her) sons, grandsons and great-grandsons (daughters) are purified. (114)

Pituah shata-gunam punaym sahstram maatur-ev ch,
Bhaginee-dasha-saahstram sodare dattam-akshayam(115)
N chaiv-opadravaa daaturn vaa naraka-yaatanaah,
Mrityu-kaale n ch bhaym yama-doota-sam-udbhavam(116)
Udaaro dhaarmikah saumyah praapyaa api vipulm dhanam,
Trinaavan manyate taarkshya aatmaanm vittamapyatha(117)
Ko garvah kriyate taarkshya kshanaa-vi-dhvnshi-bhir naraiah,
Daanm vittaadritm vaachah keerti-dharmau tathaa-a-ayusah,
aropakaranam kaayaadasatah saaram-uddhritam(118)

Anything given on behalf of father has a hundred-fold merit; on behalf of the mother, a thousand-fold; on behalf of the sister, ten-thousand fold and on behalf of sibling, it is inexhaustible. (115) There are no troubles and no torments of Narak for the one who resorts to Daan and no fear caused by the Yam-doots at the time of death. (116) The Udaar (liberals), Dharmik and gentle people after acquiring the wealth in abundance, treat their body and the wealth like a wooden straw. (117) O Garuda! What to take pride of a body which can disappear in moments. Therefore, the objective of life should be to use wealth for Daan; speech for truth; life for glory of Ishwara and Dharma; the body for welfare while keeping away from untruth. (118)

**Annadi-nidhano Devah Shankh Chakra Gadaa-dharah,
Akshayah pundree-kaakash Preta-mokshya-prado-bhav.**

***

81

CHAPTER 9

*WHAT SHOULD A DYING PERSON DO DURING LAST HOURS AND
THE REQUIRED OBSERVANCES; IMPORTANCE OF TULSI,
SAALIGRAM AND OTHERS*

GARUD UVAACH

Kathitm   bhavataa   samyag-daanama-atura-kaalikam,
Mriya-maanaasy yat-kritym 2tad-idaaneem vad prabho(1)

SHREEBHAGAVAANUVAACH

Shrnau taarkshya pravakshyaami deha-tyaagasy tad-vidhim,
Mritaa yen vidhaanen sad-gatim yaanti maanavaah(2)
Karma-yogaad-yadaa dehee munchit-yatraa nijm vapuah,
Tulasee-san-nidhau kuryaan-manadaalm gomayen tu(3)
Tilaansh-chaiv vikeeryaath darbhaamsh-chaiv vi-nikshipet,
Sthaapayed-aasane shubhre shaalag-raama-shilaam tadaa(4)
Shaalag-raama-shilaa yatraa paapa-dosha-bhayaapahaa,
Tat-sannidhaana-maranaan-muktir-jantoah sunishchitaa(5)
Tulasee-vitapa-chchhaayaa yatra-asti bhava-taapahaa,
Tatrauv maranaan-muktiah sarvadaa daana-durlabhaa(6)

GARUD SAID-You have spoken at length about the Daan
given for the departed. Tell now, O Prabho, about the duties
of a dying person. (1) **BHAGWAN SAID-** Listen, O Taarkshya,
I will explain the observances for one leaving the body and by
what rites, human beings obtain **Sad-gati** after death. (2) As a
result of accumulated karma, the **Dehi** (dweller in the body)
leaves the physical body, then, one should make a Mandal
with cow dung, near to a Tulsi (holy basil) tree. (3) Spread
Til (sesame seeds) in the Mandal and put Darbha-grass, and
then have the Saaligrama placed on the cleaned **Aasana** (seat).
(4) **Saaligrama** removes all types of fear and the ill effects of
Paap. Mokshya is certain for the being that dies near it. (5)
Dying under the shade of the **Tulsi** (remover of Bhav Taap),
gives Mokshya which is difficult to obtain even by Daan. (6)

Tulasee-vitapa-sthaanm   grihe   yasya-avatisthate,
Tad-grihm teertha-roopm hi n yaanti yama-kinkraah(7)
Ropanaat paalanaat sekaad dhyaana-sparshana-keertanaat,
Tulasee dahate paapm nrinaam janma-arjitm khag(8)
Tasyaa dalm mukhe kritvaa tila-darbha-asane mritah,
Naro vishnau-puram yaati putraaheeno-apy-asnshayah(9)
Tilaah   pavitraas-tri-vidh   darbhaash-cha   tulaseer-api,
Narn   nivaarayantyete   durgatim   yaantama-aturam(10)
Mam   sveda-sam-udbhootaa   yat-aste   paavanaas-tilaah,
Asuraa   daanavaa   daityaa   vi-dravanti   tilaistatah(11)
Darbhaa vibhootir-me taarkshya mam roma-sam-udbhavaah,
Atas-tat-sparshanaadev svargm gachchhanti maanavaah(12)
Kusha-moole sthito brahmaa kusha-madhye janaardanah,
Kusha-agre shankaro devs-tryo devaah kushe sthitaah(13)
Atah   kushaa   vahni-mantraa-tulasee-vipra-dhenavah,
Naite nir-maalyataam yaanti kriya-maanaaah punah punah(14)
Darbhaah pindaeshu nir-maalyaa braahmanaaah preta-bhojane,
Mantraa gaus-tulasee neeche chitaayaam ch hutaashanah(15)

A home in which the Tulsi is planted, is like a Tirtha (holy place).
The Yam-doots do not come near that home. (7) O Bird, the Paap
accumulated during past births get burnt out just by planting it,
nurturing, watering, and meditating, touching or just by reciting
its name. (8) The person who dies with a Tulsi leaf in mouth,
while seated on the Asana having Til and **Darbha-grass** on it,
goes to Vishnu-pur (abode of Vishnu) unfailingly, even though
has no offspring. (9) Til, Darbha-grass and Tulsi are three holy
things and they save a dying person from Dur-gati. (10) Since
the Til has germinated from My sweat, therefore, it is holy; hence
Asuras, Daanavas and Daityas run away from Til. (11) The
Darbha grasses, carry my majesty, O Taarkshya, it has come
from my body pores; hence merely by touching them, one
achieves Swarga (heaven). (12) Similarly, Brahmaa is seated at
the root of the **Kush-grass**; in the middle of the kush is
Jaanardana (BhagwanVishnu); at the tip of the kusa is
Sankara (Bhagwan Shiva). The three Deva are seated in the
kush grass. (13) Hence Kush, fire, Mantras, Tulsi, Purohita
(priest) and cows do not lose their purity by being used again and
again. (14) Darbha-grass becomes impure once it has been offered
along with Pind; Purohit, by eating the offerings to the Pret, the
garland becomes impure by removing it; mantras, cows and Tulsi,
when used lowly; and fire becomes impure, on cremation. (15)

83

Gomayen-opalipte   tu   darbhaastaranaa-snskrite,
Bhootale hya-aturm kuryaad-antarikshm vi-varjayet(16)
Brahmaa vishnaush-ch rudrksh-ch sarve devaa hutaashanah,
Manadaal-opari tishthanti tasmaat-kurveet manadaalam(17)
Sarvatraa vasudhaa pootaa lepo yatraa n vidyate,
Yatraa lepah kritas-tatraa punar-lepen shuddhyti(18)
Raaksasaash-ch pishaachaash-ch bhootaah pretaa yama-anugaah,
Alipta-deshm khatvaayaam-antarikshe vishanti ch(19)
Ato-agni-hotraam shraaddhm ch brahma-bhojym sura-archanam,
Manadaalen vinaa bhoomyaama-aturm naiv kaarayet(20)
Lipta-bhoomyaamatah kritvaah svarnaa-ratnm mukhe kshipet,
Vishnaoah paad-odakm dadyaach-chhaalag-raama-sva-roopinaah(21)
Shaalag-raama-shilaa-toym yah pibed bindu-maatraakam,
S sarva-paapa-nir-mukto vaikunatha-bhavanm vrajet(22)
Tato   gangaa-jalm   dadyaan-mahaa-paataka-naashan,
Sarva-teertha-krita-snaana-daana-punaya-fala-pradam(23)

The dying person should be laid on the ground cleaned with cow-dung and with darbha-grasses spread over; it not supported in the air (couch). (16) Brahmaa, Vishnu, Rudra (Shiva), all the Devaas, and Sacrificial Fire are seated upon the **Mandal**. Therefore, Mandal should be prepared (so that they all may sit on it comfortably). (17) The earth is pure everywhere. If there is a stain in the ground, it should be cleaned away by plastering again with cow dung. (18) The Raakshyas, Pishaach, Bhoot, Pret and Yam-doot (demons, goblins, elementals, spooks, and the Doot of Yam) enter upon an un-plastered (with cow-dung) place; and a cot and sky (above the ground). (19) Therefore, neither perform **Agnihotra** (fire oblation to Ishwara), Shraddh, feeding of Purohits, worship of deities, nor place the dying person on the ground, without Mandal. (20) Place the dying person on the ground plastered with cow-dung, put gold and jewels in the mouth of dying person, and give him the **Charanaa-mrit** (holy water of the feet of Vishnu) received from the Saaligrama-shila which is symbol of Vishnu. (21) Whosoever takes even a drop of the water of Saaligram shila, is absolved of all the Paap and goes to the Vaikuntha (abode of Vishnu). (22) Thereafter, Gangajal (holy water of Ganga), the effacer of grave Paap, should be given to the dying one, which gives Punya (rewards) equal to holy bath in all the Teerths and Daan-Punya put together. (23)

Chaandraayanam chared-yastu sahstram kaaya-shodhanam,
Pibedysh-chaiv gangaambhah samau syaataamubhaavapi(24)
Aginm praapy yathaa taarkshya toola-raashir-vinashyati,
Tathaa gangaa-ambu-paanen paatakm bhasmasaad bhavet(25)
Yastu sooryaanshu-santaptm gangaayaah salilm pibet,
S sarva-yoni-nir-muktah prayaati sadanm hareah(26)
Nadyo jala-avagaahen paavayanteetaraan-janaan,
Darshanaat-sparshanaat-paanaat-tathaa gangeti keertanaat(27)
Punaatyapunayaan-purushaan shatasho-ath sahstrashah,
Gangaa tasmaat-pibet-tasy jalm snsaara-taarakam(28)
Gangaa gangeti yo brooyaat-praanaaiah kanatha-gatair-api,
Mrito vishnau-puram yaati n punar-jaayate bhuvi(29)
Utkraamadbhish-cha yah praanaaiah purushah shraddhayaa-anvitah,
Chintayen-manasaa gangaa so-api yaati paraam gatim(30)
Ato dhyaayennimed gangaam snsmaret-taj-jalm pibet,
Tato bhaagavatm kinchi-chhirinauyaan-moksha-daayakam(31)
Shlokm shloka-ardhapaadm vaa yo-ante bhaagavatm pathet,
N tasy punara-avrittir-brahma-lokaat-kadaa-chan,
Ved-opanisadaam paathaa-ch-chhiva-vishnaustavaad-api(32)

Performance of a thousand Chandraayan fasts to purify the body and to take a sip of Ganga-jal is of equal Punya. (24) O Taarkshya! just as a heap of cotton wool is destroyed by getting fire, similarly, by taking **Ganga-jal**, one's Paap are reduced to ashes. (25) Who takes the Ganga-jal, heated by the sun rays, is freed from all rebirths and goes to **Vaikunth** (the abode of Hari). (26) A person is purified by taking a holy dip in other rivers, but one is purified by merely seeing, touching, drinking or remembering Ganga. (27) Ganga sanctifies hundreds and thousands of virtuousless people. Therefore, one should take Ganga-jal which liberates from the ocean of transmigration. (28) Who recites "Ganga, Ganga" while life is flickering in the throat, goes straight to **Vishnupur** (abode of Vishnu) after death, and is not reborn again on the earth. (29) At the time of death, who contemplates with faith, about the Ganga, is liberated. (30) Thus, mediate, bow, remember Ganga, and then take its water. Then by listening, even a bit of Bhaagvat Puraan, bestows Mokshya. (31) Who recites a verse or half or quarter of a verse of Bhaagvat Puraan or Gita in the last moments never returns on this earth from Brahmlok; (32)

Omkaara-poorvm saayujym praapnuyaan naa-atraa snshayah,
Namo bhagavate vaa sudevaayeti japan-narah(33)
Praanaa-prayaanaa-samaye kuryaad-ana-shanm khag,
Dadyaada-atura-snnyaasm viraktasy dvi-janmanah(34)
Snnyastam-iti yo brooyaat-praanaaiah kanatha-gatair-api,
Mrito vishnau-puram yaati n punar-jaayate bhuvi(35)
Evm jaata-vidhaanasy dhaarmikasy tathaa khag,
Oordhva-ch-chhidrena gachchhanti praanaas-tasy sukhen hi(36)
Mukhm ch chakshusee naase karnaau dvaaraanai sapt ch,
Ebhyah sukritino yaanti yoginas-taalu-randhratah(37)
Apaanaanmilita-praanaau yadaa hi bhavatah prithak,
Sookshmee-bhootvaa tadaa vaayur-vi-nishkraamati puttalaat(38)
Shareerm patate panchaan-nirgate marut-eeshvare,
Kaalaa-hatm pataty-evm niraa-dhaaro yathaa drumah(39)
Nir-vicheshtm shareerm tu praanaair-muktm jugupsitam,
Asprishym jaayate sadyo durgandhm sarva-ninditam(40)
Tridha-avasthaa shareerasy krimi-vida-bhasma-roopatah,
Kim garvah kriyate dehe kshanaa-vidhvnsi-bhir-naraiah(41)

Recitation of **Veda and Upanishada**, recitation of **Vishnu-Shiv-Strotra**; reciting **"Om"** Mantra first and then **'Namo Bhagvate Vasudevay'** mantra, are liberating. There is no doubt in it. (33) When the life breath is leaving the body, one should take the fast, O Bird, discarding the worldly things, the wise should take **Sanyaasa** (giving up attachment to worldly things and objects). (34) When life is flickering in the throat, one who says "I take Sanyaasa," goes to Vishnu-pur after death, and is never re-born on the earth. (35) Who is Dharmik and has thus performed the rites, O Bird, his life breaths easily pass through the higher opening. (36) The mouth, two eyes, two nostrils and two ears, are the seven gateways through which the life of Sukriti (doers of goods deeds) passes away. In case of Yogis, it passes through an opening on the head. (37) As the life joins the air and separates from the body, then, becoming subtle, the life-breath departs from the inert body. (38) Stricken by the time, when the Ishwara of life breath (Marutiswar) departs, the body falls like the unsupported tree. (39) Left by the vital breath, the motionless body, becomes detestable and unfit to touch; foul smells soon arise in it, and it is condemned by everybody. (40) The body which has only three type of plight —worm, dung and ashes- then, how can one take pride in a body which is perishable in moments. (41)

Prithivyaam leeyate prithvee aapsh-chaiv tathaa jale,
Tejas-tejasi leeyet sameer-astu sameeranae(42)
Aakaashsh-cha tathaa-a-akaashe sarva-vyaapee ch shankrah,
Nitya-mukto jagat-saakshee aatmaa deheshv-ajo-amarah(43)
Aatmaa nityo-avyayah satyah sarvagah sarvabhrin mahaan,
Aprameyah svayn-jyotira-graahyo manasa-api yah(44)
Sachchida-ananda-roopo-asau sarva-praanai-hridi sthitah,
Vinashyatsv-api bhaavesu n vinashyati karhichit(45)
Nainm chhindanti shastraanai nainm dahati paavakah,
N chainm kledayantyaapo n shosayati maarutah(46)
Vaasaansi jeernaani yathaa vihaay navaani grihnaati naro-aparaanai,
Tathaa shareeraanai vihaay jeernaanyanyaani snyaati navaani dehee(47)
Sarv-endriya-yuto jeevah shabda-adi-vishayair-vritah,
Kaama-raaga-adi-bhir-yuktah karma-kosha-samanvitah(48)
Punaya-vaasanayaa yukto nirmite sven karmanaa,
Pravishets nave dehe grihe dagdhe yathaa grihee(49)

(Among the five elements of body) the earth (soil) is dissolved into earth; likewise water into water; fire is dissipated in fire; also air in the air. (42) And, similarly, ether to ether, whereas the universal Atma that is in the bodies, is eternally free like Shiva witness to the universe, birth-less, deathless and immortal. (43) Atma is eternal, it is not an occurrence, is ultimate truth, omnipresent, all pervasive, foremost supreme, beyond the reach of sense organs, self illuminated, beyond reach of mind, and is unbounded. (44) It is like **Sat-Chit-Anand** (truth, consciousness and bliss) and stays in the hearts of all creatures. It does not disappear with the extinction of the matter. (45) Neither the Atma can be destroyed by weapons nor can it be burnt by fire. Neither it can be damped by water, nor can the air dry it up. (46) Like the human beings who replace the worn out cloths by the new ones, similarly, the embodied replaces the old worn out body by a new one. (47) The embodied, possessing all the sense objects, surrounded by sound and other desires, clinging to lust and attachment, enveloped by the cells of karma; (48) Consisting of good tendencies, created by its own karma, the embodied enters a new body as does a householder whose house has been burnt. (49)

Tadaa vimaanamaadaay kinkinaeejaalamaali yat,
Aayaanti deva-dootaash-cha lasach-chaamara-shobhitaah(50)
Dharma-tattva-vidah praagyaah sadaa dhaarmika-vallabhaah,
Tadainm krita-kritym svar-vimaanen nayanti te(51)
Su-divya-deho virajaambarstrk su-varnaa-ratnaa-bharanaai-rupetah,
Daana-prabhaavaats mahaanu-bhaavah praapnoti naakm sur-poojya-maanah(52)
Tasmaachch prachyutaa raagyaamanyesaam ch mahaatma-naam,
Jaayante neerujaam gehe sad-vritta-pari-paalakaah(53)

In case of Dharmik people, resplendent with flashing plumes, Dev-doots arrive, bringing a Vimana decorated with beautiful Jhaalar. (50) The Doots knowing the true meaning of Dharma and who are the Dharmik and beloved people, carry them, in their own Vimana. (51) By virtue of Daan, the righteous person getting in a sublime body with shining garments and beautiful garlands, adorned with ornaments made of gold and diamond attains Swarga and is honoured by the Sura. (52) After enjoying the rewards of their virtuous deeds in the Swarg, the Dharmik are reborn on earth in the families of kings, and other great people, free of difficulties, and again follow the path of Dharma. (53)

Annadi-nidhano Devah Shankh Chakra Gadaa-dharah,
Akshayah pundree-kaakash Preta-mokshya-prado-bhav.

CHAPTER 10

*DIVINE EMOTIONAL HOMAGE TO THE DEPARTED, POST DEATH
RITES, PRET CONDITION, COLLECTION OF THE MORTAL
REMAINS AND THEIR IMMERSION, NARAYAN BALI, PANCHAK,
REWARDS OF PIND DAAN*

GARUD UVAACH

Deha-daaha-vidhaanm ch vad sukritinaam vibho,
Praayshchittm dur-mriteah kim pachaka-adi-mritasy ch(1)

SHREE-BHAGAVAAN-UVAACH

Shrinau taarkshya pravaksyaami sarvamev-audhrva-daihikam,
Yat-kritvaa putraa-pautraash-cha muchyante paitrika-ad-rinaat(2)
Kim dattair-bahu-bhir-daanaiah? Pitror-antyeshtima-acharet,
Tena-agnishtoma-sadrisham putraah falama-vaapnuyaat(3)
Tadaa shokm pari-tyajy kaarayen-munadaanm sutah,
Samasta-baandhavair-yuktah sarva-paapa-vimuktaye(4)
Maataa-pitror-mritau yen kaaritm munadaanm n hi,
Aatmajah s kathm gyeyah snsaaraarnaava-taarakah(5)

GARUD SAID -Tell me, O Prabhu! The procedure of cremation
of the Sukriti. What are the atonements for unnatural death
and the death in Panchak? (1) **BHAGWAN SAID**- Listen, O
Taarkshya! I will tell you all about the 'Aurdhva-dehik' rites,
by performing which the offspring is released from the Pitr-
rin (debt to ancestors). (2) Why to give numerous Daans but
one should perform the Antyeshthi (last rites) for parents.
The son who does so, gets reward equal to that of performing
of Agnistoma Yagya. (3) The son, abandoning sorrow of death,
should get his head shaved, along with all his relatives, to
remove all Paap. (4) The son who does not get his head
shaved upon the death of the mother or the father, how can
he be called a son, who helps in swimming through the
ocean of Sansaar (release from the cycle of birth and death). (5)

Ato munadaanam-aavashym nakha-kaksha-vi-varjitam,
Tatah sa-baandhavah snaatvaa dhauta-vastranai dhaarayet(6)
Sadyo jalm samaaneey tatastm snaapayech-chhavam,
Manadaayech-chandanaiah strag-bhir-gngaa-mrittikayaa-athavaa(7)
Naveena-vstraiah snchchhaady tadaa pindam sa-dakshinaam,
Naama-gotraam sam-uchchaary sanklpena-apasavyatah(8)
Mrityu-sthaane shavo naam tasy naamnaa pradaapayet,
Ten bhoomir-bhavet-tushtaa tad-adhisthaatri-devataa(9)
Dvaara-deshe bhavet-paanthastasy naamnaa pradaapayet,
Ten naivopa-ghaataay bhoota-kotishu dur-gataah(10)
Tatah pradakshinaam kritvaa poojaneeyah snusha-adi-bhiah,
Skandhah putrona daatavyas-tadaa-anyair-baandhavaiah sah(11)
Dhritvaa skandhe sva-pitarm yah shma-shaanaay gachchhati,
So-ashva-medha-falm putro labhate ch pade pade(12)
Neetvaa skandhe sva-pristhe-anke sadaa taaten laalitah,
Tadaiv tad-rinaan-muchyen-mritm sva-pitarm vahet(13)

The head must be got shaved, except the nails and the hair of the armpits. Thereafter, having bathed alongwith his kinsmen, one must put on washed clothes. (6) The corpse should be bathed with clean water and adorned with garland and with **Chandan** (sandal-paste) or the clay of Ganga. (7) Having covered the body with new cloths, offer Pinda and Dakshina (donation), pronounce own name and Gotra, thereafter, make a Sankalp (resolve) placing **Janeuo** (sacred thread) on the right shoulder (Apasavya). (8) Offer Pind in the name of Shav (dead body) at the place of death. By doing so, the earth and its presiding Devtas are pleased. (9) At the doorway, offer Pinda in the name of 'Paanth' (traveler); by doing so, the crores of evil spirits reached to the condition of Durgati, can do no harm. (10) Afterwards, the daughter-in-law and others should take **Parikrama** (circumambulate) around it and pay tributes. Then the son, along with the other relatives should bear it on their shoulders. (11) The son who carries the body of his parent to the cremation ground on his shoulders, gets reward of "Ashavmedh Yagya" at every steps. (12) The parents bring up their offspring by carrying them on their shoulder; the son pays off that debt by carrying his dead parent on the shoulders. (13)

Tato-ardha-maarge vishraamm sammaarjyaabhyuksy kaarayet,
Snsnaapy bhoota-sngyaay tasmai ten pradaapayet(14)
Pishaachaa raakshasaa yakshaa ye chaa-anye dikshu snsthitaah,
Tasy hotavya-dehasy naiva-ayogyatva-kaarakaah(15)
Tato neetvaa shmashaaneshu sthaapayed-uttaraa-mukham,
Tatraa dehasy daaha-arthm sthalm snshodhayed-yathaa(16)
Sammaarjy bhoomim snlipyol-likhyoddhrity ch vedikaam,
Abhyuksyopasamaadhaay vahnim tatraa vidhaanatah(17)
Pushpa-akshatairatha-abhyachry devm kravyaada-sngyakam,
Lomabhya-stvanuvaaken homm kuryaad-yathaa-vidhi(18)
Tvm bhoota-bhrijja-gadyonistvm bhoota-pari-paalakah,
Mritah saansaarikastasmaadenm tvm svargatim nay(19)
Iti sampraarthayitvaa-agnim chitaam tatrauv kaarayet,
Shree-khanadaa-tulasee-kaashthaiah palaasha-ashvattha-daaru-bhiah(20)
Chitaam-aaropy tm pretm pindaau dvau tatraa daapayet,
Chitaayayam shava-haste ch preta-naamnaa khag-eshvar,
Chitaa-moksha-prabhritikm pretatvam-upajaayate(21)

Reaching the halfway to the cremation ground, the dead body should be given rest on a clean surface. Having bathed the corpse, offer Pind in the name of "Bhoot". (14) Due to this oblations, the Pishaach, Rakhasyas, Yaksh (demons and fiends and the goblins) in different directions, do not cause obstructions to the body which is to be sacrificed. (15) Then, the body should be taken to the cremation-ground and laid down keeping its head to the north. A place should be cleaned for cremation of the body. (16) Clean the ground and plaster it with cow-dung, erect an altar, sprinkle the water on it and lit the fire the way as prescribed in Vedas. (17) The "Kravyaad Agni" (the fire for cremation) should be worshipped with flowers and **Akshyat** (unbroken rice). Thereafter, oblation of body be made to Fire with the procedure as laid down in Vedas while chanting Veda hymn "Lomebhay swaha." (18) "O Kravyaad Agni, you are like the womb for the body made of five elements; you are the supporter of beings, nourisher of creatures. This one belonging to the mortal world, is dead, lead him to Swarga!" (19) After praying to the fire, erect a funeral pyre with Tulsi, Chandan (sandal wood) and with the wood of Palash and Pipal. (20) O Supreme Birds, having placed the dead body on the funeral pyre, offer two Pind in the name of the departed; one in the hand of the dead and the other in the name of "Pret", on the funeral Pyre. From the time it is released on the funeral pyre, the condition as "Pret" begins. (21)

91

Ke-api tm saadhakm praahuah preta-kalpa-vido janaah,
Chitaayaam ten naamnaa vaa preta-naamnaa-athavaa kare(22)
Ityevm panchabhiah pindaaiah shavasya-ahuti-yogyataa,
Anyathaa chopa-ghaataay poorvokta-aste bhavanti hi(23)
Prete dattvaa pancha pindaan hutamaadaay tm trinaaiah,
Agnim putraastadaa dadyaann bhavet-panchakm yadi(24)
Apet veet vi ch sarpataato-asmaa etm pitaro lokamakran,
Ahobhirabhiraktubhivryaktm yamo dadaatyavasaanamasmai(25)
Av bhrij punaragne pitribhyo yast aahutshchrati svadhaabhih,
Ayurvasaan up vetu shesah sm gachchhataam tanvaa jaatavedah(26)
Ushantastvaa ni dheem hyushantah sami-dhee-mahi,
Ushannushat aa vah pitghn havise attave(27)
Sm gachchhasv pitribhiah sm yamen-eshtaapoorten parame vyoman,
Hitvaayaavadyn punarastamehi sm gachchhasv tanvaa suvarchaah(28)
Udeerataamavar ut paraas unmadhyamaah pitarah somyaasah,
Asum y iiyuravrikah rritagyaaste no-avantu pitaro havesu(29)

As per scholars of "Pret-kalpa," the departed is known as "Saadhak" till the time of placing on the funeral Pyre. After that, is known as "Pret." Therefore, the Pind should be offered with these nomenclatures. (22) Thus, by offering five Pinda, the dead body is qualified to be consigned to flames; otherwise, the above-mentioned, come to attack upon him. (23) The son, having offered five Pinda to the Pret, should ignite the fire with the straw, provided there are no Panchaks, (and pronounce loudly): (24) "O evil Spirits! Get away from here, leave this place. The ancestors have selected this place for him. The Yam has allotted him this place to rest, which is full of water, days and nights. (25) O holy Fire! Lead this dead person to forefathers. This, who is offered to you, is wandering around in all directions, O Jatveda (fire for oblation of the body), may this Atma get a new life, get eatables till old age, and get a new **Vayabya** (made of air) body. (26) O Fire! We, who love you, have placed you here and got you ignited, please invoke our dear forefathers, who love us, and may they accept the offerings. (27) O departed! Go and join your forefathers, the Yam and the Supreme in the sublime paradise. Return to your home leaving all your Paap behind here in this world. May you be filled up with divine splendor and enter into a new body. (28) Soma, lower, middle and upper category, loving forefathers may please come forward, and also those forefathers who have obtained eternal life or have taken a form of Atma. May they be merciful and come forward as they are compassionate and are conversant with seasons. The forefathers, whom we have invoked, may protect us. (29)

Ye anagnidagdhaa ye anagnidagdhaa madhye divah svadhayaa maadayante,
Tebhiah svaraal suneetimetaam yathaavashm tanvm kalpayasv(30)
Mainamagne vi daho maabhi shocho maasy tvachm chiksipo maa shareeram,
Yadaa shritm krinaavo jaatavedo-athemenm pr hinautaat pitribhyah(31)
Shartm yadaa karasi jaatavedo-aathemenm pari dattaat pitribhyah,
Yadaa gachchhaatyasuneetimetaamathaa devaanaanvashaneerbhavaati(32)
Up sarp maatarm bhoomimetaa muruvyachasm prithiveem sushevaam,
Oornaamradaa yuvatirdaaksinaavat esaa tavaapaatu nirrriterupasthaat(33)
Uchchhvanchasv prithivi maa nibaadhathaah soopaayanaasmai bhav soopavanchanaa,
Maataa putraam yathaa sichaa-abhyenm bhoom oornauhi(34)
Soorym chaksurgachchhatu vaatamaatmaa dyaam ch gachchh prithiveem ch dharmanaa,
Apo vaa gachchh yadi tatraa te hitamosadheesu prati tisthaa shareeraiah(35)

O Fire! Those put to flame along with our forefathers, those not put to flames, and those who take pleasure being in the company of forefathers, please arrange for a charming and splendid body according to the wishes of the departed so that it is inspired in the new life. (30) O Fire! Please take care, kindly do not burn this departed, do not harm and scorch from all sides, do not throw his flesh here and there; O **Jatveda** (fire deity of funeral), when you reduce him to ashes, then send him to our forefathers, where there is no pain, where there is no death. (31) O Jatveda! When you completely reduce him to ashes, hand him over to the forefathers. When he follows the way which leads him to the new life, may it be that which happens with the wishes of Deva (deities). (32) (With reference to those being buried), O Departed! go to the splendid and beautiful mother earth. Who has given you this new earth and kept you safe from the womb of death, may the earth become like tender velvet. (33) O Earth! Be light weight, do not press him, quench him and please become a smooth refuge for him. O mother Earth! Take care of this departed the same way as the mother nurses her child in her lap. (34) May your eyes be directed towards the Sun, may your breath go towards the air, may you lead to Swarga or earth in accordance with your Karma or may you go to water, if you are happy there; as is the fate, if you may become a plant, then, enter into medicinal plants, along with full body parts. (35)

Yn tavamagne samadahastamu nirvaapayaa punah,
Kiyaambvatraa rohatu paakadoorvaa vayalkashaa(36)
Sheetike sheetikaavati hlaadike hlaadikaavati,
Manadaookyaa-asu sngam imn svagnin harsay(37)
Parm mrityo anuparehi panthaam yaste sv itaro devayaanaat,
Chaksusmate shrinavate te braveemi maa nah prajaam reerisomot veeraan(38)
Yathaahaanyanupoorvm bhavanti yath rritav rritubhiryanti saadhu,
Yathaa n poorvamaparo jahaatye vaa dhaataraayoonsi kalpayaisaam(39)
Aa rohataayurjarasm vrinaanaa anupoorvm yatamaanaa yatisth,
Ih tvastaa sujanimaa sajosaa deerghamaayuah karati jeevase vah(40)
Upasnhar tasmaat tvamenm vargm nayaa-amrit,
Iti kravyaadamabhyachry shareeraahutimaacharet(41)
Panchikeshu mrito yastu n gatim labhate narah,
Daahas-tatraa n kartavyah krite-anya-maranam bhavet(42)
Aadau kritvaa dhanistha-ardham-etan-nakshatraa-panchakam,
Revaty-antm n daaher-ahm daahe ch n shubhm bhavet(43)

O Jatveda! Now extinguish the fire with which you have burnt for cremation. From the ashes of the dead body, may grass and plants grow all around the place of cremation. (36) O tender plant, O soft-soft plant, O life giving medicinal plant, mix up with the exhilarating frog, make the fire rejoicing. (37) O Death! go to that way which belongs to you, which is different from the divine vehicle. I am addressing you keeping eyes and ears wide open; do not give pain to our offspring, do not harm our brave children. (38) O Ishwar! Safeguard the people who are alive in the same way as days pass by in a certain sequence; as the seasons pass in a sequence so that the younger ones do not leave their elders behind. (39) O living people! May you achieve old age and have long life. May the benevolent give you happy and long life. (40) Take it unto yourself towards Swarga. Now worship the Kravyaad Fire and consign the departed to the fire. (41) The one who dies in Panchaks (astrologically inauspicious time period) does not achieve Mokshya (if cremated without eradication of Panchak evils). That person should not be cremated in Panchak then; if cremated, another person may die. (42) The time starting from the latter half of Dhanistha constellation and ending with Revati is not a suitable time for cremation. If cremation takes place, some inauspicious thing may happen. (43)

Grihe haanir-bhavet-tasy riksheshveshu mrito hi yah,
Putraanaam gotrinaam cha-api kshchid-vighnah prajaayate(44)
Athavaa riksha-madhye hi daahah syaad-vidhi-poorvakah,
Tad-vidhim te pravakshyaami sarva-dosha-prashaantaye(45)
Shavasy nikate taarkshya nikshipet-puttalaastadaa,
Darbha-mayaamsh-cha chatur riksha-mantra-abhi-mantriaataan(46)
Tapta-hemm prakartavym vahanti riksha-naama-bhiah,
'pretaajayat' mantrona punar-homastu samputaiah(47)
Tato daahah prakartavyastaish-cha puttalakaiah sah,
Sapindaanadine kuryaattasy shaantividhim sutah(48)
Tila-paatraam hiranaym ch roopym ratnm yathaa-kramam,
Ghrita-poornam kaansya-paatraam dadyaad-dosha-prashaantaye(49)
Evm shaanti-vidhaanm tu kritvaa daahm karoti yah,
N tasy vighno jaayet preto yaati paraam gatim(50)
Ardhe dagdhe-athavaa poornae sfotayet-tasy mastakam,
Grihasthaanaam tu kaashthen yateenaam shree-falem ch(51)
Praaptaye pitri-lokaanaam bhittvaa tad-brahma-randhrakam,
Aajya-ahutim tato dadyaan-mantronaa-anen tat-sutah(52)

Harm befalls on the house of those who die in the Riksa and some trouble arises for the offsprings and Gotra (Clan). (44) However, I will explain to you the rites for the warding off all the ills effects, in case cremation takes place during Panchak period. (45) O Taarksya! place four Puttal (effigies) made of Darbha grass and consecrated with Riksa mantras, near the Shav. (46) Purified gold should be used and sacrifice performed with Riksa mantras, with the mantra "Pretaa-jayat". (47) Cremation along with the Puttals (effigies) should be performed and the son, on the day of the offering of the Pinda, should perform the Shanti-vidhan (pacificatory rites). (48) To ward off ills of Panchak, donate sesamum, gold, silver, diamonds, bronze vessel and a filled with Ghee, in a sequence. (49) Thus, who performs the cremation procedure after the Shanti-vidhan (pacificator rites), does not face any obstacle and the Pret attains Param-gati. (50) When the body is half or fully burnt, the skull should be split open. In the case of Grihasta (householders), it should be done with wooden (bamboo) stick, in that of ascetics, with a coconut (this process of skull splitting is called "Kapaal-mochan Kirya"). (51) For attainment of the abode of the forefathers, having split open the Brahmaa-randhra, the son should make an Aahuti (oblation) of Ghee with this mantra- (52)

Asmaattvamabhijaato-asi   tvadaym   jaayataam   punah,
Asau   svargaay   lokaay   svaahaa   jvalatu   paavak(53)
Evam-aajya-ahutim dattvaa tila-mishraam samantraakaam,
Roditavym   tato   gaadhm   yen   tasy   sukhm   bhavet(54)
Daahaad-anantarm kaarym streebhiah snaanm tatah sutaiah,
Til-odakm   tato   dadyaan-naama-gotropa-kalpitam(55)
Tatas   teshoopavisteshu   puraanaagyah   sukrit   svakah,
Shokaapanodm kurveet snsaara-anityataam buravan(56)
Maanushye   kadalee-stambhe   asaare   saara-maarganaam,
Karoti   yah   s   sammoodho   jala-budbuda-sannibhe(57)
Panchadhaa sambhritah kaayo yadi panchatvamaagatah,
Karmabhiah sva-shareerotthais-tatraa kaa parivedanaa(58)
Gantraaee   vasumatee   naasham-udadhir-daivataani   ch,
Fena-prakhyah kathm naashm martya-loko n yaasyati(59)
Evm   snshraavayet   tatraa   mridu-shaadvala-snsthitaan,
Te-api snshruty gachchheyur-grihm baala-purah-saraah(60)

"O Fire! You are born from Him; He is born through you and
going to you again. He is an offering to Swarga-Lok (heaven-
realm) through you. O Fire, blaze forth!" (53) Chanting Vedic
Mantras an oblation of sesamum and Ghee may be made.
Thereafter, the son (son represent both son and daughter)
should weep loudly which will make the departed calm. (54)
After cremation, the women should bathe first, then the
sons, and offer Tilanjali (water mixed with sesamum)
pronouncing the name of the gotra. (55) (After funeral) when
the family and friends sit in a pure place, a scholar amongst
them should relieve them off from their sorrow by telling the
uncertainty of the world and say: (56) "The one who ascribes
meaning to a body, which is like a trunk of banana lacking
substance and a body which is like a drop of water; is a
mindless person. (57) If a body made of **Panch-boot** (five
elements) has been merges with the same due to karma of
that body, then why to repent and weep? (58) The earth is
not permanent, oceans are not permanent, deities are also
not permanent, then why the foam like body in the Mrityu-
lok shall not perish. (59) While sitting in a soft grassy lawn,
the sorrow reliever (scholar) or priest may say so to the
bereaved people. Listening to this sorrow relieving sermon,
the bereaved may return to their homes keeping younger
ones ahead. **(the modal discourse on condolence meeting
is given at the end of these chapters).** (60)

Praashayen-nimba-patraanai mritakasy gunaan vadet,
stree-jano-agre grihm gachchhet-prishthato nara-sanchayah(61)
Grihe snaanm punah kritvaa go-graasm ch pradaapayet,
Patraa-valyaam ch bhujeeyad grihaannm naiv bhaksayet(62)
Mritaka-sthaanamaalipy dakshina-abhi-mukhm tatah,
Dvaadashaahaka-paryantm deepm kuryaad-ahar-nisham(63)
Soorye-astamaagate taarkshya shmashaane vaa chatush-pathe,
Dugdhm ch mrinamaye paatre toym dadyaad dina-traayam(64)
Apakva-mrina-maym paatraam ksheera-neera-pra-pooritam,
Kaastha-traaym gunaair-baddhm dhritvaa mantram pathed-imam(65)
Shmashaanaa-anala-dagdho-asi parityakto-asi baandhavaiah,
Idm neeram-idm kseeramatraa snaahi idm pib(66)
Chaturthe sanchayah kaaryah sa-agnikaish-cha nir-agnikaiah,
Triteeye-ahni dviteeye vaa kartavysh-chaa-virodhatah(67)
Gatvaa shmashaana-bhoomim ch snaanm kritvaa shuchir-bhavet,
Oornaa-sootraam vestayitvaa pavitraaeem paridhaay ch(68)

They should eat the leaves of the neem-tree and recount
the virtues of the departed. From the cremation ground,
the women folk shall go ahead followed by men. (61) After
reaching home, take bath once again. Give food to the cow
and then eat in a leaf-plate; but do not eat the stale food
stored in the house. (62) Having plastered the place of death
with cow-dung, he should be there facing south while
keeping a lamp burning throughout the day and night, upto
the twelfth day. (63) O Taarkshya, for three days at
sunset, offer milk and water in an earthen pot, at the
cross-roads or in the cremation-ground. (64) Keeping near
an unbaked earthen pot filled with milk and water and
bound with-three wooden pieces, he should recite this
mantra: (65) "You have been consigned to flames of fires
in the cremation-ground. You have been forsaken by
relatives. Here is the water to take bath, this is the milk
for you to drink." (66) After taking into consideration the
inauspicious and **Nishidh days** (forbidden days), **Asti-
sanchay** (collection of mortal remains) should be done
on the fourth day by those who perform fire sacrifices at
home; and on the second or the third day for those who
do not. (67) After going to the cremation ground, get
purified by taking a bath and wrap a woolen shawl. Then,
wearing the **"Pavtri"** (a sacred ring made of kusha grass
which is worn in the third finger of the right hand); (68)

97

Dadyaach-chhmashaana-vaasi-bhyastato maasa-balim sutah,
Yamaay tveti-mantrona tistrah kuryaat-pari-kramaah(69)
Tato dugdhen chaa-abhyuksy chitaa-sthaanm khag-eshvar,
Jalen sechayet-pshchaad-uddhared-asthi-vrindakam(70)
Kritvaa palaasha-patroshu ksaalayed-dugdha-vaari-bhiah,
Snsthaapy mrinamaye paatro shraaddhm kuryaad-yathaa-vidhi(71)
Trikonam sthanadailm kritvaa go-mayen-opalepitam,
Dakshina-abhi-mukho dikshu dadyaat-pindaa-traaym trishu(72)
Punjee-krity chitaa-bhasm tatraa dhritvaa tri-paadukaam,
Sthaapayet-tatraa sa-jalamana-achchhaady mukhm ghatam(73)
Tatas-tanadaula-paaken dadhi-ghrita-samanvitam,
Balim pretaay sajalm dadyaan-mishtm yathaa-vidhi(74)
Padaani dash panchaiv ch-ottarasyaam dishi vrajet,
Gartm vidhaay tatra-asthi-paatraam snsthaapayet-khag(75)
Tasy-opari tato dadyaat-pindam daaha-arti-naashanam,
Gartaad-uddhrity tat-paatraam neetvaa gachchhej-jalaashayam(76)
Tatraa prakshaalayed-dugdha-jalaad-asthi punah punah,
Charchayech-chandanenaath kumkumen vishesatah(77)

The son should make oblation of black lentil to the inhabitants of the cremation ground while reciting the mantra beginning with "Yamaay-twa" and take three Parikarma. (69) O Supreme of Birds, now sprinkling milk and water over the place of the funeral pyre and, thereafter, begin to pick up the pile of bones. (70) Keeping the bones on Palaash leaves, wash them with milk and water and put them into an earthen pot. Thereafter, perform Shraaddh as prescribed. (71) A triangular altar may be erected at the place for Shraaddh, and the place should be plastered with Gomay (cow dung, milk and ghee mixed together) while, facing south, should offer three Pinda, in the three directions. (72) Place a three-legged stool above the ashes collected from the pyre and keep a Ghat (jar) containing water with mouth uncovered, on the stool. (73) Now, an oblation of cooked rice with curd and ghee, water and sweet meals should be offered to Pret as prescribed. (74) O Bird, then walk fifteen steps in the north and digging a pit there, place the jar of bones in it. (75) Thereafter, offer a Pinda over the Pit which destroys the pain of combustion, take the vessel from the hole and carry it to a water reservoir. (76) In the reservoir wash the bones with milk and water repeatedly and paste them with sandal-paste and especially with saffron. (77)

Dhritvaa samputake taani kritvaa ch hridi mastake,
Parikramy namas-krity gangaa-madhye vinikshipet(78)
Antar-dashaahm yasya-asthi gangaa-toye nimajjati,
N tasy punaraa-vrittir-brahma-lokaat-kadaa-chan(79)
Yaa-vad-asthi manushyasy gangaa-toyeshu tishthati,
Taa-vad-varsha-sahstrani svarga-loke maheeyate(80)
Ganga-jala-ormi snsprishy mritakm pavano yadaa,
Sprishate paatakm tasy sady ev vinashyati(81)
Aaraadhy tapaso-agrena gangaam deveem bhageerathah,
Uddhaara-arthm poorvajaa-naam aanayad brahma-lokaatah(82)
Trishu lokeshu vikhyaatm gangaayaah paavanm yashah,
Yaa putraan-sagarasyaitaan-bhasma-akhyaananayad-divam(83)
Poorve vayasi paapaani ye kritvaa maanavaah gataah,
Gangaayaam-asthi-patanaat-svarga-lokm prayaanti te(84)
Kshchid vyaadho maha-aranaye sarva-praanai-vihinsakah,
Singhen nihato yaa-vat-prayaati naraka-alaye(85)
Taavat kaalen tasya-asthi gangaayaam patitm tadaa,
Divym vimaanama-aruhy s gato deva-mandiram(86)

Put the bones into box, touch it with your heart and head and take a round of it and then immerse them into the middle of Ganga. (78) Whose bones are immersed in Gangajal (water of Ganga) within ten days, never returns from Brahm-Lok. (79) As long as the bones of human beings, remains in the water of Ganga, he remains in the Swarga for that many thousands of years. (80) Even if the dead is touched by the wind which has flown over Ganga, all his Paap are annulled at once. (81) The divine Ganga was brought on the earth from Brahm-Lok by Bhagirath, with great devotion and austerities, for the Mokshya of to his ancestors. (82) The sacred glory of Ganga is famous in all the three realms. That very Ganga had led to Swarga the sixty thousand descendents of Sagara who were reduced to ashes by the curse of Kapil Muni. (83) Who have committed Paap during their previous births, if their bones are immersed in Ganga, they will go to Swarga. (84) Once a hunter in a great forest, the killer of all sorts of creatures, was killed by a lion. He was being led to Narak. (85) Coincidentally, his bones got dropped into Ganga by a crow, he went to the Swarga, aboard on the divine aircraft. (86)

99

Atah svaym hi sat-putro gangaayaam-asthi paatayet,
Asthi-sanchayanaad-oordhvm dasha-gaatraam samaacharet(87)
Ath kshchid-videshe vaa vane chairabhaye mritah,
N labdhas-tasy dehsh-che-chchhrinauyaad-yad-dine tadaa(88)
Darbha-puttalakm kritvaa poorva-vat-kevalm dahet, Tasy bhasm
Samaadaay gangaa-toye vinikshipet(89)
Dasha-gaatra-adikm karm tad-dinaadev kaarayet,
S ev divaso graahyah shraaddhe saanvatsara-adike(90)
Poornae garbhe mritaa naaree vidaary jatharm tadaa,
Baalm nishkaasy nikshipy bhoomau taamev daahayet(91)
Gangaa-teere mritm baalm gangaayaa-mev paatayet,
Anye deshe kshiped bhoomau sapta-vinshati-maasajam(92)
Atah parm dahet-tasy gangaayaam-asthi nikshipet,
Jala-kumbhsh-cha daatavym baalaanaam-ev bhojanam(93)
Garbhe nashte kriyaa na-asti dugdhm deym mrite shishau,
Ghatm ch paayasm bhojym dadyaad baalavipat-tishu(94)

Therefore, the obedient son should himself immerse the bones in the Ganga. After the bones are collected, he should perform the Dasgaatra rites (formation of ten body parts). (87) If someone dies in a foreign country or in a forest or killed by dreaded thieves and his body is not found, then, on the day when this information was received; (88) An effigy of Darbha grass be made and it should be cremated as explained above, and then collect its ashes and immerse them into the water of Ganga. (89) The ten-day's rites should be performed from that day and that date should be noted for performing the annual Shraddh. (90) If a woman dies in the fullness of pregnancy, take out the child from her womb and the dead child should be buried in the earth, and she alone be cremated. (91) When a child dies on the bank of Ganga, he should simply be immersed in Ganga; if a child, up to the age of twenty-seven months, dies in a foreign country, he should be buried in the earth. (92) In the case of death of a child older than 27 month, he should be cremated and his bones immersed in Ganga. A pot filled with water should be donated and food should be served to the children only. (93) If the embryo is destroyed, no rites are needed. In case of death of a fetus only milk should be distributed. If an infant of three years (Baalak) dies, then one should offer a Ghat filled with water, kheer and eatables. (94)

Kumaare ch mrite baalaan kumaaraanev bhojayet,
Sa-baalaan-bhojayed-vipraan pauganadae sa-vrate mrite(95)
Mritsh-cha panchamaad-oordhvama-vratah savrato-api vaa,
Paayasen gudaena-api pindaan-dadyaad-dash kramaat(96)
Ekaadashm dvaadashm ch vrish-otsarga-vidhim vinaa,
Mahaa-daana-viheenm ch pauganadae krityama-acharet(97)
Jeevamaane ch pitari n pauganadae sapindaana,
Atas-tasy dvaadashaahaany-ekoddishtm samaacharet(98)
Shishuraadantajananaad baalah syaad yaa-vad-aashikham,
Kathyate sarva-shaastreshu kumaaro mauni-bandhanaat(99)
Svalpaat-karma-prasngaachcha svalpaad-vishaya-bandhanaat,
Svalpe vayasi dehe ch kriyaam svalpaamap-eechchhati(100)
Kishore tarunae kuryaach-chhayyaa-vrisha-makha-adikam,
Pada-daanm mahaa-daanm go-daanam-api daapayet(101)
Yatee-naam chaiv sarveshaam n daaho n-odaka-kriyaa,
Dasha-gaatra-adikm teshaam n kartavym suta-adi-bhiah(102)

If a child upto five Kumar dies, one should feed the young and children. If a Pogand (upto 10 years) who is Upaneet (sacred thread ceremony done) dies, one should have the purohit and the children fed. (95) When a five year old dies, whether Upaneet or not, one should offer ten Pinda, along with Kheer and Jaggery. (96) Barring Eakaadas (eleventh day), Dwaadas (twelfth day), Varsho-utsarg (releasing of a bull), and the Maha-daan (great donation), one should perform all other the rites for a Pogand. (97) If Pogand dies while his father is alive, there is no need to perform "Sapindi", but perform the "Eakodisht" (rites directed for one) on the twelfth day. (98) The infant is called ' Shishu' till the teething. The child is known as Baal till Shikha is not there, thereafter, with the thread ceremony he is known as 'Kumar' in all the scriptures (Balika and Kumari in case of girls). (99) The number of prescribed rites is less in the case of the children as they have less attachment of sense-objects. Therefore, their other actions are also less. (100) When one dies in the boyhood and in the youth, donation of a cot, the Varsho-utsarg (release of bull) and other rites should be performed; and the Paad-daan (donation of shoes), the great Daan and the Godaan should be made. (101) In the case of death of the ascetics (sanyaasi), cremation is not done. Therefore, there is no Paad-daan, Mahaa-daan, Go-daan and ten days rites are also not performed for them by their son. (102)

Danadaa-grahanaa-maatrona naro naaraayanao bhavet,
Tri-danadaa-grahanaat-teshaam pretatvm naiv jaayate(103)
Gyaanin-astu sadaa muktaah svaroopa-anubhaven hi,
Ataste tu pradattaanaam pindaanaam naiv kaanksinaah(104)
Tasmaat-pinda-adikm teshaam naiv n-odakama-acharet,
Teertha-shraaddhm gayaa-shraaddhm pitri-bhaktyaa samaacharet(105)
Hnsm param-hnsm ch kutee-chaka-bahoodakau,
Etaan snnyaasinas-taarkshyaa prithivyaam sthaapayen-mritaan(106)
Gangaadeenaam-abhaave hi prithivyaam sthaapanm smritam,
Yatraa santi mahaa-nadyas-tadaa taasvev nikshipet(107)

Merely holding of Dand (a sacred stick held by saadhus and Sants) makes one Naarayana and holding of Tri-dand absolves them of Pret condition. Because by carrying the three-fold stick, they never go into the Pret condition. (103) The knowledgeable have the realization of their own true nature. Hence they are always unattached and they do not expect pinds. (104) Therefore, Pinda and water is not to be offered to them, but if the offspring are devoted to their parents, they should perform Teerth, Shraddh and Gaya Shraddh. (105) O Taarksya, the four types of Sanyaasis (ascetics)— the Hansa, Paramhansa, Kutichaka, Bahudaka – must only be buried in the earth upon death. (106) In the absence of Ganga or other rivers, the bodies of Sanyaasis should be buried in the earth. Where great rivers exist, they should be immersed into them. (since immersion is prohibited by Law, therefore, they may be buried) (107)

**Annadi-nidhano Devah Shankh Chakra Gadaa-dharah,
Akshayah pundree-kaakash Preta-mokshya-prado-bhav.**

***

CHAPTER 11

*INESCABILITY OF DEATH, DEATH NO REASON FOR SORROW,
THE DASHGAATRA KARM, COMPETENCY TO PERFORM THE
KRIYA (RITES) AND THE PROCEDURE (VIDHAN)*

GARUD UVAACH

Dasha-gaatraa-vidhim broohi krite kim sukritn bhavet,
Putra-abhaave tu kah kuryaad-iti me vad keshav(1)

SHREEBHAGAVAANUVAACH

Shrinau taarkshyaa pravakshyaami dasha-gaatraa-vidhim tav,
Yad-vidhaay ch sat-putro muchyate paitrikaad-rinaat(2)
Putraah shokm parityajy dhritima-asthaay saattvikeem,
Pituah pinda-adikm kuryaad-ashru-paatm n kaarayet(3)
Shlesma-ashru baandhavair-muktm preto bhunkte yato-avashah,
Ato n roditavym hi tadaa shokaan-nirarthakaat(4)
Yadi varsha-sahstraanai shochate ahar-nishm narah,
Tathaapi naiv nidhanm gato drishyet karhichit(5)

GARUDA SAID Tell me, O Keshav, what is the procedure
to perform Dashgatra rites and what are the merits of
their performance? Also tell me as to who should perform
these rites, in the absence of son? (1) **BHAGWAN SAID-**
Listen, O Taarkshya! I will tell you the procedure of
Dashgatra rites and by performing it a good son is released
of the 'Pitri-rin' (obligations towards departed ancestors).
(2) Renouncing the sorrow of death the son should keep
patience and become **Saatvik**. He should offer Pind, etc.,
to the parent but should not shed tears. (3) The tears of
kith and kin have to be swallowed by the Pret (departed).
Therefore, they should not weep; similarly, mourning is also
meaningless. (4) The departed will not appear again even if
the death is mourned day-night for thousands of years. (5)

103

Jaatasy hi dhruvo mrityur-dhruvm janm mritasy ch,
Tasmaad-aparihaarye-arthe n shokm kaarayed budhah(6)
N hi kashchid-upaayo-asti daivo vaa maanusho-api vaa,
Yo hi mrityu-vashm praapto jantuah punariha-avrajet(7)
Avashym bhaavi-bhaavaanaam pratee-kaaro bhaved-yadi,
Tathaa duahkhair-n yujyeran nala-raama-yudhisthiraah(8)
Naayamatyanta-snvaasah kasyachit kenachit sah,
Api svasy shareerena kimutaanyah prithag-janaiah(9)
Yathaa hi pathikah kshchich-chhaayaama-ashrity vishramet,
Vishramy ch punar-gachchhet tad-vad-bhoota-samaagamah(10)
Yat-praatah snskritm bhojym saaym tachch vinashyati,
Tad-anna-rasa-sampushte kaaye kaa naam nityataa(11)
Bhaishajyam-etad-duahkhasy vichaarm pari-chinty ch,
Agyaana-prabhavm shokm tyaktvaa kuryaat kriyaam sutah(12)
Putra-abhaave vadhooah kuryaad bhaarya-abhaave ch sahodarah,
Shishyo vaa braahmanaasy-aiv sapindao vaa samaacharet(13)

Death is certain for those who are born and likewise birth is also certain for those who die. Therefore, the wise should not grieve over the inevitable. (6) There is no way by which Deva (deities) or human beings can revive a dead creature. (7) Had there been a redressal for averting the inevitable, then Nala, Shri Ram (in His human act) and Yudhisthar would not have experienced the miseries of death. (8) Nobody is permanent company for others in this world. Our own body is like a momentary dream, what to talk of others. (9) As a traveler rests under the shade of a tree for a while and then departs again, similar is the coming of beings in this world. (10) Even the best of food eaten in the morning, is destroyed by evening, then how can there be permanence in a body which is sustained by the same food? (11) This thought is the remedy of miseries. Therefore, the son should perform the Kriya giving up the sorrow which arises due to the ignorance. (12) In the absence of a son, the wife should perform the Kriya. In the absence of wife, the sibling or a pupil or a priest or the Sapindi should perform them. (13)

Jyeshthasy vaa kanishthasy bhraatuaha putraushcha pautraakaiah,
Dasha-gaatra-adikm kaarym putraa-heene nare khag,
Asagotraah sagotro vaa yadi straaee yadi vaa pumaan,
Prathame-ahani yah kuryaat s dashaahm samaapayet(14)
Bhraatranaam-ekajaataanaamekshchet putraa-vaan bhavet,
Sarve te ten putrona putrinao manura-braveet(15)
Putraah pautraah prapautro vaa tad-bhraataa bhraatri-santatiah,
Sapindaana-santatir-vaa-api kriyaarhaah khag gyaatayah(16)
Sarveshaam putraa-heenaanaam mitraah pindam pradaapayet,
Kriyaa-lopo n kartavyah sarva-abhaave purohitah(17)
stree vaa-ath purushah kashchid-ishtasy kurute kriyaam,
Anaatha-preta-snskaaraat koti-yagya-falm labhet(18)
Pituah putrona kartavym dasha-gaatra-adikm khag,
Mrite jyesthe-apy-ati-snehaan-n kurveet pitaa sute(19)
Bahavo-api yadaa putraa vidhim-ekah samaacharet,
Dasha-gaatraam sapindaatvm shraaddha-anya-anyaani shodaash(20)

The person who has no son, his Dash-gaatra should be performed by his younger or elder brother or by their sons or grandsons, O Bird. Man or woman from the same clan or a different clan can perform these rites but whosoever performs the first day's rites, should continue for ten days. (14) If only one of the brothers from the same father has a son, they all are considered to have a son. Manu said so. (15) O Bird! son, grandson, great grandson, brother, offspring of the brothers of the departed or the offspring of Sapinda and others can perform the Kriya. (16) A friend may offer Pindas for all those who have no sons. But the rite should not be escaped. If there is nobody else, the Purohit may perform them. (17) A woman or a man who performs the Kriya for a friend, gets the reward of tens of millions of Yagya by performing this sacrament for a helpless departed. (18) The Dash-gaatra rites for the father **(the word father symbolizes both father and mother)** should be performed by the son, O Bird. But, if the eldest son dies, the father should not perform the rite whatsoever excessive affection he might have for the deceased, being the eldest. (19) If there are many sons, only one shall perform Dash-gaatra, Pind offerings and the other sixteen Shraddh. (20)

Ekenaiv tu kaaryaanai snvibhakta-dhaneshv-api,
Vibhaktaistu prithak-kaarym shraaddhm saanvatsara-adikam(21)
Tasmaaj-jyeshthah suto bhaktyaa dasha-gaatraam samaacharet,
Eka-bhojee bhoomi-shaayee bhootvaa brahma-parah shuchiah(22)
Sapta-vaarm pari-kramy dharanaeem yat-falm labhet,
Kriyaam kritvaa pitur-maatus-tat-falm labhate sutah(23)
Aarabhy dasha-gaatraam ch yaa-vad dvai-vaarshikm bhavet,
Taavat putraah kriyaam kurvan gayaa-shraaddha-falm labhet(24)
Koope tadaage vaa-a-araame teerthe devaalaye-api vaa,
Gatvaa madhyamayaame tu snaanm kuryaad-amantraakam(25)
Shuchir-bhootvaa vriksha-moole dakshina-abhi-mukhah sthitah,
Kuryaach-ch vedikaam tatraa go-mayen-opalipyataam(26)
Tasyaam parnae darbha-maym sthaapayet kaushikm dvijam,
Tm paadya-adi-bhir-abhyarchy pranaamed-ataseeti ch(27)
Tad-agre ch tato datvaa pinda-arthm kausham-aasanam,
Tasy-opari tatah pindam naam-gotropa-kalpitam(28)

Even if the wealth has been divided, only one son will perform these rites. But the annual Shraddh should be performed severally if the wealth has been distributed. (21) Therefore, the eldest son should perform ten-days' rites with full devotion, eating one meal a day, sleeping on the floor, remaining puritan and devoted to Brahmn (ultimate reality). (22) The son gets the same rewards for the performance of the rites for the father and mother as is obtained by sacred **Pari-krama** (circumbulating) of the mother earth seven times. (23)The son who performs all the prescribed Kriya for one year, beginning with the ten-days' rites, gets such reward as is acquired by performing Shraddh at the holy Gaya. (24) He should take bath in a well or a pond, in a garden, at a sacred place, or in a temple, between nine and twelve noon, without reciting Mantras. (25) After getting purified, be seated facing southward at the bottom of a tree, prepare an altar there, plastered with cow-dung. (26) Spread the leaves as mat over the alter, get a Dvija made of Darbha and Kusha grass seated on the altar, perform the ablution with water and worship it while offering Pranaam (salutation) and say "Atasi". (27) Spread KusHa grass in front of the alter for offering Pind, thereafter, offer the Pind uttering the name and Gotra of the departed. (28)

Dadyaat tanadaula-paaken yava-pishten vaa sutah,
Usheerm chandanm bhringa-raaja-pushpm nivedayet,
Dhoopm deepm ch naivedym mukha-vaasm ch dakshinaam(29)
kaaka-annm payasoah paatre vardha-maana-jala-anjaleen,
Pretaaya-amuka-naamme ch mad-dattam-upa-tisthatu(30)
annm vstran jalm dravyam-anyad vaa deeyate ch yat,
Preta-shabden yad-dattm mritasyaanantya-daayakam(31)
Tasmaada-adi-dinaadoordhvm praak-sapindaee-vidhaanatah,
Yoshitah purushasya-api preta-shabdm samuchcharet(32)
prathame-ahani yat-pindao deeyate vidhi-poorvakam,
Tenaiv vidhinaannen nav pindaan pradaayapayet(33)
Navame divase chaiv sapindaaiah sakalair-janaiah,
Taila-abhynga prakartavyo mritaka-svarga-kaamyayaa(34)
Bahiah snaatvaa griheetvaa ch doorvaa-laajaa-samanvitaah,
Agratah pramadaam kritvaa samaa-gachchhen-mrita-alayam(35)
Doorvaa-vat kula-vriddhiste laajaa iv vikaasataa,
Evam-uktvaa tyajed gehe laajaan doorvaa-samanvitaan(36)

The son should offer Pinda made of cooked rice or of barley meal. He should dedicate Usira-root, **Chandan** (sandal paste), the flowers of Mograa, incense, a lamp, eatables, mouth-freshner and Dakshina (donation). (29) With crow-food, milk and water filled jar and handfuls of castor-oil in a pot and say, "May the Pret, named so and so, get this food offered by me." (30) The food, clothes, water, wealth or other things, when given with appellation as 'Pret'; the departed gets infinite benefits. (31) Therefore, the Pinda to the departed woman or man should be offered with the appellation of 'Pret' right from the first day in accordance with Sapinda rites. (32) The procedure with which the first Pinda is offered should be followed for subsequent nine Pinda. (33) On the ninth day, all the Sapindi relatives should massage their bodies with oil, wishing the departed to attain Swarga. (34) After taking bath, proceed to the home of departed while keeping women folk ahead taking Durba grass and parched rice in hands. (35) In the home of the departed, they should say, "May his family expand like the Durba grass and expand like the parched grain." And then strew the mixed-Durba grass and parched grain in the house. (36)

Dashame-ahani maansen pindam dadyaat khageshvr,
Maashena tan-nisedhaadvaa kalau n pala-paitrikam(37)
Dashame divase kshaurm baandhavaa-naam ch munadaanam,
Kriyaa-kartuah sutasya-api punar-munadaanama-acharet(38)
Mishta-annair-bhojayedekm dineshu dashasu dvijam,
Praarthayet preta-muktim ch harim dhyaatvaa krita-anjaliah(39)
Atasee-pushpa-snkhaashm peeta-vaasa-samachyutam,
Ye namasyanti govindm n teshaam vidyate bhayam(40)
Anaadi-nidhano devah shankh-chakra-gadaa-dharah,
Akshayyah punadaareeka-akshah! Preta-moksha-prado bhav(41)
Iti sampraarthanaa-mantraam shraaddha-ante pratyahm pathet,
Snaatvaa gatvaa grihe datvaa go-graasm bhojanm charet(42)

On the tenth day, O Khageswar, a Pind of Masa (black lentil) should be given since meat is forbidden in the Kaliyuga, at the Shraddh for the ancestor. (37) The kinsmen should shave their head, on the tenth day. The son who performs the rites must again have a complete shave. (38) The priests should be offered sweets and foods on tenth day. He should, with folded hands, meditate and pray to Hari (Vishnu) for the release of the departed. (39) Fear does not grip those who pray to Vishnu, the eternal yellow clad Govind (Krishna or Vishnu), who is as charming as flower of Atasi. (40) May Bhagwan Vishnu, who is without beginning or end, one who is adorned with **Shankh** (Conch), **Chakra** (disc) **Gadaa** (club) & **Padma** (Lotus), (symbolizing sound, time, energy and beauty). Become giver of Mokhsya to the departed. (41) This mantra should be repeated with devotion every day at the conclusion of Shraddh. Thereafter, take bath, go to home and give "Gaugrass" (food to cow) and have meal for self. (42)

**Annadi-nidhano Devah Shankh Chakra Gadaa-dharah,
Akshayah pundree-kaakash Preta-mokshya-prado-bhav.**

CHAPTER 12

EKAADASH KARMA (ELEVENTH-DAY RITES), DAAN (DONATIONS, CHARITY), VARSHO-UTSARG (RITES FOR RELEASE OF THE BULL), UTTAM SHODASHI, SAPINDIKARAN, NARAYAN-BALI, ETC.

GARUD UVAACH

Ekaadasha-dinasya-api vidhim boorahi sur-eshvar!
Vrish-otsarga-vidhaanm ch vad me jagad-eeshvar!(1)

SHREEBHAGAVAANUVAACH

Ekaadashe-ahni gantavym praatarev jala-ashaye,
Aurdhvadehi-kriyaa sarvaa karanaeeyaa prayatnatah(2)
Nimantraayed braahmanaansh-cha veda-shaastraa-paraayanaan,
Praarthayet preta-muktim ch namas-krity krita-anjaliah(3)
Snaana-sandhya-adikm kritvaa hyaachaaryo-api shuchir-bhavet,
Vidhaanm vidhi-vat kuryaad-ekaadasha-din-ochitam(4)
Amantram kaarayech-chhraaddhm dashaahm naam gotraatah,
Ekaadashe-ahni pretasy dadyaat-pindam samantraakam(5)

GARUDA SAID O **Sureshwara** (Ishwar of Sura), tell me the procedure of Ekadash(the rites of the eleventh day) and, O **Jagdiswara** (Ishwara of the universe), explain to me the procedure of **Varsho-utsarg** (release of a bull). (1) **BHAGWAN SAID-** In the early morning on the **Ekadas** (eleventh day), go to a water-reservoir and perform **Aurdhva-dehik** with all efforts. (2) Invite Purohit who is well-versed in Vedas and Shastra, and offering Namaskar with folded hands, pray for the Mukti (release) of the departed. (3) The **Acharya Purohit** (preceptor) should also become purified by taking bath and performing the Sandhyaa, etc., he should conduct the Ekadash karma as per the prescribed procedure. (4) The Shraddh should be performed with the name and Gotra, without the use of mantras till the tenth day; and on the eleventh day, offer a Pind to the departed while chanting the mantras. (5)

Sauvarnam kaarayed-vishnaum brahmaanam raupyakm tathaa,
Rudras-taamra-mayah kaaryo yamo loha-mayah khag!(6)
Paschime vishnau-kalashm gng-odaka-samanvitam,
Tasy-opari nyased-vishnaum peeta-vstrena veshtitam(7)
Poorve tu brahma-kalashm ksheer-odaka-samanvitam,
Brahmaanam sthaapayet-tatraa þeta-vstrena veshtitam(8)
Uttarasyaam rudra-kumbhm pooritm madhu-sarpishaa,
Shree-rudrm sthaapayet-tatraa rakta-vstrena veshtitam(9)
Dakshinaasyaam yama-ghatam-indr-odaka-samanvitam,
Krishnaa-vstrena snveshty tasy-opari yamn nyaset(10)
Madhye tu manadaalm kritvaa sthaapayet kaushikm sutah,
Dakshina-abhi-mukho bhootvaa-apasavyen ch tarpayet(11)
Vishnaum vidhim shivm dharmm veda-mantraush-cha tarpayet,
Homm kritvaa charet-pshchaach-chhraaddhn dasa-ghata-adikam(12)
Go-daanm ch tato dadyaat-pitr-rinaan taaranaay vai,
Gaur-eshaa hi mayaa dattaa preetaye te-astu maadhav(13)
Upabhuktm tu tasya-aseed-vstr-abhooshanaa-vaahanam,
Ghrita-poornam kaansya-paatraam sapta-dhaanym tad-eepsitam(14)

A golden image of Vishnu, a silver one of Brahma, a copper one of **Rudra** (Shiva) and an iron one of Yama (pronounced as Yam) should be prepared, O Bird. (6) The **Vishnu-kalash** (urn or finial), a pot filled with water of Ganga and upon it the image of Vishnu, clad in yellow robes should be placed in the west. (7) The **Brahm-kalash**, a pot full of milk and water for Brahma and upon it the image of Brahma should be placed in the east direction, clad in white robes upon it. (8) The **Rudra-kalash** should be kept in the north along with honey and ghee and the image of Rudra, clad in red robes, should be placed on it. (9) In the south, place the "**Yam-kalash**" filled with rain-water; and upon it place the image of Yama, clad in black robes. (10) The son should make a south facing **Mandap** (pavilion) in the middle and place kusha grass on it. He should become **Apasvya** (sacred thread shifted to right shoulder) and give **Tarpan** (libation). (11) Offer Tarpan to Vishnu, creator Brahma, to Shiva and to Dharma-raj (Yama) while chanting Vedic mantras. Followed by Homa (offering to Ishwara through fire), then perform "Dash-ghat" and other Shraddh. (12) Thereafter, **Godaan** (donation of cow) should be done for redemption from **Pitr-rin** (obligation to ancestors) while expressing the following "O Madhav (Vishnu) this cow is offered by me. May this please you." (13) The clothes, ornaments, vehicles and all that which the departed used during lifetime, may be offered as Daan alongwith a brass vessel filled with ghee, the seven grains and all other things which departed liked, when alive. (14)

Tila-ady-ashta-mahaa-daanam-anta-kaale n chet kritam,
Shayyaa-sameepe dhritva-itad-daanm tasyaah pradaapayet(15)
Pretasy pratimaa-yuktaa sarv-opakaranaair-vritaa,
Preta-shayyaa mayaa hyeshaa tubhym vipr niveditaa(16)
Itya-achaaryaay daatavyaa braahmanaay kutumbine,
Tatah pradakshinaee-krity pranai-paty visarjayet(17)
Evm shayyaa-pradaanen shraaddhen navakaa-dinaa,
Vrish-otsarga-vidhaanen preto yaati paraam gatim(18)
Ekaadashe-ahini vidhinaa vrish-otsargm samaacharet,
Heena-anga-roginan baalm tyaktvaa kuryaat-sa-lakshanaam(19)
Eshtavyaa bahavah putraa yady-eko-api gayaam vrajet,
Gaureem vivaahayet kanyaam neelm vaa vrisham-utsrijet(20)
Ekodashe-ahni sampraapte vrisha-alaabho bhaved-yadi,
Darbhaiah pishtastu sampaady tm vrishm mochayed budhah,
Vrish-otsarjana-velaayaam vrisha-alaabhah kathnchan,
Mritikaabhistu darbhair-vaa vrishm kritvaa vimochayet(21)
Raurava-adishu ye kechit pachyante yasy poorvajaah,
Vrish-otsargena taan sarvaans-taarayed-eka-vinshatim(22)

If the Sesamum, etc., eight **Maha-daan** (great donations) were not made during the last days of departed, then all these should be donated placing along the Shayya daan. (15) "For the departed, this Shayya (bedding) alongwith other things and the image is donated by me to you, O Vipra (preceptor)." (16) With these words, give it to a Acharya **Purohit** (preceptor) having a **family** (Grihast) to support; thereafter taking **Pari-krama** (moving in a circle round preceptor) do **Pranam** (salute) to him and present it as **Dakshina** (virtuous fee one can afford). (17) By this gift of the Shayya, Sraddhaas of the ninth and other days, and by the rite of the release of a bull, the deceased gets, Param-gati (speed to supreme i.e. Mokshya) .(18) On the eleventh day **Varsho-utsarg** should be performed as prescribed. The bull should not be lacking any of the limbs or should not be ailing or too young but should be the one having proportionate features. (19) One should desire for many sons (here the word son denotes to daughter as well) so that even one of them may go to Gaya to perform the rites or conduct the marriage of virgin Gauri or release a bull of Neel-vrish. (20) In case a bull is not available on the day of release, a symbolic bull made of Kusha-grass or barley flour or of clay, may be dedicated. (21) Twenty one generations get liberated if the Varsho-utsarg is performed for ancestors who are in the "Raurava" and other Narak. (22)

111

Tasmaat pitri-vimukty-arthm vrisha-yagym samaacharet,
Yath-okten vidhaanen kuryaat sarvm prayatnatah(23)
Grahaanaam sthaapanm kritvaa tat-tan-mantraustu poojanam,
Homm kuryaad yathaa-shaastrm poojayed-vrisha-maatarah(24)
Vatsm vatseem samaanaayy badhneeyaat kankrnam tayoah,
Vaivaahyen vidhaanen stambhama-aropayet tadaa(25)
Snaapayech-ch vrishm vatseem rudra-kumbh-odaken ch,
Gandha-maalyaish-cha sampoojy kaarayech-ch pradakshinaam(26)
Trishoolm dakshinae paarshve vaame chakrm pradaapayet,
Tm vimuchya-anjalim baddhvaa pathen-mantraam-imm sutah(27)
Dharmas-tvm vrisha-roopena brahmanaa nirmitah puraa,
Tav-otsarga-pradaanen taarayasv bhava-arnaavaat(28)
Iti mantraan-namas-krity vatsm vatseem sam-utsrijet,
Varado-ahm sadaa tasy preta-mokshm dadaami ch(29)
Tasmaad-esh prakartavyas-tat-falm jeevato bhavet,
Aa-putraastu svaym kritvaa sukhm yaati paraam gatim(30)

Therefore, perform the rites for the release of a bull for the Mokshya of ancestors. With all out efforts, the rites should be performed according to the prescribed procedure. (23) **Havan** (offerings to Ishwar through fire) should be performed in accordance with Shastra after establishment of the Graha (planets) and worship should be done with their respective mantras. The mother of bull, should also be worshipped. (24) Bring together a calf and bull calf and bind them together with a marriage string in accordance with marriage ceremony, and then tie them to a post. (25) Bath the calf and bull calf with the Rudra Pot and having worshipped them with fragrances and garlands, take the **Parikrama** (circumbulation). (26) The bull should be marked with the trident of Shiva in the sourthern side on the back and with **Chakra** (discus of Vishnu) on the left side on the back. Before releasing the bull, the son should recite this mantra, with folded hands: (27) "You are Dharma in the form of a bull. You were formerly created by Brahma. Your release will lead to Mokshya of the departed from this ocean of existence." (28) After offering Namaskar to (Dharma through) calf and bull calf with the above mantra, they should be released. Whosoever does this, O Garuda! shall always be the granted boons by Me and shall bestow Mokshya to the Pret. (29) The merits of release of bull during life time are the same as that of post death. The sonless person should do it himself so that he is blessed with happiness in this life and attains Paramgati after death. (30)

Kaartika-adau shubhe maase ch-ottaraayanaage ravau,
Shukla-pakshe-athavaa krishnae dvaadashya-adi tithau tathaa(31)
Grahanaa-dvitaye chaiv punaya-teerthe-ayana-dvaye,
Vishuvad-dvitaye ch-api vrish-otsargm samaacharet(32)
Shubhe lagne muhoorte ch shuchau deshe samaahitah,
Brahmanam tu samaahooy vidhigym shubha-lakshanaam(33)
Japair-homais-tathaa daanaiah prakuryaad-deha-shodhanam,
Poorva-vat sakalm kritym kuryaad-dhoma-adi-laksanaam(34)
Shaala-graamm ch snsthaapy vaishnaavm shraaddham-aacharet,
Aatma-shraaddhm tatah kuryaad-dadyaad-daanm dvi-janmane(35)
Evm yah kurute pakshin-na-putraasya-api putraa-vaan,
Sarva-kaama-falm tasy vrish-otsargaat-prajaayate(36)
Putra-abhaave tu patnee syaad dauhitro duhita-api vaa,
Putroshu vidya-maaneshu vrishm na-anyen kaarayet(37)
Evm kritvaa vrish-otsargm kuryaach-chhraaddhaani shodaash,
Sapindaeekaranaadarvaak tadahm kathayaami te(38)

In the month of Kartika and in other auspicious months, when the Sun is in Uttarayan; on the **Dwadashi** (twelfth day) in the **Shukla Pakshya** (waxing moon); or the **Krishna Pakshya** (waning moon) and similar other days; (31) In the two eclipses; at a sacred Teerth; on **Vishnu Sankranti** (equinoctial) and **Ayan Sankranti** (solstitial points), one should perform the Varsho-utsarga. (32) In the auspicious **Lagna** (ascendance) and **Muhurt** (time) and in a holy place, a Purohit well conversant with the performance of the rites and bears a good moral character, should be invited. (33) The body should be purified by **Jaap** (repetition of the name of Ishwara), Homa and Daan and Havan and other rites should be performed as described earlier. (34) The Vaisnava Shraaddh should be performed after enshrining of **Saaligram** (the iconic fossilized icons symbolizing the universal principle of Lord Vishnu) and then perform the Shraddh for self and give Daan to the Dvija. (35) O Bird, whosoever performs Varsho-utsarg whether having a son or not, all his wishes are fulfilled. (36) Varsho-utsarg should be performed by wife or the son of a daughter in the absence of a son, else the daughter will perform it. But if a son is available, no one else should do it. (37) Thus, after having performed the rites for Varsho-utsarg, sixteen Shraddh should be performed. What is to be done before performing the **Spindi-karna** (ritual for reception for the Pret into the community of the Pitr or ancestors), I will tell you about that. (38)

113

Sthaane dvaare-ardha-maarge ch chitaayaam shava-hastake,
Asthi-sanchayane shastho dash pindaa dashaahniikaah(39)
Malinm shodaashm chaitat prathamm pari-keertitam,
Anyach-ch shodaashm madhye dviteeym kathayaami te(40)
Prathamm (shree) vishnaave dadyaat dviteeym shree-shivaay ch,
Yaamyaay parivaaraay triteeym pindaam-utsrijet(41)
Chaturthm soma-raajaay havya-vaahaay panchamam,
Kavya-vaahaay shasthm ch dadyaat kaalaay saptamam(42)
Rudraay cha-ashtamm dadyaan-navamm purushaay ch,
Pretaay dashamm chaiv ekadashm vishnaave namah(43)
Dvaadashm brahmanae dadyaad-vishnaave ch traayo-dasham,
Chatur-dashm shivaayaiv yamaay dasha-panchakam(44)
Dadyaat tat-purushaayaiv pindam shodaashakm khag,
Madhym shodaashakm praahuretat tattva-vido janaah(45)
Dvaadash prati-maaseshu paakshikm ch tri-paakshikam,
Nyoona-shaana-maasikm pindam dadyaan-nyoona-abdikm tathaa(46)
Uttamm shodaashm chaitan-mayaa te parikeertitam,
Shrapayitvaa charum taarkshyaa kuryaad-ekaadashe-ahani(47)

At the place where the death took place; at the threshold; half-way to cremation ground; at the funeral pyre; in the hand of the corpse and at the time of the collection of the mortal remains; these six, and the ten Pindas are to be offered in ten days, (39) The first sixteen Pind are called "**Malin** (impure) **Shodashi**" (sixteen). Next, I will tell you about the procedure of "**Madhayam** (middle) Shodashi Pind. (40) Offer the first Pinda to Vishnu, the second to Shri Shiva and the third to the family of Yama. (41) The fourth to Moon, the fifth to Agni (the bearer of oblations to the deities), the sixth to the bearer of oblations to the ancestors and the seventh to **Kaal** (death); (42) The eighth to Rudra, give the ninth to **Purusa** (the eternal universal principle), the tenth to the **Pret**, and the eleventh to Bhagwan Vishnu; (43) Give the twelfth to Brahma, the thirteenth to Vishnu, the fourteenth to Shiva; the fifteenth to Yama; (44) Give the Shodas (sixteenth) Pind to Tat-Purusa. O Bird! These are called the middle sixteen by men who know the truth. (45) The Pinds should be given in each one of the twelve months, on the fortnight, the third fortnight, before the six months and also before the year. (46) O Taarkshya, I have told you about the "**Uttam**(best) **Shodshi**." On the eleventh day, offer the Pind with Kheer preparations. (47)

Chat-vaarin-shat tathaiva-ashtau shraaddhm pretatva-naashanam,
Yasy jaatm vidhaanen s bhavet-pitri-panktibhaak(48)
Pitri-pankti-pravesha-arthm kaarayet shodaasha-traayam,
Etach-chhraaddha-viheenshchet preto bhavati susthiram(49)
Yaavann deeyate shraaddhm shodaasha-traaya-sngyakam,
Sva-dattm para-dattm ch taa-van-naivopatisthate(50)
Tasmaat-putrona kartavym vidhinaa shodaasha-traayam,
Bharturyaa kurute patnee tasyaah shreyo hy-anantakam(51)
Samparetasy yaa patyuah kurute ch-aurdhva-daihikam,
Kshayaahm paakshikm shraaddhm saa sateety-uchyate mayaa(52)
Upakaaraay saa bhartur-jeevatyesaa pati-vrataa,
Jeevitm safalm tasyaa yaa mritm svaaminm bhajet(53)
Ath kshchit pramaaden mriyate vahin-vaari-bhiah,
Snskaara-pramukhm karm sarvm kuryaad-yatha-vidhi(54)
Pramaadaad-ichchhayaa vaapi naagaad-vaa mriyate yadi,
Pakshayor-ubhayor-naagm panchmeeshu pra-poojayet(55)
Kuryaat pishtamayeem lekhyaam naaga-bhoga-akritim bhuvi,
Archayet taam sitaiah puspaiah sugandhaish-chandanen ch(56)

These forty-eight Shraddh destroy the Pret condition of departed. The one, for whom these are performed, as per prescribed procedure, joins the assembly of Pitr. (48) For the entry into the assembly of Pitr, the three **Shodshi** (sixteens) should be performed; if deprived of Shraddh, the Pret condition remains firm. (49) In case Shodas-traya Shraddh are not performed either by himself or by another, one certainly does not join the Pitr. (50) Therefore, the Shodas-traya should be performed by the son, as prescribed. But if the wife performs them for the husband, she achieves infinite rewards. (51) A wife who performs the **Aurdhva-dehic**, the annual and the fortnightly Shraddh, is called by me, "Sati (truthful)." (52) The life of a wife who lives for the benefaction of her husband is successful, as she remembers her dead husband. (53) For those who die due to drowning, by fire or due to negligence. The sacrament and other rites should be performed as prescribed. (54) If a person is killed due to carelessness or by choice or by a snake, then in their cases worship of a serpent may be performed on the **fifth day** (Panchmi) of both the fortnights (Shukla and Krisna Pakshya). (55) Carve out an image of a serpent upon the ground with rice-flour and worship with white flower having sweet-smell and sandal-paste; (56)

Pradadyaad dhoopa-deepau ch tanadaulaansh-cha tilaan-kshipet,
Aama-pishtm ch naivedym ksheerm ch vi-nivedayet(57)
Sau-varnam shaktito naagm gaam ch dadyaad dvi-janmane,
Krita-anjalistato brooyaat preeyataam naagaraadaiti(58)
Punas-teshaam prakurveet naaraayanaa-balim kriyaam,
Tayaa labhante svarga-vaasm muchyante sarva-paatakaiah(59)
Evm sarva-kriyaam kritvaa ghatm sa-annm jala-anvitam,
Dadyaad-aabdn yathaa-sankhyaan pindaan vaa sa-jalaan kramaat(60)
Evam-ekaadashe kritvaa kuryaat-saapindaanm tatah,
Shayya-apa-daanaam daanm ch kaarayet sootake gate(61)

Incenses, lamps, rice, sesamum and uncooked rice-flour and milk should be offered to the serpent. (57) If one's financial position permits, an image of serpent made of gold and a cow be donated to a Dvija. Then one should pray, with folded hands, by saying - "May the King of Serpents be pleased." (58) Thereafter, **Narayana-bali rites** (the rites performed for those who died of unnatural death) should be performed, by which they are absolved of all the Paap and get abode in Swarga. (59) Thus, after performing all the rites, one should donate every day a Ghat (pot) with food and water until the end of the year, or offer three hundred sixty Ghat, water oblation and Pind, each. (60) After the performance of the eleventh day's rites and release from Sutaka, the Sapindi Shraddh may be performed on twelfth day and the Pinds for all the ancestors, donation of Shayya, a pair of Pada (footwear) and other offerings, gifted. (61)

**Annadi-nidhano Devah Shankh Chakra Gadaa-dharah,
Akshayah pundree-kaakash Preta-mokshya-prado-bhav.**

CHAPTER 13

SUTAK (IMPURITY) PERIOD, SAPINDI SHRAADDH, GAYA SHRAADDH AND IMPORTANCE OF DAAN (DONATIONS AND CHARITY)

GARUD UVAACH

GARUDSapindaana-vidhim boorahi sootakasy ch nirnaayam,
Shayya-apa-daanaam saamagreem teshaam ch mahimaam prabho(1)
Shrinau taarkshyaa pravaksyaami saapindaya-ady-akhilaam kriyaam,
Preta-naam parityajy yayaa pitri-ganae vishet(2)

SHREEBHAGAVAANUVAACH

N pindao milito hyeshaam pitaamaha-shiva-adishu,
Nopatisthanti daanaani putraur-dat-taany-anekadhaa(3)
Ashuddhah syaat-sadaa putro n shuddhyti kadaachan,
Sootakm n nivartet sapindaee-karanam vinaa(4)
Tasmaat-putrona kartavym sootaka-ante sapindaanam,
Sootaka-antm pravakshyaami sarveshaam ch yathochitam(5)

GARUD SAID-Tell me O Prabho! the procedure to perform Sapindi Shraddh and the rules on **Sutak** (temporary impurity associated with death, **Shayya-daan** (donation of bed), **Pad-daan** (donation of footwear) and donation of other things and the importance thereof. (1) **BHAGWAN SAID**- Listen, O Taarkshya! I will tell you about the entire Sapindan and all the other rites by performing of which, the departed leaves Pret-yoni and joins the assembly of **Pitr** (ancestors). (2) Till the Pindas of departed are not combined with the **Pitamah** (dead ancestors who are in the form of Aditya, Vasu and Rudra), he cannot receive the various Daans made by the sons. (3) Without performing Sapindi rites, the son always remains impure as the condition of Sutak persists without **Sapindee-karan**. (4) Therefore, it is the duty of the son to perform Sapindan at the end of Sutak. I will tell you the right course of action to be followed for removal of Sutak. (5)

Ubhayatraa dashaahaani kulasyaa-annm vi-varjayet,
Daanm prati-graho homah svaadhyaaysh-cha nivartate(6)
Dashaahen sapindaastu shuddhynti preta-sootake,
Tri-raatrona sakulyaastu snaatvaa shuddhynti gotraajaah(7)
Chaturthe dasha-raatraam syaat-shana-nishaah punsi panchime,
Shasthe chaturahah proktm saptame ch dina-traayam(8)
Astame dinam-ekm tu navame prahara-dvayam,
Dashame snaana-maatraam hi mritakm janma-sootakam(9)
Deshaantara-gatah kshchich-chhrinauyaadyo hyanir-dasham,
Yach-chheshm dasha-raatraasy taa-vad-evaa-shuchir-bhavet(10)
Ati-kraante dashaahe tu tri-raatraama-shuchir-bhavet,
Samvatsare vyateete tu snaana-maatraad-vi-shuddhyti(11)
Aadya-bhaaga-dvaym yaa-van-mritakasy ch sootake,
Dviteeye patite cha-adyaat-sootakaach-chhuddhir-ishyate(12)
Vaak-pradaane krite tvatraa gyeyam ch-obhayatas-trayaham,
Pitur-varasy ch tato dattaanaam bharturev hi(13)

For ten days, avoid food of that family where birth or death has taken place. During this period, Daan, Homa, sacrifice and study of sacred scriptures is also prohibited. (6) The **Sapinda relatives** (blood relatives in the direct line of descent, generally of five generations) are purified from the death related impurity in ten days, the members of same Kul in three nights, and the people of the Gotra are purified merely by taking bath. (7) Sutak remains for ten nights, upto fourth generation; for six nights, up to the fifth generation; four days, upto the sixth generation; and for three days, up to the seventh generation. (8) To the eighth generation, for a single day; to the ninth generation, a quarter of a day and to the tenth generation, merely till bathing, lasts the impurity of death and birth. (9) If a person dies in another country and one hears of death, then the **Sutak** lasts for the ten days from the day the news of death is heard. (10) If the news of death is heard after the lapse of ten days, one is purified after three nights. If the news of death is heard after a year, one gets purified just by taking a bath. (11) If a second death takes place just during the currency of first Sutak, then the purification from the first Sutak will purify for the second one as well. (12) If it takes place after the betrothal ceremony, impurity for three days exists in both the families. But after marriage, only the husband's family is affected by Sutak. (13)

118

Aadanta-jananaat-sady   aachailaannaishikee   smritaa,
Tri-raatraama-avrataadeshaad dasha-raatraamatah param(14)
Guhaa-vahni-praveshe   ch   deshaantara-mriteshu   ch,
Snaanm sachailm kartavym sadyah shauchm vidheeyate(15)
Aama-garbhaash-cha ye jeevaa ye ch garbhaad vi-niahshritaah,
N teshaam-agni-snskaaro naa-a-ashauchm n-odaka-kriyaa(16)
Shilpinah   kaaravo   vaidyaa   daasee-daasaas-tathaiv   ch,
Raajaanah shrotriyaash-chaiv sadyah-shauchaah prakeertitaah(17)
Satraaee ch mantraa-pootsh-cha aahita-agnir-nripas tathaa,
Eteshaam sootakm na-asti yasy chechchhanti vaadaavaah(18)
Sarvesaamev   varnaanaam   sootake   mritake-api   vaa,
Dashaahaach-chhuddhirityes kalau shaastrsy nishchayah(19)
Aasheer-vaadm deva-poojaam pratyutthaana-abhi-vandanam,
Parynke shayanm sparshm n kuryaan-mrita-sootake(20)
Sandhyaam daanm japm homm svaadhyaayn pitri-tarpanaam,
Brahma-bhojym vratm naiv kartavym mrita-sootake(21)

If an infant, who has not yet cut his teeth, dies, purification is immediate; before **Mundan** (tonsure), one night; before the **Janeu** (sacred thread) ceremony, three nights and afterwards ten nights. (14) Taking bath and changeover to washed cloths would be enough to purify from the Sutak of accidental death inside the tunnel, death in an unknown place, death due to fire, etc., and death in alien place. (15) No cremation is required for immature fetus born due to miscarriage and infant who is born dead; there is also no Sutak in these cases and even bathing and sprinkling of water for purification is also not required. (16) Artisans, architects, doctors, service class people, rulers, priests who study and teach the Vedic scriptures regularly - all of them get immediately purified with a bath in case of any Sutak. (17) One who is purified by daily Japa, Vedic mantras, who offers Homa (fire sacrifice) and the king, are not affected by impurity. (18) In Kaliyug, the Sutak period on account of death and birth is for ten days for all the castes. It is the judgment of the Shastra. (19) Blessing others, worshiping the Dev, reception of guest, sleeping on a bed and touching others, should not be done during Sutak. (20) Sandhya, Daan, Jaap, Homa, **Swaadhyay** (self study of scriptures), offerings to the forefathers, feeding to Brahmins and the observance of fasts should not be performed during the Sutak. (21)

119

Braahmana-arthe vipannaa ye naareenaam go-graheshu ch,
Aahaveshu vipannaanaam-eka-raatraam-ashauchakam(22)
Vratino mantraa-pootasy sa-agnikasy dvijasy ch,
Brahma-nishthasy yatino n hi raagyaam ch sootakam(23)
N teshaam-ashubhm kinchad vipraanaam shubha-karmanai,
Anaatha-preta-snskaarm ye kurvanti narottamaah(23.1)
Vivaah-otsava-yagyeshu jaate ch mrita-sootake,
Tasy poorva-kritm chaa-annm bhojym tan-manura-braveet(24)
Sootake yastu grieehaanti tadagya-anaann doshabhaak,
Daataa doshama-vaapnoti yaachakaay dadann-api(25)
Prachchhaady sootakm yastu dadaaty-annm dvijaay ch,
Gyaatvaa grihnaanti ye vipraah dosha-bhaajastu ev hi(26)
Tasmaat-sootaka-shuddhyrthm pituah kuryaat-sapindaanam,
Tatah pitri-ganaaiah saardhm pitri-lokm s gachchhati(27)

For those who died for the safety of devotees (Sant, Sanyaasi, Saadhu, Pujari, Purohit, Brahmin), safety of women, protection of cows and in a war for the protection of Dharma, there is Sutak for only one day and one night. (22) Those observing Vrit (vows), who are purified by mantras or are Agnihotri (resorting to fire offerings), Dvija, one who is Brahmn-nisht (absorbed in the Brahmn), an ascetic or a king are not affected by Sutak. (23) Those who are engaged in **Shubh-karm** (auspicious deeds), are helpful to knowers and who perform the last rites of departed destitute and orphans, such people are never unpurified. (23.1) As declared by Manu, during the course of a marriage, festival or a Yagya, if an impurification happens due to a death or a birth, then the food prepared before impurification, can be eaten. (24) If someone accepts food and other Daan due to ignorance from a family having Sutak, he or she is not a defaulter. But after knowing about the impurification, if food is accepted, both the donor and the receiver are equally at fault. (25) One who offers food to Dvija, hiding own impurification status, and the Vipra accepts it despite the knowledge of Sutak, both are the defaulters. (26) Therefore, for the purification from Sutak, one should perform the Sapindan of the parent. With this, the deceased goes to the **"Pitralok"** (world of the ancestors) and joins them. (27)

Dvaadashaahe tripakshe vaa shana-maase vatsare-api vaa,
Sapindaee-karanam proktm munibhis-tattva-darshibhiah(28)
Mayaa tu prochyate taarkshyaa shaastr-dharma-anusaaratah,
Chaturnaamev varnaanaam dvaadashaahe sapindaanam(29)
Anityatvaat-kali-dharmaanaam punsaam chaiv-aayushah kshayaat,
Asthiratvaach-chhareerasy dvaadashaahe prashasyate(30)
Vrata-bandhotsa-vaadeeni vratasy-odyaapanaani ch,
Vivaaha-adi bhavennaiv mrite ch grihamedhini(31)
Bhikshur-bhikshaam n grihnati hantakaaro n grihyate,
Nitym naimittikm lupyed-yaa-vat-pindam n melitah(32)
Karma-lopaat pratyavaayee bhavet-tasmaat-sapindaanam,
Nir-agnikah sa-agniko vaa dvaadashaahe samaacharet(33)
Yat-falm sarva-teertheshu sarva-yagyeshu yat-falam,
Tat-falm samavaapnoti dvaadashaahe sapindaanaat(34)
Atah snaatvaa mrita-sthaane gomayen-opalepite,
Shaastr-okten vidhaanen sapindaeem kaarayet(35)

As declared by Manu, the Sapindan rites should be performed on the twelfth day, the third fortnight, the sixth month or at the end of the year. (28) As per the scriptures, the Sapindan rites for all the four castes should be on the twelfth day, O Taarkshya! (29) The twelfth day is recommended because of the uncertainties in pursuing the Dharma in Kaliyug and because of the instability of the body. (30) On demise of a Grihastha (householder), Upanayan (scared thread) ceremony, Utsav (festival), Vrit Udyaapan (conclusion of a fast), Vivaah (marriage), etc., should not be performed. (31) The Bhikshu is not to accept alms, guests are not to be entertained. The **Nitya-karma** (daily, obligatory duties like sandhya, etc.), **Naimittik-karma** (ceremonies to be performed for special occasions like 16 sanskaar, etc.), of **Grishasta** are to be avoided till the performance of Sapinda rites. (32) The interception in Nitya and Naimittik karma brings peccancy. Therefore, the Sapindan rites should be performed on the twelfth day, with or without with fire. (33) Punya which is achieved by pilgrimage of all the Teerth (sacred bathing-places) or the Punya which is achieved by performing all the Yagya, the same reward is achieved by performing the Sapindan on the twelfth day. (34) Therefore, Sapindi rites should be performed as prescribed in the scriputers after taking bath and cleaning and plastering, with cow-dung, the spot where death took place. (35)

Paadya-aghya-achamaneeya-adyair-vishve-devaansh-cha poojayet,
Kupitre vikirm dattvaa punaraap upa-sprishet(36)
Dadyaat-pitaamahaadeenaam treen pindaansh-cha yathaa-kramam,
Vasu-rudra-arka-roopaanaam chaturthm mritakasy ch(37)
Chandanais-tulasee-patraur-dhoopair-deepaiah su-bhojanaiah,
Mukha-vaasaiah su-vstraish-cha dakshinaabhish-cha poojayet(38)
Preta-pindam tridhaa kritvaa su-varnaasy shalaakayaa,
Pitaamaha-adi-pindaeshu melayettm prithak prithak(39)
Pitaamahyaa samm maatuah pitaamaha-samm pituah,
Sapindaee-karanam kuryaad-iti taarkshyaa matm mam(40)
Mrite pitari yasyaath vidyate ch pitaamahah,
Ten deyaas-trayah pindaaah pra-pitaamaha-poorvakaah(41)
Tebhysh-cha paitrikm pindam melayettm tridhaa kritam,
Maatary-agre prashaantaayaam vidyate ch pitaamahee(42)
Tadaa maatrika-shraaddhe-api kuryaat-paitrika-vad-vidhiah,
Yadvaa mayi mahaa-lakshmyaam tayoah pindam ch melayet(43)

The **Visva-dev** (all the 33 categories of deities holding the universe) should be worshipped with water, arghya, achaman, Thereafter, having offered Pinds to other departed ones, one should sip the water. (36) Three Pinds should be offered to grandfather, great grandfather and great great grandfather (or mother's line as applicable) in the form of Vasu, Rudra and Arka and the fourth Pind to the deceased. (37) Worship with sandal-paste, leaves of the holy Tulsi, incenses, lamps, delicious dishes, mouth-freshner, decent cloths and Dakshina (virtuous fee-one can afford as donations). (38) Divide the Pind for the departed into three parts with the help of a thin bar of gold. Merge them separately with the three Pinds given to the grandfather, great grandfather and great great grandfather. (39) Sapindan for the mother should be with the grandmother's and that of father with the grandfather's side. It is my opinion, O Taarkshya. (40) In case the father dies while the grandfather is alive, the three Pinds should than be offered to the great grandfather and his ancestors. (41) The father's Pind, divided into three parts should be merged with their Pinds. If the mother dies before the grandmother; (42) The Shraddh of mother should be performed in the same way as that of the father; one should mix the Pind with both Vishnu (as father) and great Lakshmi (as mother). (43)

Aputraayaah striyaah kuryaat-patiah saapindaana-adikam,
Shvashrva-adibhiah sahaivaa-asyaa sapindaee-karanam bhavet(44)
Bhatrra-adi-bhi-stribhiah kaarym sapindaee-karanam striyaah,
Naitan-mam matm taarkshyaa patyaa saapindayam-arhati(45)
Ekaam chitaam sama-aroodhau dampatee yadi kaashyap,
Trinaam-antaratah kritvaa shvashuraadestadaacharet(46)
Ek ev sutah kuryaada-adau pindaadikm pituah,
Tad-oodhrvm ch prakurveet satyaah snaanm punsh-charet(47)
Sarveshaam putraa-heenaanaam patnee kuryaat sapindaanam,
Rritvijaa kaarayed vaa-api purohitamatha-api vaa(48)
Kritvaa sapindaanm taarkshyaa prakuryaat-pitri-tarpanaam,
Udaaharet-svadhaa-kaarm veda-mantrauah samanvitam(49)
Atithim bhojayet-pshchaad-dhanta-kaarm ch sarvadaa,
Ten tripyanti pitaro munayo deva-daanavaah(50)
Graasa-maatraa bhaved bhikshaa chatur-graasm tu puskalam,
Puskalaani ch chat-vaari hanta-kaaro vidheeyate(51)

The husband should perform the Sapindan rites for his sonless wife. This Sapindan for her is performed along with her mother-in-law and others. (44) O Taarkshya, in my opinion the Sapindan rite for a woman should not be performed along with that of her husband, her father-in-law and grand father-in-law because the Sapindan for woman should be performed with that of woman and man with that of man. (45) O Kashyap! If husband and wife have to be cremated in the same funeral pyre, then, having placed grass between them, and with that of the mother-in-law and father-in-law respectively. (46) Only one son should perform the Pind, etc., first for the father, after that, having bathed again, for the mother. (47) A wife should perform the Sapindan rites of her husband in case they do not have a son. Or she may get it performed by a priest or a Purohit. Otherwise a pupil may perform it. (48) After the Sapindan rites, O Taarkshya! Tarpan to the Pitr should be done. "Swadhakaram" should be recited for Tarpan along with Vedic mantras. (49) Thereafter, food should be offered to the guest who should perform "**Hantkaar**" (hantkar signifies gratification). By this, the Pitr, the Munis, the Dev and the Danavas are satisfied. (50) A mouthful is called Bhikshya (alms), four mouthfuls are Pushkal (abundance). And four Pushkals are called "Hanta-kaara." (51)

Sapindayaam vipra-charanaau poojayech-chandana-aksataiah,
Daanm tasmai pradaatavyam-akshayya-tripti-hetave(52)
Varsha-vrittim ghritm cha-annm suvarnam rajatm sugaam,
Ashvam gajm rathm bhoomim-aachaaryaay pradaapayet(53)
Tatshcha poojayen-mantrauah svasti-vaachana-poorvakam,
Kumkuma-aksata-naivedyair-grahaan-deveem vinaayakam(54)
Aachaaryastu tatah kuryaad-abhishekm sa-mantraakam,
Baddhvaa sootraam kare dadyaan-mantraa-pootaans-tatha-aksataan(55)
Tatshcha bhojayed vipraan-mishta-annair-vividhaiah shubhaiah,
Dadyaat-sa-dakshinaam tebhyah sa-jala-annaan dvi-shada-ghataan(56)
Vaarya-ayudha-pratodastu danadaastu dvija-bhojanaat,
Sprista-vyaan-antarm varnaaiah shudhyeran te tatah kramaat(57)
Evm sapindaanm kritvaa kriyaa-vstraanai santyajet,
Shukla-ambara-dharo bhootvaa shayyaa-daanm pradaapayet(58)
Shayyaa-daanm prashnsanti sarve devaah savaasavaah,
Tasmaach-chhayyaa pradaatavyaa maranae jeevite-api vaa(59)
Saara-daaru-mayeem ramyaan su-chitraush-chitritaam dridhaam,
Patta-sootraur-vitanitaam hema-patraur-alankritaam(60)

During the Sapinda rites, worship the feet of Purohit with Chandan (sandal-paste) and Akshat and give Daan to him for unending gratification of Pitrs. (52) Give Ghee, Grains, Gold, Silver, milch cow, a horse, an elephant, a chariot and a piece of land (this is with reference to kings or wealthy persons) to the Purohit for one year's subsistence. (53) Then worship Navagriha, Devi and Ganesh with Mantra, Kum-kum (saffron), Akshyat, Naivedaya after performing Swasti-vaachan. (54) Then the Purohit should do Abhisekh with Mantras, tie the **Rakshya sutra** (safety thread) in the wrist of Yajman (one performing rites) and present the Akshyat consecrated with mantras. (55) Then feed the priests and Purohit with various delicious foods along with sweets and give them Dakshina and twelve Ghats filled with water and grains. (56) After offering food to the Dvij, a Brahmin should get purified by touching water, Khastriya by a weapon, Vaishya by scale and Sudra by touching a rod. (57) Once the Sapinda rites are performed, the clothes worn during the Sapindan rite, should be cast off; and white cloths be put on. Thereafter, a Shayya should be donated. (58) All the Devas, including Indra, praise the Daan of a Shayya. Therefore, a Shayya should be donated, after death or during life time. (59) Made of the best wood, elegantly painted with beautiful pictures, sturdy, covered with silken cloth, ornamented with golden leaves; (60)

Hnsa-toolee-prati-chchhannaam shubha-sheersopadhaanikaam,
Prachchhaadana-patee-yuktaam pushpa-gandhaiah su-vaasitaam(61)
Divya-bandhaiah su-baddhaam ch su-vishaalaam sukha-pradaam,
Shayyaam-evm vidhaam kritvaa hyaastritaayaam nyased-bhuvi(62)
Chhatram deepa-alaym raupym chaamara-asana-bhaajanam,
Bhrngaarm karakaa-darshm pancha-varnaa-vitaanakam(63)
Shayanasy bhavet kinchid-yichcha-anyad-upakaarakam,
Tat-sarvm paritastasyaah sve sve sthaane niyojayet(64)
Tasyaam snsthaapayed-dhaimm harim laksmee-samanvitam,
Sarva-abharanaa-snyuktama-ayudha-ambara-snyutam(65)
streenaan ch shayane dhritvaa kajjalaa-lakta-kumkumam,
Vstram bhooshaadikm yachch sarvamev pradaapayet(66)
Tato viprm sapatneekm gandha-pushpair-alnkritam,
Karna-anguleeyaa-bharanaaiah kanatha-sootraush-cha kaanchanaiah(67)
Ushnaeesam-uttareeym ch cholakm paridhaay ch,
Sthaapayet sukha-shayyaayaam laksmee-naaraayana-agratah(68)
Kumkumaiah pushpa-maalaabhir-harim laksmeem sam-archayet,
Poojayel-loka-paalaansh-cha grahaan deveem vinaayakam(69)
Uttara-abhi-mukho bhootvaa griheetvaa kusuma-anjalim,
Uchchaarayed-imm mantraam viprasy puratah sthitah(70)

The mattress stuffed with swam like white soft cotton together with a pillow and bed cover having fragrance of flowers sprinkled on it. (61) A bed, well bound with sublime strips, well nit, broad and cozy should be placed on the ground covered with cloth. (62) An umbrella, a row of lamps, currency, an oxtail fan, an Aasan to sit, a vessel, a water-pot, a mirror and a canopy of five colors; (63) Anything that is useful for a bed room should be placed around the bed in their proper places. (64) Place, a **Murti** of Hari and Lakshmi together, made of gold, on it with all the ornaments, weapons and clothes. (65) In case of the departed being a woman, place the Collyrium, Vermilion, Kumkum, clothes, ornaments and all other necessary things on the Shayya as additions. (66) Thereafter, adorn the Purohit alongwith his wife, with flowers and fragrances, with ear and finger ornaments and golden necklace; (67) Attired and wearing a turban, upper body cloths (waskat) and Dhoti and a stoll, should be seated on the comfortable Shayya facing Lakshmi and Narayana. (68) Worship Hari and Laksmi with Kumkum and flower. And garland and worship Lok-pal, Graha (planets), Devi and Ganesha. (69) Thereafter, facing north and offering flowers from palms, pronounce this mantra, standing in front of the Purohit; and his wife (purohit and his wife representing Shri Vishnu and Shri Laxmi) (70)

Yathaa krishna tvadeeya-asti shayyaa ksheeroda-saagare,
Tathaa bhooyaadashoonyeym mam janmani janmani(71)
Evm puspa-anjalim vipre pratimaayaam hareah kshipet,
Tatah s-opaskarm shayyaa-daanm snkalpa-poorvakam(72)
Dadyaad vrat-opadestre ch gurave brahma-vaadine,
Grihaana braahmanaainaam tvm ko-adaad-iti keertayan(73)
Aandolayed dvijm laksmeem harim ch shayane sthitam,
Tatah pradakshinaee-krity pranai-paty vi-sarjayet(74)
Jeevamaanah sva-hasten yadi shayyaam dadaati yah,
S jeevmsh-cha vrish-otsargm parvanaeeshu samaacharet(75)
Deshm kaalm tathaa-a-atmaanm dravym dravya-prayojanam,
Upapattim-avasthaam ch gyaatvaa karm samaacharet(76)
Iyam-ekasy daatavyaa bahoo-naam n kadaachan,
Saa vibhaktaa ch vikreetaa daataarm paatayatyadhah(77)
Paatre pradaay shayanm vaanchhitm falama-apnuyaat,
Pitaa ch daataa tanayah paratroh ch modate(78)

"Just like your Shayya in Ksheer Sagar, O Krishna! May this bed be available for me from births to births." (71) Saying so, make oblation of flowers on the Priest and the image of Hari, then, donate the Shayya alongwith its accessories, with the resolve. (72) After giving Daan to preachers who preach divine ways, the Guru who believes in one Brahmn and give away the Shayya to purohit and say, "O Brahmin, receive these." Then the Brahmin should receive all these by saying "Kodaat" (who gives so nicely). (73) Rock the Shayya while the Purohit, Lakshmi and Hari are seated on it and then having taken their Pradakshina (circumbulating around) and take their leave, while offering Pranam. (74) If someone donates Shayya on his own behalf while still living, it should be performed on a festive day along with Varsho-utsarg. (75) But a person should perform any Karm (rite) giving consideration to place, time, his condition, availability of money with him, the aim for which money is being used and the outcome. (76) The Shayya should be given to only one person and never to many. Division of it between Purohits or its sale brings downfall of donor. (77) The wishes are fulfilled by donating a Shayya to the deserving one. Parent and the donor both remain happy in this world and in Parlok. (78)

Yad-vaapee nirjale deshe yad-daanm nirdhane dvije,
Praanainaam yo dayaam dhatte s bhaven-naaka-naayakah(79)
Go-grahe desha-vidhvnse deva-teertha-vipatsu ch,
Uttamaa-adhama-madhyasy baadhya-maanasy dehina,
Aatmaanm tatraa santyajy svarga-vaasm labhech chiram(80)
Uda-kumbha-pradaanen kinkaraas triptimaapnuyuah,
Kaartike ch chatur-dashyaam deepa-daanm sukhaay vai(81)
Graasa-maatraam niyamato nitya-daanm karoti yah,
Chatush-chaamar snyukt vimaanenaa-adhi-gachchhati(82)
Bhootm bhavym bhavishym ch paapm janma-traaya-arjitam,
Prakshaalayati tat sarvm vipra-kanya-opanaayanaat(83)
Chhatr-opaanaha-vstraanai mudrikaa ch kamanadaaluah,
Aasanm panch-paatraanai padm sapta-vidhm smritam(84)
Danadaen taamra-paatrona hyaama-annair-bhojanair-api,
Arghya-yagyopaveetaish-cha padm sampoornaataam vrajet(85)
Anen pada-daanen dhaarmikaa yaanti sdgtim,
Yama-maargm gataanaam ch pada-daanm sukha-pradam(86)
Aatapas-tatraa vai raudro dahyate yen maanavah,
Chhatraa-daanen suchchhaayaa jaayate tasy moordhani(87)

The one who got a water point constructed in draught hit place, the one whose donations reach to poor Purohits, the one having mercy towards creatures, will become leader of Swarga. (79) One who protects cowshed, saves country from destruction, protects Gurus and Priests, temples and pilgrim places, women and children, attains Mokshya. (80) The Yam-doots are satisfied with the donation of water pots. To light the lamps on the Chaturdashi of Kartik-maas, gives happiness. (81) The one who donates even a single bite of food every day, goes to Swarga, escorted in a Vimaan decorated with four Chaamar. (82) One can wash off all Paap pertaining to past, present and future and also the Paap accumulated in the past three births by supporting the Upanayan ceremony of a Vipra girl. (83) An umbrella, footwear, clothes, a ring, Kamandal (a water-pot), an Asaan (seat) and Panch-patra are called the **Sapta-pada** (seven kinds of Padas). (84) This **Pada** is complete with walking stick, vessel, uncooked cereals, delicacies, Arghya and Yagyopweet (sacred thread). (85) By this Padadaana the Dharmik obtains Sad-gati and at the same time this Pada-daana gives comfort to those who have gone to the **Yam-marg** (path to Yam). (86) There is scorching heat in Yamlok by which the humans get burnt, but the Daan of an umbrella provide shade above their heads. (87)

Ati-kanataka-snkeernae   yama-lokasy   vartmani,
Ashva-aaroodhaash-ch te yaanti dadante yady-upaanahau(88)
Sheet-oshnaa-vaata-dukhaani tatraa ghoraanai khechar,
Vstra-daana-prabhaavena   sukhm   nistarate   pathi(89)
Yama-dootaa mahaa-raudraah karaalaah krishnaa-pingalaah,
N peedaayanti tm maarge mudrikaayaah pradaanatah(90)
Bahu-gharma-samaakeernae   nir-vaate   toya-varjite,
Kamanadaalu-pradaanen   trisitah   pibate   jalam(91)
Mrit-oddeshen yo dadyaaj-jala-paatraam ch taamrajam,
Prapaa-daana-sahstrasy yat-falm so-ashnute dhuravam(92)
aasane   bhojane   chaiv   datte   samyag-dvi-jaataye,
Sukhen bhunkte paatheym pathi gachchhan shanaiah shanaiah(93)
Evm   sapindaana-dine   dattvaa   daanm   vidhaanatah,
Bahoon sam-bhojayed-vipraan yah shvapaaka-adikaan-api(94)
Tatah   sapindaanaad-oordhvamarvaak-snvatsaraad-api,
Prati-maasm pradaatavyo jala-kumbhah sapindaakah(95)
Kritasy   karanam   na-asti   preta-kaaryaad-rite   khag,
Preta-arthm tu punah kuryaad-akshayya-tripti-hetave(96)
Ato   vishesm   vakshyaami   maasikasya-abdikasy   ch,
Paakshikasy vishesm ch vishesha-tithishu mrite(97)

The Yam-marg is full of piercing thorns, the Daan of shoes enable them to ride a horse. (88) O Garud! The extreme cold, heat and wind lead to miseries, but the Daan of clothes helps the traveler to go along the way happily. (89) The Yam-doots are very terrible, fierce and of yellow and dark color, the daan of ring saves from the pains inflicted by Doots. (90) Due to extreme heat there is scarcity of air and water in Yam-marg. But, by the Daan of a water pot, one drinks water when thirsty. (91) Who gives a water-vessel made of copper on behalf of departed, certainly enjoys the fruit equal to construction of thousands of wells (for charity). (92) Through appropriate Daan of a Aasaan and food to Purohit, one makes the path of traveler comfortable while the departed enjoys the provisions. (93) Thus, after making Daan on the day of Sapindan in accordance with the prescribed procedure, feed the various Vipras and also lower and other outcasts. (94) Thereafter, between the Sapinda and the annual rites, give a Ghat with Pind every month. (95) Nothing is repetition in case of the rites for departed, O Bird! repetition for the departed, brings unfading satisfaction. (96) Now, I will tell you, specially, about the monthly, the annual and the fortnightly rites on account of death taking place on special days. (97)

Paurnaa-maasyaam mrito yastu chaturthee tasy oonikaa,
Chatuthryaam tu mrito yastu navamee tasy oonikaa(98)
Navamyaam tu mrito yastu riktaa tasy chatur-dashee,
Ity-evm paakshikm shraaddhm kuryaad-vinshatime dine(99)
Ek ev yadaa maasah sankraanti-dvaya-snyutah,
Maasa-dvaya-gatm shraaddhm mala-maase hi shasyate(100)
Ekasmin-maasi maasau dvau yadi syaataam tayor-dvayoah,
Taavev paksau taa ev tithayasnitraashadev hi(101)
Tithy-ardhe prathame poorvo dviteeye-ardhe tad-uttarah,
Maasaaviti budhaish-chintyau mala-maasasy madhyagau(102)
Asnkraante ch kartavym sapindaee-karanam khag,
Tathaiv maasikm shraaddhm vaarshikm prathamm tathaa(103)
Snvatsarasy madhye tu yadi syaad-adhi-maasakah,
Tadaa traayodashe maasi kriyaa pretasy vaarshikee(104)
Pinadaa-vajryam-asankraante snkraante pindaa-snyutam,
Prati-snvatsarm shraaddham-evm maasa-dvaye-api ch(105)
Evm snvatsare poornae vaarshikm shraaddham-aacharet,
Tasminn-api visheshena bhojaneeyaa dvijaatayah(106)

The one who dies at the full moon, the rites fall on the fourth day. If one dies on the fourth day, the rites fall on the ninth. (98) In case one dies on the ninth day, the monthly rites will be on Rikta - fourteenth. In these cases one should perform the fortnightly Shraddha on the twentieth day. (99) In case, in a regular month, two Sankraantis occur in one month (called **Kshya-maas**), the month being double, Sraddha for both months should be performed in **Mal-maas**. (100) If there are two month in one month, the Pakshya and date for both the months should be treated as the same. (101) If it falls in the first half of the day, it should be taken as previous and for second half as latter. This is how the middle month of Mal-maas, it is understood by the wise. (102) The Sapindikaran rites, O Bird, should be performed when there is no Sankraanti in a particular month; similar will be in the case of the monthly, the annual and the first Shraddha. (103) If there is "**Adhimaas**" (an additional month) during a year, then the annual rites for the departed should be performed in the thirteenth month. (104) When there is no Sankraanti, the rites should be performed without Pinda and when there is sankraanti, with Pind. Thus the annual Shraddh should be performed in both months. (105) At the end of the year, the annual Shraddh should be performed and in that all may be fed, specially the Dvija. (106)

129

Kuryaat snvatsaraad-oodhrvm shraaddhe pindaa-traaym sadaa,
Ekoddishtm n kartavym ten syaat-pitri-ghaatakah(107)
Teertha-shraaddhm gayaa-shraaddhm gajach-chhaayaam ch paitrikam,
Abda-madhye n kurveet grahanae n yuga-adihsu(108)
Yadaa putrona vai kaarym gayaa-shraaddhm khag-eshvar,
Tadaa snvatsaraad-oodhrvm kartavym pitri-bhaktitah(109)
Gayaa-shraaddhaat pramuchyante pitaro bhava-saagaraat,
Gadaa-dhara-anugrahena te yaanti paramaam gatim(110)
Tulasee-mnjareebhish-ch poojayed-vishnau-paadukaam,
Tasyaalavaala-teertheshu pindaan dadyaad-yathaa-kramam(111)
Uddharet sapt gotraanai kulam-ek-ottarm shatam,
Shamee-patraa-pramaanaen pindam dadyaad gayaa-shire(112)
Gayaam-upety yah shraaddhm karoti kula-nandanah,
Safalm tasy taj-janm jaayate pitri-tushtidam(113)
Shrooyate cha-api pitri-bhir-geetaa gaathaa khag-eshvar,
Iksvaakor-manu-putraasy kalaap-opa-vane suraiah(114)

After the annual Shraaddh, offer three Pinds at the Shraddh, but Ekodisht (ceremony for one only) should not be done; by doing it one becomes the destroyer of his forefathers. (107) The Tirth Shraddh, Gaya Shraddh and the Gajachhaya Shraddh, for the fathers should not be performed till the completion of one year, nor at eclipses, nor on Yuga days. (108) When the son wants to perform the Gaya Sharadda, O Khageswar, it should only be performed after **Samvatsar** (a year), with dedication to the forefathers. (109) The forefathers are freed from the **Bhav-sagar** (ocean of existence) by performing the Shraddh at Gaya and by the grace of Vishnu, they obtain **Param Gati** (speed to supreme i.e, Mokshya). (110) Worship the feet of Vishnu with Tulsi Manjari (leaves of holy basil) and offer Pind at Teerth with due procedure. (111) One who offers Pind at Gaya, even of the size of Sami leaf, redeems over seven of his Gotra and one hundred and one Kula. (112) The proud son of family performs the Shraddh at Gaya, his life becomes fruitful due to satisfaction of the forefathers. (113) O Khageswar, the forefathers hear a song sung by the Sura (benevolent ones) overheard by Iksayaaku the son of Manu, in the garden of Kalaapa, in which they say: (114)

Api naste bhavishyanti kule sanmaarga-sheelinah,
Gayaamupety ye pindaan daasyantyasmaakama-adaraat(115)
Evam-aamushmikeem taarkshyaa yah karoti kriyaam sutah,
S syaat sukhee bhaven-muktah kaushikasya-atmajo yathaa(116)
Bharadvaaja-atmajaah sapt bhuktvaa janma-paramparaam,
Kritvaa-api govadhm taarkshyaa muktaah pitri-prasaadatah(117)
Sapta-vyaadhaah dashaarna-eshu mrigaah kaalnjare girau,
Chakra-vaakaah sharad-dveepe hnsaah sarasi maanase(118)
Te-api jaataah kuru-kshetre braahmanaa veda-paaragaah,
Pitri-bhaktyaa ch te sarve gataa muktim dvija-atmajaah(119)
Tasmaat sarva-prayatnen pitri-bhakto bhaven-narah,
Ih loke pare vaapi pitri-bhaktyaa sukhee bhavet,
Pitu-maatri-samm loke na-asty-anyad daivatm param,
Tasmaat sarva-prayatnen poojayet pitarau sadaa(120)
Etat-taarkshyaa mayaa-a-akhyaatm sarvam-ev-audhrva-daihikam,
Putraa-vaanchhaa-pradm punaym pitur-mukti-pradaayakam(121)

"Will there not be someone in your family who, treading the right path, will go to Gaya and offer us Pindas, with due respect?" (115) Son, who thus, performs the Aamusmik rites for Parlok, O Taarkshya! becomes happy and liberated, like the son of Kausika. (116) The seven sons of Bharadwaj, having experienced a series of births, were liberated by the blessings of the Pitr (fore-fathers), O Taarkshya, although they had killed a cow. (117) Those seven sons were born as hunters in the country of Dasarnas; in the next birth they were born as deer on the mountain of Kalinjira; subsequently, the Chakravaka birds in Sarad-dwipa and the swans in the Manasa lake; (118) They were born as Brahmins, learned in Vedas, in Kurukeshtra, and all these sons of the Dvija attained Mokshya due to devotion to the forefathers. (119) Therefore, with every effort one should become devoted to Pitr (forefathers), because by devotion to the forefathers one becomes happy in this as well as in **Par-lok** (the other world). There is no greater deity in this world than the mother and father. Therefore, with all efforts one should serve them. (120) Thus, O Taarkshya, I have described all about Aurdhva-dehik rites which earns Punya; satisfying the desires of the offspring and giving Mokshya to the forefathers at the same time. (121)

131

Nirdhano-api narah kshchidyah shrinaoti kathaamimaam,
So-api paapa-vi-nir-mukto daanasy falama-apnuyaat(122)
Vidhinaa kurute yastu shraaddhm daanm mayoditam,
Shrinauyaad gaarudam cha-api shrinau tasya-api yat-falam(123)
Pitaa dadaati sat-putraan go-dhanaani pitaamahah,
Dhana-daataa bhavet-so-api yastasy pra-pitaamahah(124)
Dadyaad-vipulam-anna-adym vriddh-astu pra-pitaamahah,
Triptaah shraaddhen te sarve dattvaa putraasy vaanchhitam(125)
Gachchhanti dharma-maargaish-cha dharma-raajasy mandiram,
Tatraa dharma-sabhaayaam te tisthanti parama-adaraat(126)

SOOT UVAACH

Evm shree-vishnaunaa proktam-aurdhva-daana-sam-udbhavam,
Shrutvaa maahaatmyam-atulm garudo harsama-agatah(127)

A poor person is absolved from Paap, just by hearing this narration, and earns the Punya equal to making the Daan for the fore-fathers, without even making any. (122) Now, listen about reward for the one who performs the Shraddh and Daan with due procedure, as described by me, and also hears the Garuda Purana: (123) The father (mother) bestows true offspring; the grandfather (grand-mother), wealth of cows (movable property) and great grandfather (great-great-mother) give riches. (124) Gratified by the Shraddh, the great-great-grandfather (great-great-grand mother) gives food in abundance; they all grant the desires of offspring (125) They go to the mansion of the Dharam-raaj, following the path of Dharma, and there they are seated, highly respected, in the assembly of Dharma. (126) **SUTA SAID** Having heard the words of Bhagwan Vishnu on the incomparable greatness of Aurdhva-dehik rites and Daan, Garuda went into raptures. (127)

**Annadi-nidhano Devah Shankh Chakra Gadaa-dharah,
Akshayah pundree-kaakash Preta-mokshya-prado-bhav.**

CHAPTER 14

THE GRANDEUR OF YAMLOK, AN ACCOUNT OF THE CASTLES OF
CHITRAGUPTA AND OTHERS, ARCHITECTURE OF THE ASSEMBLY
OF DHARMRAAJ, WELCOME OF VIRTUOUS IN THAT ASSEMBLY

GARUD UVAACH

Yamalokah kiyan-maatraah? Kee-drishah? Ken nirmitah?
Sabhaa ch kee-drishee tasyaam? Dharm aaste ch kaiah sah?(1)
Ye dharma-maargair-gachchhanti dhaarmikaah dharma-mandiram,
Taan dharmaan-api maargaansh-cha mam-aakhyaahi dayaa-nidhe(2)

SHREEBHAGAVAANUVAACH

Shrinau taarkshyaa pravaksyaami yad-agamym naarada-adi-bhiah,
Tad-dharma-nagarm divym mahaa-punayairavaapyate(3)
Yaamya-nairritayor-madhye purm vaivasvatasy yat,
Sarvm vajra-maym divyam-abhedym tat-sura-asuraiah(4)
Chaturstrm chatur-dvaaram-uchcha-praakaara-veshtitam,
Yojanaanaam sahstram hi pramaanaen tad-uchyate(5)
Tasmin pure-asti subhagm chitraa-guptasy mandiram,
Pancha-vinshati-snkhyaakair-yojanair-vistritaayatam(6)

GARUDA SAID What is the extent of **Yamlok** (realm of
Yam)? How does it looks? Who was the architect? How
does the assembly looks like, and with whom does
Dharamraj reside? (1) How do the **Dharmik** (adherents of
Dharma) reach the **Dharam-mandir** (temple of Dharma);
tell me about those Dharmik ones and the Dharmik paths,
O **Dayanidhi** (treasure of compassion). (2) **BHAGWAN SAID-**
Listen, O Taarkshya! the way from which Narada and other
Divine Rishis enter in this **Dharm-nagar** (city of Dharam),
is the celestial path, accessible to those having great
merits. (3) Between the south and south-west direction,
lies the city of Yamraj, son of Vivaswata. It is celestial,
built of diamonds and is resplendent, impermeable to the
Sur or Asur (benevolent and malevolent spirits). (4) The
city is square shaped, having four gateways, surrounded
by fort like high ramparts and measuring a thousand Yojan.
(5) In that city, is the very beautiful mansion of Chitragupta,
which extends to twenty-five Yojan. (6)

Dash-ochchhritm mahaa-divym loha-praakaara-veshtitam,
Pratolee-shata-snchaarm pataakaa-dhvaja-bhooshitam(7)
Vimaana-gana-snkeernam geeta-vaaditraa-naaditam,
Chitritm chitraa-kushalair-nirmitm deva-shilpi-bhiah(8)
Udyaan-opavanaiah ramym naanaa-vihaga-koojitam,
Gandharvair-apsaro-bhish-cha samantaat pari-vaaritam(9)
Tat-sabhaayaam chitraa-guptah sva-asane parama-adbhute,
Snsthito ganaayeda-ayur-maanushaa-naam yathaa-tatham(10)
N muhyati kathanchit s sukrite dush-krite-api vaa,
Yad-yen-opaarjitm karm shubhm vaa yadi vaa-ashubham(11)
Tat-sarvm bhunjate tatraa chitraa-guptasy shaasanaat,
Chitraa-gupta-alayaat praachyaam jvarasya-asti mahaa-griham(12)
Dakshinaasyaam ch shoolasy lootaa-visfotayos-tathaa,
Pshchime kaala-paashah syaad-ajeernaasya-aruches-tathaa(13)
Udeechyaam raaja-rogo-asti paanadau-rogas-tathaiv ch,
Aishaanyaam tu shiro-artiah syaad-aagneyyaam-asti moorchchhanaa(14)
Atisaaro nairririte tu vaayavyaam sheeta-daahakau,
Evama-adi-bhir-anyaish-cha vyaadhibhiah pari-vaaritah(15)
Likhate chitraa-guptastu maanushaanaam shubha-ashubham,
Chitraa-gupta-alayaad-agre yojanaanaam ch vinshatiah(16)

Having heavenly appearance and height of up to ten Yojan with hundreds of streets decorated with flags and banners and is surrounded by iron walls. (7) It has numerous **Vimaan** (spacecrafts which were used by Devas to visit earth) resounding with melodious songs and music, decorated by skilful painters and constructed by the best of divine architects. (8) Pleasant with flowery gardens and orchards and chirping of various birds; every part of it is inhabited by celestial Gandharva and Apsara. (9) Chitragupta, while seated on his sublimely awesome throne in that assembly, deliberates upon the life span of human beings. (10) Chitragupta is never subjective in distinguishing between good and evil deeds, and whoever has done virtuous or evil karma; (11) The person has to experience the consequences of all the deeds by order of Chitragupta. To the east of the abode of Chitragupta, is the grand house of Jwara. (12) In the south, are the houses of Rheumatic, Dermatomsis and Acne and Pimples. To the west, are those of the noose of Death, Dyspepsia and sourness. (13) In the north, there is Tuberculosis and Jaundice likewise, to the north-west, Headache; to the south-east, Epilepsy. (14) To the south-west, is Dysentery; to the north-west, cold and heat. The house of Chitragupta is surrounded by the houses of these and other diseases. (15) Chitragupta records the good and evil Karma of people. Twenty Yojanas ahead of the abode of Chitragupta; (16)

Pura-madhye mahaa-divym dharma-raajasy mandiram,
Asti ratna-maym divym vidyuj-jvaala-arka-varchasam(17)
Dvi-shatm yojanaanaam ch vistaaraayaamatah sfutam,
Panchaashach-ch pramaanaen yojanaanaam sam-uchchhritam(18)
Dhritm stambha-sahstraish-cha vaidoorya-manai-manadaitam,
Kaanchina-alankritm naanaa-hamrya-praasaada-snkulam(19)
Shaaradaabhranibhm rukma-kalashaiah su-manoharam,
Chitraa-sfatika-sopaanm   vajra-kuttima-shobhitam(20)
Muktaa-jaala-gavaakshm ch pataakaa-dhvaja-bhooshitam,
Ghanataanaka-ninaadaadhym hema-toranaa-manadaitam(21)
Naanaa-a-ashchrya-maym svarnaa-kapaata-shata-skunlam,
Naanaa-druma-lataa-gulmair-nish-kanataiah su-viraajitam(22)
Evama-adi-bhir-anyaish-cha bhooshanaair-bhooshitm sadaa,
Aatma-yoga-prabhaavaish-cha nirmitm vishva-karmanaa(23)
Tasminn-asti   sabhaa   divyaa   shata-yojanamaayataa,
Arka-prakaashaa bhraajisnauah sarvatah kaama-roopinaee(24)
Na-ati-sheetaa n cha-aty-ushnaa manaso-atyanta-harshinaee,
N shoko n jaraa tasyaam kshut-pipaase n cha-apriyam(25)

In the middle of the city, is the very stunning celestial mansion of the Dharamraj. Bejeweled and resplendent, it looks like jewel, and splendid like lightning and rays of the sun. (17) It is spread in two hundred Yojan in extent and measures fifty Yojan in height. (18) It is supported by thousands of pillars, decorated with gemstones and adorned with golden vases, ornamented with gold, and is full of palaces, mansions and temples. (19) Pleasant like sky of autumn with beautiful crystal stairways having walls painted beautifully and the floor having diamond carvings. (20) With windows having strings of pearls, the mansion is decorated with flags and banners. Sweet reverberating blissful melodies, sounds of bells and drums; with the castles embellished with golden fringes. (21) Full of various wonders; with hundreds of golden doors; vivacious with trees, flowering plants and creepers without thorns. (22) This mansion is always decorated with these and other embellishments. The city was created by the **Vishvakarmaa** (architect of the universe) by his **Atma-yog** (revelation from Atma). (23) In the palace is the divine assembly hall which is **Kamrupani** (the place which changes the form with the wishes of Dharam-raaj) which is a thousand yojana in extent, splendid like the Sun and full of light. (24) The place is neither hot nor cold and it is most delightful to the heart as no sorrows and no old age is there and no problems of hunger and thirst and nothing is unpleasant. (25)

135

Sarve kaamaah sthitaa yasyaam ye divyaa ye ch maanushaah,
Rasa-vachch prabhootm ch bhakshym bhojym ch sarvashah(26)
Rasa-vanti ch toyaani sheetaany-ushnaani chaiv hi,
Punayaah shabdaadayas-tasyaam nitym kaama-fala-drumaah(27)
Asam-baadhaa ch saa taarkshyaa ramyaa-kaamaagamaa sabhaa,
Deergha-kaalm tapastaptvaa nirmitaa vishva-karmanaa(28)
Taam-ugra-tapaso yaanti suvrataah satya-vaadinah,
Shaantaah snnyaasinah siddhaah pootaah pooten karmanaa(29)
Sarve bhaa-svara-deha-aste-alnkritaa virajaa-ambaraah,
Sva-kritaiah karmabhiah punayais-tatraa tishthanti bhooshitaah(30)
Tasyaam s dharmo bhagavaana-asane-anupame shubhe,
Dasa-yojana-visteernae sarva-ratnaiah su-manadaite(31)
Upa-vishtah sataam shreshtha-shchhatraa-shobhita-mastakah,
Kunadaala-alankritah shree-maan mahaa-mukuta-manadaitah(32)
Sarva-alnkaara-snyukto neela-megha-sama-prabhah,
Baalavyajana-hastaa-bhir-apsaro-bhish-cha veejitah(33)
Gandharvaa-naam samoohaash-cha snghashsh-cha-apsaro-ganaaah,
Geeta-vaaditraa-nritya-adyaiah paritah sevayanti tam(34)

All the desirable things which exist on the earth or in **Dev-lok** (realm of Deities) are available here. The eatables and drinks are in plenty and everywhere and are as per taste. (26) The water, whether warm or cold tastes sweet; pleasant sounds reverberates all around and there are **Kalp-vriksh** (tree which fulfills all the desires). (27) O Taarkshya, that assembly have no barriers, it is enchanting and fulfills desires. This was created by Vishvakarma by his continuous hard work for a long time. (28) Those who have done great **Tapas** (penance), who are truth-speaking, those in peace, Sanyasi, **Siddha** (enlightened, perfected masters, yogis) and purified by good karma (**karma yogi**) can only reach that city. (29) All inhabitants have glowing looks and are adorned with graceful garments and remain there ornamented due to their own **Punyas** (meritorious karma). (30) The Dharam-raaj is seated in the matchless throne at the middle of the assembly which extends to ten Yojana and is decorated with various jewels. (31) Dharam-raaj, who is the supreme in the assembly, is ornamented with ear-rings and splendid grand crown. There is Chhatar (canopy) over him. (32) Adorned with all ornaments, there is a radiant glow around him like that of the luster of blue cloud and he is fanned by Apsaras holding soft woolen fans in their hands. (33) Group of **Apsara** (celestial musicians) surround him and entertain him with songs, music and dances. (34)

Mrityunaa   paasha-hasten   kaalen   ch   baleeyasaa,
Chitraa-gupten   chitrona   kritaanten   nisevitah(35)
Paasha-danadaa-dharair-ugraiaha nidesha-vasha-varti-bhiaha,
Aatma-tulya-balair-naanaa-subhataiah   pari-vaaritah(36)
Agnishvaattaash-cha pitarah somapaash-ch-oshmapaash-cha ye,
Svadhaa-vanto barhishado moortaa-amoortaash-cha ye khag(37)
Aryama-adyaah   pitri-ganaa   moorti-mantas-tatha-apare,
Sarve te munibhiah saardhm dharma-raajam-upaasate(38)
Atrir-vashishthah   pulaho   dakshah   kraturatha-angiraah,
Jaamad-agnyo bhrigush-chaiv pulastya-agastya-naaradaah(39)
Ete   cha-anye   ch   bahavah   pitri-raaja-sabhaa-sadah,
N shakyaah pari-snkhyaatum naamabhiah karmabhis-tathaa(40)
Vyaakhyaabhir-dharma-shaastraa-naam nirnaetaaro yathaa-tatham,
Sevante   dharma-raajm   te   shaasanaat-paramesthinah(41)
Raajaanah   soorya-vnsheeyaah   soma-vnshyaas-tatha-apare,
Sabhaayaam dharma-raajm te dharm-agyaah pary-upaasate(42)
Manur-dileepo   maan-dhaataa   sagarsh-cha   bhageerathah,
Ambareesho-anaranaysh-cha muchukundo nimiah prithuah(43)
Yayaatir-nahushah   purur-dushyantsh-cha   shivir-nalah,
Bharatah shantanuah paanadauah sahstra-arjun ev ch(44)

Mrityu, with a noose in hand; powerful Kala and Chitragupta, the recorder of fate, are in his service. (35) Attended by various fierce Doots who are equal to him in prowess, bearing awful nooses and rods are ever ready to do his bidding. (36) Agnishva, Pitris, Somapas and Ushmapas, Swadhav and the powerful Barhisads with form and formless, are the councilors present. (37) The Aryam and other Pitr, hosts of progenitors and others having forms wait and pray upon the Dharam-raaj, the Munis; (38) Rishi Atri, Vasistha, Pulaha, Daksa, Kratu, Angira, Jamadagni and also Bhrigu, Pulastya, Agastya, Narada; (39) These and many others are the members of the assembly of the Dharam-raj, the king of Pitr. It is impossible to enumerate all of them either by their names or their karma. (40) The exponents and commentators of the Dharama-shastras serve the Dharam-raaj and the adjudicators by order of **Parame-sthin** (supreme power- Brahmn) (41) In the assembly, the kings of the **Surya-vanshi** (solar lineage) and **Chandra-vanshi** (lunar lineage) work on behest of Dharamraj. (42) Manu, Dilipa, Mandata, Sagara, Bhagiratha, Ambarisha, Anaranya, Muchakunda, Nimi, and Prithu; (43) Yayati, Nahusa, Puru; Dusmanta, Sibi, Nala, Bharata, Santanu, Pandu, and also Sahasrarjuna; (44)

Ete raaja-rshayah punayaah keerti-manto bahu-shrutaah,
Istvaa-ashva-medhair-bahu-bhir-jaataa dharma-sabhaa-sadah(45)
Sabhaayaam dharma-raajasy dharm ev pra-vartate,
N tatraa paksha-paato-asti na-anritm n ch matsarah(46)
Sabhyaah sarve shaastr-vidah sarve dharma-paraayanaaah,
Tasyaam sabhaayaam satatm vaivasvatam-upaasate(47)
Iidrishee saa sabhaa taarkshyaa dharma-raagyo mahaatmanah,
N tm pashyanti ye paapaa dakshinaen pathaa gataah(48)
Dharma-raaja-pure gantum chatur-maargaa bhavanti ch,
Paapi-naam gamane poorvm s tu te pari-keertitah(49)
Poorva-adi-bhir-tri-bhir-maargairye gataa dharma-mandire,
Te vai su-kritinah punayais-tasyaam gachchhanti taan-shrinau(50)
Poorva-maargastu tatr-aukah sarva-bhoga-samanvitah,
Paari-jaata-taru-chchhaaya-achchhaadito ratna-manadaitah(51)
Vimaana-ganaa-sankeernao hnsa-avali-viraajitah,
Vidruma-araama-snkeernaah peeyoosha-drava-snyutah(52)
Ten brahma-rshayo yaanti punayaa raaja-rhsayo-amalaah,
Apsaro-ganaa-gandharva-vidyaa-dhara-mahoragaah(53)
Devata-araadhakaash-cha-anye shiva-bhakti-paraayanaaah,
Greeshme prapaadaanarataa maaghe kaastha-pradaayinah(54)

These **Raj-rishi** (royal sages), meritorious, famous, well-read in Vedas, having performed many Asvamedh Yagyas, are in the assembly of Dharam-raaj. (45) Dharma alone prevails in the assembly of the Dharam-raaj. There is no prejudice, no untruthfulness or lies and no jealousy. (46) All those assembled are scholars of the scriptures; all are devout to justice and Dharma; and in that assembly they continuously wait upon Vaivasvata Dharam-raaj. (47) O Taarkshya, such is the assembly of the Mahatma Dharamraj. However, the Paapi, who go by the southern path, are not able to see it. (48) There are four ways leading to **Dharamraaj-pur** (city of Dharam-raaj). The way for the Paapi has already been described to you. (49) Who go into the Temple of Dharam-raj from the other three gateways, are the **Sukriti** (doer of good deeds). By their **Punya** (meritorious deeds), they go into it. Now listen about them: (50) One of them is the eastern way, full of all worldly comforts and enjoyments, way is covered with the shade of **Parijata** trees; and paved with jewels; (51) Numerous Vimaanas, the swans floating in beautiful lakes full of the essence of the nectar, bounded by trees and pleasure-gardens. (52) By that way go the holy Brahmrishis and the pious Rajrishis, the Apsaras, Gandharvas, Vidhyadhar and Mahoarag. (53) Worshippers of the Devtas, the devotees of Shiva, those who make provision of potable water in summer, and who give fuel for warmth in winter. (54)

Vishraamayanti varshaasu viraktaan daana-maanatah,
Dukhitasya-amritm broote dadate hya-ashraym tu ye(55)
Satya-dharma-rataa ye ch krodha-lobha-vi-varjitaah,
Pitri-maatrishu ye bhaktaa guru-shushrooshanae rataah(56)
Bhoomidaa grihadaa godaa vidyaa-daana-pradaayakaah,
Puraanaa-vaktri-shrotaarah paaraayanaa-paraayanaaah(57)
Ete su-kritinsh-cha-anye poorva-dvaare vishanti ch,
Yaanti dharma-sabhaayaam te susheelaah shuddha-buddhayah(58)
Dviteeyast-oottaro maargo mahaa-ratha-shatair-vritah,
Nara-yaana-samaa-yukto hari-chandana-manadaitah(59)
Hnsa-saarasa-snkeernash-chkra-vaakopa-shobhitah,
Amrita-drava-sampoornaas-tatraa bhaati sarovarah(60)
Anen vaidikaa yaanti tathaa-abhyaa-gata-poojakaah,
Durgaa-bhaanvosh-cha ye bhaktaas-teertha-snaataash-cha parvasu(61)
Ye mritaa dharma-sangraame-ana-shanen mritaash-cha ye,
Vaaraanaasyaam go-grihe ch teertha-toye mritaa vidheah(62)
Braahmana-arthe svaami-kaarye teertha-kshetroshu ye mritaah,
Ye mritaa deva-vidhvnse yoga-abhyaasen ye mritaah(63)

Who respectfully provide shelter to ascetics in their houses during the rains and give Daan to them; those who give solace to the people in distress, and provide shelter to them, (55) Who are devoted to **Satya-dharma** (Dharma of truth); those free from anger and greed; those devoted to father and mother, those taking pleasure in the service of Gurus, (56) Who give Daan of land, houses, cows; who impart teaching; who narrate and listen Puranas; who are expert in recitation of Vedas. (57) These all Sukritis and others go to the Assembly of Dharam-raaj through eastern gate. They are gentle and of pure intelligence. (58) The second is the northern path. It is populated with hundreds of great chariots, palanquins and is paved by heavenly Hari-chandan trees; (59) It is full of swans, Saras crane and Chakva ducks and has fascinating lakes full of nectar like water. (60) Those who are learned in Vedas, who honor guests, worship Bhagwati **Durga** and **Bhanu** (sun deity) and those who take holy dip during **Parva** (sacred days) in Teerth. (61) Those who die in **Dharam-sangram** (war for the protection of Dharma), and those who die due to fasting for solemn vow, those who die in Kashi, those who die in **Goushala** (cow pen), those who are accidentally drowned in the sacred waters of Teerth; (62) Those who die for the **Brahmins** (protection of priests, knower, Sadhu-sant), in the service of Ishwara, at the Teerth and for the protection of Temples, Devta and holy Teerth, by the will of the Devta; those who die in the practice of Yoga.(63)

Sat-paatraa-poojakaa nitym mahaa-daana-rataash-cha ye,
Pravishanty-uttare dvaare yaanti dharma-sabhaam ch te(64)
Triteeyah pshchimo maargo ratna-mandira-manadaitah,
Sudhaa-rasa-sadaa-poornaa-deerghikaa-bhir-viraajitah(65)
Airaa-vata-kul-abhootamatta-maatnga-sankulah,
Uchchaiah-shravasam-utpanna-haya-ratna-samanvitah(66)
Etena-atma-paraa yaanti sach-chhaastra-pari-chintakaah,
Ananya-vishnau-bhaktaash-cha gaayatraaee-mantraa-jaapakaah(67)
Para-hinsaa-para-dravya-para-vaada-paraan-mukhaah,
Sva-daara-nirataah santah sa-agnikaa veda-paathakaah(68)
Brahma-charya-vrata-dharaa vaana-prasthaas-tapasvinah,
Shree-paada-snnyaasa-paraah sama-loshta-ashma-kaanchanaah(69)
Gyaan-vairaagya-sampannaah sarva-bhoota-hite rataah,
Shiv-vishnau-vrata-karaah karma-brahma-samarpakaah(70)
Rinaais-tri-bhir-vi-nirmuktaah pancha-yagya-rataah sadaa,
Pitrnaam shraaddha-daataarah-kaale sandhyaam-upaasakaah(71)
Neecha-sanga-vi-nir-muktaah sat-sngati-paraayanaaah,
Ete-apsaro-ganaair-yuktaa vimaana-vara-snsthitaah(72)

Who regularly honor the deserving and give Maha-Daan, reach
that Dharam-Sabha through the northern gate. (64) The third
Pathway is from the western side. It has beautiful buildings
decorated with jewels, and beautified with ponds, always filled
with the essence of nectar. (65) Numerous uninhibited elephants
belonging to the family of Eravata and horses sprung from Uche-
hshrava are decorated with jewels. (66) From this way go the knower
of **Atma-tatva** (elements of Atma), those who contemplate on true
scriptures, those exclusively devoted to Vishnu, those who do the
Japa of Gayatri-mantra; (67) Those who turn away from violence
against others, wealth of others, and vilification of others; those
faithful to their wives; the noble minded; Agnihotri and those
who pursue Vedas; (68) **Brahmchari** (One who is observer of the
vow of celibacy); vanprasthi, **Tapasavi** (doing penance); the
austere; devotees of **Sri-paad** (Vishnu); **sanyasi** (ascetic); those
who look equally upon gold, stone and earth; (69) Those who
have attained knowledge and the dispassionate; who are dedicated
to the welfare of all living beings; those devoted to Shiva and
Vishnu and those who dedicate all their actions to Brahmn, (70)
Those who are absolved from three-fold debts; who are regular in
the performance of Panch-yagya; those who perform Sraddha for
the forefathers; those who perform the Sandhya upasana at the
proper times; (71) The ones who abstains from the company of
the wicked, keep **Sat-sang** (company of truthful) these,
accompanied by number of Apsaras, ascend the best of Vimanas. (72)

Sudhaa-paanm prakurvanto yaanti te dharma-mandiram,
Pravishanti pshchima-dvaare yaanti dharma-sabha-antare(73)
Yamas-taana-agataan dristvaa svaagatm vadate muhuah,
Sam-utthaanm ch kurute teshaam gachchhati sam-mukham(74)
Tadaa chatur-bhujo bhootvaa shnkh-chakr-gada-asi-bhrit,
Punaya-karma-rataa-naam ch snehaan-mitraa-vada-acharet(75)
Singhaasanm ch dadate namas-kaarm karoti ch,
Paada-arghm kurute pshchaat poojyate chandana-adi-bhiah(76)
Namas-kur-vantu bhoah sabhyaa gyaaninm parama-adaraat,
Esh me manadaalm bhittvaa brahma-lokm prayaasyati(77)
Bho bho buddhi-mataam shresthaa naraka-klesha-bheeravah,
Bhavadbhiah saadhitm punayair-devatvm sukha-daayakam(78)
Maanushm durbhalm praapy nitym yastu n saadhayet,
S yaati narakm ghorm ko-anyas-tasmaad-achetanah?(79)
Asthirena shareerena yo-asthiraish-cha dhana-adi-bhiah,
Snchinoti sthirm dharmm s eko buddhi-maan narah(80)
Tasmaat sarva-prayatnen kartavyo dharma-sngrahah,
Gachchhadhvm punayavat-sthaanm sarva-bhoga-samanvitam(81)

They inhale nectar and go to the abode of Dharma and entering from the western gate, go to the Dharam-sabha. (73) Seeing their entry, Yama rises from his seat and comes forward to receive them with repeated welcome. (74) Then, assumes His **Chaturbhuja Mudra** (four arms), holding **Sankh** (conch), **Chakra** (discus), **Gada** (mace) and **Pushp** (flower) and with **Varad-hasta** Mudra, He is friendly and affectionate with those who delight in doing meritorious deeds. (75) He offers them the throne and offers Namaskar to them. Putting water on their feet, he honors them with sandal-paste on their forehead. (76) "O members of the assembly! Offer your Namaskar to these knowers with great reverence. They, departing from my **Mandal** (Yamlok), will go to **Brahmn-lok** (realm of Brahma). (77) O, Best of the wise, who avoid the Paap leading to pains of Narak; you have attained divinity, the state of **Aanand** (bliss) by your Punya. (78) It is rare to attain human state. But one who getting human birth does not dedicate himself to Dharma, goes to a dreadful Narak. Who can be more foolish than him? (79) One who realizing the impermanent nature of human life, accumulates Dharma, using the perishable wealth with him, is a wise person. (80) Therefore, with all means in possession, one should accumulate Dharma. O Punya-atma! Go to the **Vaikunth** (realm of Vishnu) which abounds in all enjoyable things. (81)

141

Iti dharma-vachah shrutvaa tm pranaamy sabhaam ch taam,
Amaraiah poojya-maanaaste stooyamaanaa muneeshvaraiah(82)
Vimaana-ganaa-snkeernaaah prayaanti paramm padam,
Kechid-dharma-sabhaayaam hi tisthanti parama-adaraat(83)
Ushitvaa tatraa kalpaantm bhuktvaa bhogaana-maanushaan,
Praapnoti punaya-sheshena maanushym punaya-darshanam(84)
Mahaa-dhanee ch sarvagyah sarva-shaastra-vishaaradah,
Punah sva-atma-vichaarena tato yaati paraam gatim(85)
Etat te kathitm sarvm tvayaa prishtm yama-alayam,
Idm shrinavan-naro bhaktyaa dharma-raaja-sabhaan vrajet(86)

Hearing these **Dharma-vachan** (words of dharma), and having offered their pranaam to Dharam-raaj and the assembly, they are honored by the immortals and eulogized by the leaders of the Munis; (82) Accompanied by multitudes of Vimanas, they lead to highest destination and attain the **Param-pad** (ultimate state). Some of them remain in the assembly of Dharamraja, getting ultimate honor. (83) Having spent great times there and enjoyed super-human bliss for some **Kalpa** (ages) they obtain, as a result of their surplus merits, a human birth. (84) In the human birth they become wealthy, wise and pundit of all Shastraas. Again with the cognition about Atma, they acquire the **Param Gati** (speed to supreme i.e, Mokshya). (85) O Garuda, all this about the abode of Yama has been told as asked by you. The one who listen to this with devotion, goes to the assembly of the Dharam-raaj. (86)

**Annadi-nidhano Devah Shankh Chakra Gadaa-dharah,
Akshayah pundree-kaakash Preta-mokshya-prado-bhav.**

CHAPTER 15

BIRTH OF THE DHARM-ATMA, SHATH-CHAKRA, YOGA-DHYAN, DEVOTION TO AJAPAA, MEDITATION OF SRI-GURU AND SO ON.

GARUD UVAACH

Dharma-atmaa svargatim bhuktvaa jaayate vimale kule,
Atas-tasy sam-utpattim jananee-jathare vad(1)
Yathaa vichaarm kurute dehe-asmin-sukritee janah,
Tathaa-ahm shrotum-ichchhaami vad me karunaa-nidhe(2)
Shree-bhagavaan-uvaach
Saadhu prishtm tvayaa taarkshyaa parm gopym vadaami te,
Yasy vigyaana-maatrona sarvagyatvm prajaayate(3)
Vakshyaami ch shareerasy svaroopm paaramaarthikam,
Brahmaanadaa-gunaa-sampannm yogi-naam dhaaranaa-spadam(4)
Shat-chakra-chintanm yasmin yathaa kurvanti yoginah,
Brahma-randhre chida-ananda-roopa-dhyaanm tathaa shrinau(5)
Shuchee-naam shree-mataam gehe jaayate sukritee yathaa,
Tathaa vidhaanm niyamm tat-pitroah kathayaami te(6)

GARUDA SAID Dharmatma, having experienced the fortune of Swarga, are re-born in **Vimal-Kul** (pure clan). Tell me how they get genesis in the womb of a mother. (1) O **Karunaa-nidhi** (treasure of compassion), I wish to hear how a **Sukriti** (person of good deeds) thinks about this body. (2) **BHAGWAN SAID-** You have asked a pertinent question, O Taarkshya. I will tell you the supreme secret by knowing of which one becomes omniscient. (3) I will tell you about the Parmarthik nature of that body which possesses all the attributes of the entire universe and is meant for possession of Yogis. (4) Hear now, how the Yogis meditate upon the six Chakras within it, and upon the nature of **Sat** (Truth), **Chit** (Consciousness) and **Aananda** (bliss) in the **Brahm-randhra**, (5) How the Sukritis are born in the house of **Srimant** (those blessed by Ishwara). I will also tell you about the rites and observances for their parents. (6)

Ritu-madhye hi paapaa-naam deh-otpattiah prajaayate,
Poorva-saptakam-utsrijy tasmaad-yug-maasu snvishet(7)
Saptaaha-madhye yo garbhah s bhaven-malinaashayah,
Praayashah sambhavantyatraa putraastv-ashtaaha-madhyatah(8)
Shodaashartu-nishaah streenaam saamaanyaah samudaahritaah,
Yaa vai chatur-dashee raatrir-garbhas-tishthati tatraa vai(9)
Gunaa-bhaagya-nidhiah putraastadaa jaayet dhaarmikah,
Saa nishaa praakritair-jeevairn labhyet kadaachan(10)
Prajanaarthm mahaa-bhaagaah poojaarhaa griha-deeptayah,
Striyah shriysh-cha geheshu n vishesho-asti kshchn(11)
Shochanti jaamayo yatraa vinashyatyaashu tat-kulam,
N shochanti tu yatrautaa vardhate taddhi sarvadaa(12)
Panchame-ahani naaree-naam kaarym madhura-bhojanam,
Katum kshaarm ch teekshnaan-cha tyaajyam-ushnam ch dooratah(13)
Tat-kshetraam-ausadhee-paatraam beejm chaapyamritaayitam,
Tasminn-uptvaa narah svaamee samyak falama-vaapnuyaat(14)
Taamboola-pushpa-shree-khanadaaiah snyuktah shuchi-vstrabhrit,
Dharma-maadaay manasi sutalpm snvishet pumaan(15)

Paapi are born during the menses. Therefore, a woman should conceive only after seven days of the menstruation. (7) The genesis of embryo within seven days is impure. Pregnancy after eighth day is good. (8) The menstruation cycle of women is generally of sixteen nights. Even in that, the child born of pregnancy of fourteenth day; (9) Is of good attributes, good destiny and that child will be of Dharmik bent of mind; but only the virtuous are fortunate to get this chance. (10) The women must be revered, they are benevolent, as they bring light to home by giving birth to a child. A woman is the embodiment of prosperity and mascot of happiness. (11) The family is ruined where women face harassment. But where they are not harassed, those families always flourish. (12) The Woman (wishing to have a child) should eat sweet foods, on the fifth day of pregnancy and thereafter. Therefore, pungent, acidic, astringent and hot items should be avoided altogether. (13) The womb of a woman is like a medicine pot. The seed is like nectar in it. To achieve an appropriate result, purity of mind is a must. (14) The man, while chewing betel leaf adorned with flowers and fragrance, clean clothes and treating procreation as an act of Dharma, should unite with his wife. (15)

Nisheka-samaye   yaa-drin   nara-chitta-vikalpanaa,
Taadrik-svabhaava-sambhootir-jantur-vishati kukshigah(16)
Chaitanym beeja-bhootm hi nitym shukre-apyavasthitam,
Kaamsh-chittm ch shukrm ch yadaa hyekatvamaapnuyaat(17)
Tadaa draavama-vaapnoti yoshid-garbhaashaye narah,
Shukra-shonaita-snyogaat-pinda-otpattiah prajaayate(18)
Adho-mukhm ch-ordhva-paadm garbhaad vaayuah prakarsati,
Tale tu karayornyasy vardhate jaanu-paashveyoah(19)
Janm praapnoti punaya-atmaa grahesho-ochcha-gateshu ch,
Taj-janma-samaye vipraah praapnuvanti dhanm bahu(20)
Vidyaa-vinay-sampanno   vardhate   pitriveshmani,
Sataam   sngen   s   bhavet-sarvaagama-vishaaradah(21)
Divyaangana-adi-bhoktaa syaat-taarunaye daanavaan dhanee,
Poorvm krita-tapas-teertha-mahaa-punaya-falodayaat(22)
Tatsh-cha   yatate   nityama-atma-anaatma-vichaaranae,
Adhyaaropaa-apavaadaabhyaam kurute brahma-chintanam(23)
Asyaa-snga-ava-bodhaay   brahmanao-anvaya-kaarinaah,
Kshitya-ady-anaatma-vargasy gunaanste kathayaamyaham(24)

The nature of the one, who enters the womb, will be affected by the mental frame of the couple during union. (16) The consciousness is in the seed of embryo. The embryo is generated through combination of desire, mental frame, sperm and ovum. (17) The sperm of male meeting ovum in the interior of the womb results in the formation of body. (18) The fetus is placed upside-down in the womb of woman and pushed out by parturition force. In the womb, it develops while keeping palms nearby the toes, (19) A Punyatma (meritorious Atma) takes birth when the planets are in very suitable position. At the time of such birth Brahmins receive much wealth. (20) While growing in parents house, the child is endowed with learning and modesty, becomes skilful in all the knowledge of spirituality and science due to association with the wise. (21) As a result of meritorious deeds, penance and pilgrimages of previous births, child acquires divine looks and benevolent nature and acquires a Daani (charitable) disposition. (22) The child constantly strives to discriminate between the Atma and the non-Atma. And by the (Vedic method of) **Adhyaa-ropa** (superimposition) and **Apavaada** (exception), meditates upon Brahmn. (23) For the appropriate understanding of the pure form of Brahmn, from which one stays away due to desires for worldly attachments (liptataa) of sense objects, I will tell you about the five elements which belong to the category of non-Atma. (24)

Kshitir-vaari havir-bhoktaa vaayura-akaash ev ch,
Sthoola-bhootaa ime proktaah pindao-aym paancha-bhautikah(25)
Tvag-asthi-naadayo romaanai maansm chaiv khag-eshvar,
Ete pancha-gunaa bhoomer-mayaa te pari-keertitaah(26)
Laalaa mootraam tathaa shukrm majjaa raktm ch panchamam,
Apaam pancha-gunaaah proktaas-tejaso-api nishaa-may(27)
Kshudhaa trishaa tathaa-a-alasym nidraa kaantis-tathaiv ch,
Tejah pancha-gunam taarkshyaa proktm sarvatraa yogibhiah(28)
Aakunchanm dhaavanm ch lnghanm ch prasaaranaam,
Cheshtitm cheti panchaiv gunaa vaayoah prakeertitaah(29)
Ghosash-ch-chhidraanai gaambheerym shravanam sarva-snshrayah,
Aakaashasy gunaaah pancha gyaatavya-aste prayatnatah(30)
Mano buddhir-ahnkaarsh-chittm cheti chatushtayam,
Antah-karanaam-uddishtm poorva-karma-adhivaasitam(31)
Shrotm tvak-chaksushee jihvaa ghraanam gyaan-endriyaanai ch,
Vaak-paanai-paadapaayoopa-sthaani karm-endriyaanai ch(32)
Dig-vaata-arka-pracheto-ashvai-vahne-endr-opendra-mitraakaah,
Gyaana-karm-endriyaanaam ch devataah pari-keertitaah(33)
Idaa ch pingalaa chaiv su-shumna-akhyaa triteeyakaa,
Gaandhaaree gaja-jihvaa ch pooshaa chaiv yashasvinee(34)

Earth, water, fire, air and ether are the physical elements. This Pind (human body) is made of this **Panch-bhota** (five elements). Therefore, it is called "Panch-bhoutik." (25) The Skin, bones, nerves, pores and flesh are the five attributes of earth, O Khageswar, it is declared to you by me. (26) Saliva, urine, sperm, marrow and blood are said to be the five attributes of water. Now hear about the attributes of fire. (27) Hunger, thirst, lethargy, sleep and libido are called the five attributes of fire by Yogis, O Taarkshya. (28) Shrinking, running, jumping, stretching and sexual desire are declared the five attributes of air. (29) Speech, thought, emptiness, delusion and doubt are the five attributes of ether, which can only be understood with concerted efforts. (30) Mind, reason, arrogance and psyche these four are called the conscience, and have the impact of past Karma. (31) Ears, skin, eyes, tongue and nose are the **Gyanendriyan** (organs of knowledge). The organs of speech, hands, feet (organ of locomotion). The organs of procreation and of excretion are the **Karmendriya** (organs of action). (32) The Direction, Vayu, Surya, Pracheta, the two Asvinikumars, Agni, Indra, Upeudra, Mitra, are declared to be the organs of knowledge and action, (33) Ida and Pingala, Susumna, Gandhari, Gajajihva, Pusha and Yasavini; (34)

Almbushaa kuhoosh-cha-api shnkhinee dashamee tathaa,
Pinadaa-madhye sthitaa hyetaah pradhaanaa das naadaikaah(35)
Praanao-apaanah samaanaakhy udaano vyaan ev ch,
Naagah-koormsh-cha krikalo deva-datto dhanjayah(36)
Hridi praanao gude-apaanah samaano naabhi-manadaale,
Udaanah kanatha-deshe syaad vyaanah sarva-shareeragah(37)
Udgare naag aakhyaatah koorm unmeelane smritah,
Krikalah kshut-karo gyeyo deva-datto vijrimbhanae(38)
N jahaati mritm vaa-api sarva-vyaapee dhanjayah,
Kavalair-bhuktam-annm hi pushtidm sarva-dehi-naam(39)
Nayate vyaanako vaayuah saaraanshm sarva-naadaishu,
Aahaaro bhukta-maatro hi vaayunaa kriyate dvidhaa(40)
Snpravishy gude samyak-prithag-annm prithag-jalam,
Oordhvam-agner-jalm kritvaa kritvaa-annm ch jal-opari(41)
Agnesh-cha-adhaha svaym-praanaah sthitvaa-agnim dhamate shanaiah,
Vaayunaa dhmaayamaano-agniah prithak kittm pritha-grasam(42)
Kurute vyaanako vaayur-vishvak-sampraapayed-rasam,
Dvaarair-dvaadasha-bhir-bhinnm kittm dehaadbahiah strvet(43)
Karnaa-akshi-naasikaa jihvaa dantaa naabhir-nakhaa gudam,
Guhym shiraa vapurlom mala-sthaanaani chakshate(44)

Alambusa, Kuhu and Sankhini are the ten principal Nadis situated in the interior of the body. (35) Praana, Apaana, Samaana, Udaana and Vyana also – Naaga, Kurma, Krikala, Devadatta and Dhananjaya (various forms of vital Vayus); (36) Prana (in the heart), Apana (in the anus), Samana (in the navel), Udana (in the region of the throat), Vyana (distributed all over the body): (37) Burping is caused by Naga Vayu; opening and shutting of eyes is done by Kurma; the cause of hunger is to be known as Krikala Vayu; Yawning is caused by Devadatta; (38) The all-pervading **Dhananjaya** is the life element which does not leave even the corpse and carries all over the body the nourishment obtained by eating mouthfuls of food. (39) Vyana Vayu carries the essential part in all the Nadis. Food, as soon as eaten, is split into two by that air. (40) This Vayu separates the solid and liquid portions on entering near anus placing the water over the fire, and the solid over the water. (41) The Prana Vayu staying under the fire inflames it slowly. The fire, inflamed by the Vayu, separates the substance from the waste. (42) The Vyana air makes the essence reach all over and the waste, forced through the twelve gateways; it is thrown out from the body. (43) Ears, eyes, nostrils, tongue, teeth, navel, nails, anus, generative organs, head, trunk, hair are the places for excretion of refuse. (44)

147

Evm sarve pravartante sv-sva-karmanai vaayavah,
Upa-labhya-atmanah sattaam soorya-allokm yathaa janaah(45)
Idaaneem nara-dehasy shrinau roopa-dvaym khag,
Vyaavahaarikam-ekm ch dviteeym paaramaarthikam(46)
Tistrah kotyo-ardha-kotee ch romaanai vyaavahaarike,
Sapta-lakshaanai keshaah syur-nakhaah proktaastu vinshatiah(47)
Dvaa-trinshad-dashanaah proktaah saamaanyaad-vinataa-sut,
Maansm pala-sahstrm tu raktm pala-shatm smritam(48)
Palaani dash meda-astu tvak-palaani ch saptatiah,
Pala-dvaadashakm majjaa mahaa-raktm pala-traayam(49)
Shukrm dvi-kudaavm gyeym kudaavm shonaitm smritam,
Shashty-uttarm ch tri-shatam-asthnaam dehe prakeertitam(50)
Naadayah sthoolaash-cha sookshmaash-cha kotishah parikeertitaah,
Pittm palaani panchaa-shat-tad-ardhm shlesmanaas-tathaa(51)
Satatm jaayamaanm tu vina-mootraam cha-apramaanaatah,
Etd-gunaa-samaayuktm shareerm vyaavahaarikam(52)
Bhuvanaani ch sarvaanai parvata-dveepa-saagaraah,
Aaditya-adyaa grahaah santi shareere paaramaarthike(53)

Thus the Vayus deriving their power from the Atma are performing their functions with great regularity, just as the people do on the rising of the sun. (45) O Bird listen now, in the two-fold nature of the human body, one is **Vyaava-haarika** (Physical body) and the second **Paar-maarthika**. (46) There are thirty-five millions of pores, seven hundred thousands of hairs, and twenty nails in the Vyaava-haarik; (47) Usually there are thirty-two teeth, O son of Vinata; the flesh is one thousand *palas (one pal is little more than an ounce)* and blood is one hundred *palas*; (48) Fat is ten *palas*, skin is seven *palas*, marrow is twelve *palas*; the Mahaa-rakt (great blood) is three palas; (49) Seed is said to be two *kudavas*, ovum one *ku ava*; and there are three hundred and sixty bones in the body; (50) The **nadis**, both **Sthool** (physical) and **Sukshyam** (subtle), are in tens of million; bile is fifty palas; phlegm is half of that; (51) The urine and excreta are not measurable. These keep on changing constantly. The body which possesses these attributes is Vyava-harika. (52) All the realms and all the mountains, continents, oceans, suns and other planets are in the Paaramaarthika body (it is said that whatever is there in the universe is also in the human body and vice-versa-**Yat pinde tat- Brahmaande, Yat Brahmaande Tat Pinde**). (53)

Paaramaarthika-dehe hi shat-chakraanai bhavanti ch,
Brahmaanadae ye gunaaah prokta-aste-apy-asmin-nev snsthitaah(54)
Taanahm te pravaksyaami yoginaam dhaaranaaspadaam,
Yeshaam bhaavanayaa jantur-bhaved-vairaaja-roopabhaak(55)
Paada-adhastaat-talm gyeym paad-ordhvm vitalm tathaa,
Jaanunoah sutalm viddhi sakthi-deshe mahaa-talam(56)
Talaatalm sakthi-moole guhya-deshe rasaa-talam,
Paataalm kati-snsthm ch sapta-lokaah prakeertitaah(57)
Bhoor-lokm naabhi-madhye tu bhuvar-lokm tad-oordhvake,
Svar-lokm hridaye vidyaat kanatha-deshe mahas-tathaa(58)
Jana-lokm vaktraa-deshe tapo-lokm lalaatake,
Satya-lokm brahma-randhre bhuvanaani chatur-dashah(59)
Tri-konae snsthito merur-adhah konae ch mandarah,
Daksha-konae ch kailaasho vaama-konae hima-achalah(60)
Nishadhash-ch-ordhva-rekhaayaam dakshaayaam gandha-maadanah,
Ramanao vaama-rekhaayaam sapta-ite kula-parvataah(61)
Asthi-sthaane bhavej-jambooah shaako majjaasu snsthitah,
Kusha-dveepah sthito maanse krauncha-dveepah shiraasu ch(62)

In the Paaraamaarthika body, there are six Chakras in which the attributes of Brahma (universe) are located. Therefore, all the attributes of the universe are in human body as well. (54) I will tell you about these which are the objects of possession of Yogi. By meditating upon them, one gets absorbed in the ultimate power. (55) Atala should be considered below the feet; Vitala above the feet, Sutata in the knees, and Mahatala at the thighs; (56) At the hips, Talaatala; at the private part, Rasaatala; at the loins, Patala; these are declared to be the **Sapta-lok** (seven worlds); (57) Bhooloka is at the middle of the navel; above it, the Bhuvarloka; in the heart, Svarloka; at the throat, it should be known as Maharloka; (58) Janaloka is in the region of the mouth; Taploka, at the forehead; Satyaloka, in the Brahm-randhra. These fourteen realms are situated in Paar-maarthik body. (59) Meru (the loftiest mountain) is situated in the triangle (heart); Manda-raanchal is in the inverted triangle; Kailasaa is in the right triangle; Himachala, in the left triangle. (60) The Nisadh mountain is in the upper lines; Gandha-madana, in the lines on the right; Ramana, in the lines on the left; there are seven great mountains in all; (61) Jambu-dweep is in the place of the bones; Shaka-dweep is situated in the marrow; the Kusha-dweep is situated in the flesh; the Krauncha-dweep in the nerves; (62)

Tvachaayaam shaalmalee-dveepo gomedo roma-sanchaye,
Nakhasthm puskarm vidyaat saagaraas-tad-anantaram(63)
Kshaarodo hi bhaven-mootro ksheere ksheeroda-saagarah,
Sura-odadhiah shleshma-snstho majjaayaam ghrita-saagarah(64)
Ras-odadhim rase vidyaach-chhonaite dadhi-saagarah,
Svaad-oodo lambikaa-sthaane jaaneeyaad-vinataa-sut(65)
Naada-chakre sthitah sooryo bindu-chakre ch chandramaah,
Lochanasthah kujo gyeyo hridaye gyah prakeertitah(66)
Vishnau-sthaane gurum vidyaach-chhukre shukro vyavasthitah,
Nabhi-sthaane sthito mando mukhe raahuah prakeertitah(67)
Vaayu-sthaane sthitah ketuah shareere graha-manadaalam,
Evm sarva-sva-roopena chintayeda-atmanas-tanum(68)
Sadaa prabhaata-samaye baddha-padma-assanah sthitah,
Shat-chakra-chintanm kuryaad-yath-oktam-ajapaa-kramam(69)
Ajapaa-naam gaayatraaee muneenaam moksha-daayinee,
Asyaah sankalpa-maatrona sarva-paapaiah pramuchyate(70)
Shrinau taarkshyaa pravakshye-ahama-japaa-kramam-uttamam,
Ym kritvaa sarvadaa jeevo jeeva-bhaavm vimunchiti(71)

The Shalmali dweep is in the skin; Gomeda, in the mass of pores; Puskara, in the place of the nails; and beyond that the oceans; (63) The Saline ocean is situated in the urine; the Ksher-sagar, in milk; the Sura ocean is situated in the phlegm; in the marrow, the Ghrita ocean; (64) O son of Vintaa, the Rasa ocean is in the juices; the Dadhi ocean is known to be in the ova; the Swadu ocean in the region of the soft palate; (65) It should be known that the sun is situated in the Nada chakra; the moon is in the Bindu chakra; Mars is known to be situated in the eyes; Mercury is in the heart; (66) It should be known that the planet Jupiter is situated in the Vishnu-sthana (place of Vishnu); Venus is situated in the seed; Saturn is in the navel and Rahu in the mouth; (67) Ketu is situated in the lungs and in the body planets. Thus, one should meditate all about the whole universe in his Paarmaarthik body. (68) Everyday at dawn, sitting steadily in Padmaasana, one should meditate upon the six Chakras, in the order of Ajapaa as described above. (69) Gayatri is called **Ajapa**, the bestower of Mokshya to the Munis and; by merely thinking upon it, one is released from all Paap. (70) Listen, O Taarkshya, I will explain the best method of Ajapa, by pursuing which the individual is released from Jeevbhav, i.e, separate identity from Brahmn. (71)

Moolaa-dhaarah sva-adhishthaanm manai-poorakam-ev ch,
Anaahatm vishuddhaakhyama-agyaa-shat-chakram-uchyate(72)
Moolaa-dhaare linga-deshe naabhyaam hridi ch kanathage,
Bhruavor-madhye brahma-randhre kramaach-chakraanai chintayet(73)
Aadhaarm tu chatur-dala-anala-samm vaa-sa-anta-varna-ashraym,
sva-adhisthaanam-api prabhaakara-samm baa-la-anta-shat-patraakam,
Raktaabhm manai-poorakm dasha-dalm da-adym fa-kaara-antakm,
Patraur-dvaadasha-bhiah sv-anaahata-purm haimm ka-tha-anta-avritam(74)
Patrauah sa-svara-shodaashaiah shasha-dhara-jyotir-vishuddha-ambujam,
hn-s-ety-akshara-yugmakm dvaya-dalm raktaabha-maatra-ambujam,
Tasmaad-oordhva-gatm prabhaasitamidm padm sahstra-chchhadm,
satya-ananda-maym sadaa-shiva-maym jyotir-maym shaashvatam(75)
Ganaeshm ch vidhim vishnaum shivm jeevm gurum tatah,
Vyaapakm ch parm brahm kramaach-chakreshu chintayet(76)
Eka-vinshat-sahstraanai shat-shataany-adhikaani ch,
Aho-raatrona shvaaasasy gatiah-sookshmaa smritaa budhaiah(77)
Hn-kaarena bahir-yaati sa-kaarena vishet-punah,hanso hnseti
mantrona jeevo japati tattvatah(78)

The Mulaa-dhaara, Swaa-dhishtana, Mani-poorak, Anaahad, Visuddhi and also Aagya are called the six Chakras. (72) One should meditate upon Chakras at the Mulaadhara (at the root of the backbone), in the region of the generative organ; in the navel; in the heart; in the throat; between the eyebrows; at the top of the head; (73) The Muladhara has four petals of Lotus and is of the colour of fire. It gives Swar (sound) of the letters from Va to Sa; the Svaadhisthaana resembles the Sun, it is six-petalled and has the Swar of letters from Ba to La; the Manipooraka is red in colour and has ten petals, from Da to Pha; the Anahata is twelve-petalled, from Ka to Tha, and is golden-coloured; (74) The Visuddhi Chakkra has the moon light; sixteen petalled, has the letters Ha and Ksa, and is red in color; the one at the top of the head is the most resplendent, this lotus has a thousand petals, and is the seat of truth and bliss, ever auspicious, light-possessing and eternal. (75) In these Chakra one should meditate on Ganesa, on Vidhi, on Brahma, on Vishnu, on Shiva, on Jiva, on Guru, and on Param-Brahmn; the all-pervading in this order. (76) In a day and night, a person takes twenty one thousand six hundred breaths; this is declared as **Sukashyam Gati** of breathing by the wise. (77) The breath comes out with the sound of "Ham," and enters again with the sound of "Sa." Every human being is, indeed, always repeating the mantra. "Ham-sa, Ham-sa," (which is the mantra of the ultimate reality i.e., Brahmn) (78)

Shat-shatm ganaa-naathaay shat-sahstrm tu vedhase,
Shat-sahstrm ch haraye shat-sahstrm haraay ch(79)
Jeeva-atmane sahstrm ch sahstrm gurave tathaa,
Chida-atmane sahstrm ch japa-snkhyaan nivedayet(80)
Etaansh-chakra-gataan brahma-mayookhaan munayo-amaraan,
Satsm pradaayavettaarsh-chintayanty-aruna-adayah(81)
Shuka-adayo-api munayah shisyaan-upadishanti ch,
Atah pravrittim mahataam dhyaatvaa dhyaayet-sadaa budhah(82)
Kritvaa ch maanaseem poojaam sarva-chakreshv-ananyadheeah,
Tato guro-opadeshen gaayatraaeem-ajapaam japet(83)
Adho-mukhe   tato   randhre   sahstra-dala-pnkaje,
Hansagm shree-gurum dhyaayed-vara-abhaya-kara-ambujam(84)
Kshaalitm chintayed-dehm tat-paada-amrita-dhaarayaa,
Panch-opachaaraiah sam-poojy pranaamet-tat-staven ch(85)
Tatah kunadaalineem dhyaayeda-arohaad-avarohatah,
Shat-chakra-krita-snchaaraam sa-ardh tri-avalayaam sthitaam(86)

(Out of the twenty one thousand six hundred breaths) one should dedicate six hundred to Ganesa; six thousand to Brahma; six thousand to Hari; six thousand to Hara (Shiva). (79) A thousand for one's own Atma; a thousand for Guru; a thousand for the Chidatmaa (Brahmn). (80) Aruna and other Munis, who know about the tradition of Guru-Shishya succession, meditate upon the the rays of Brahmn emanating from the Chakras. (81) Shukdev and other Munis teach it to their pupils. Therefore, a wise person, after meditating upon the path shown by Mahatmas, should always meditate this way. (82) After carrying out the mental worship of all the Chakras with concentration of mind, one should repeat the **Ajapa-gayatri** as directed by Guru. (83) In the mental worship one should meditate on Brahmn Randhra, with the thousand-petalled lotus inverted, upon the Vishnu in Abhay Mudra (bodily gesture of Vishnu which says you be fearless) and in Varad Mudra (gesture of generosity) within the Mantra of Hamsa. (84) One should mediate and feel that his body is being bathed, in the nectar flowing from His holy feet. Having worshipped in the five-fold (Pancho-pchar) way, one should prostrate while singing His praise and offering Pranaam (salutation). (85) Then one should meditate on the Kundalini (place of light), which moves upwards and downwards, making a tour of the six chakras, placed in three-and-a-half coils. (86)

Tato dhyaayet su-shumnaakhym dhaam randhraad bahir-gatam,
Tathaa ten gataa yaanti-tad-vishnaoah paramm padam(87)
Tato mach-chintitm roopm svaym jyotiah sanaatanam,
Sada-anandm sadaa dhyaayen-muhoorte braahma-sngyake(88)
Evm guro-opadeshen mano nish-chalataam nayet,
N tu sven prayatnen tad-vinaa patanm bhavet(89)
Antar-yaagm vidhaayaivm bahir-yaagm samaacharet,
Snaana-sandhya-adikm kritvaa kuryaad-dhari-hara-archanam(90)
Deha-abhi-maaninaam-antar-mukhee-vrittir-n jaayate,
Atas-teshaam tu mad-bhaktiah su-karaa moksha-daayinee(91)
Tapo-yoga-adayo moksha-maargaah santi tathaapi ch,
Sameecheenastu mad-bhakti-maargah snsaarataamih(92)
Brahma-adi-bhish-cha sarvagyairayam-ev vi-nishchitah,
Tri-vaarm veda-shaastraanai vichaary ch punah punah(93)
Yagya-adayo-api sad-dharmaash-chitta-shodhana-kaarakaah,
Fala-roopaa ch mad-bhaktistaam labdhvaa na-ava-seedati(94)

Thereafter, one should meditate on the place called Susumna, which goes out of the Randhra; thereby one goes to the highest state of Vishnu (divinity). (87) One should always meditate, in Brahm-muhurt (dawn), on My form (Bhagwan Vishnu), as self-illumined, eternal and ever-blissful. (88) Under the instruction of a Guru, without whom you would fail, you should control the fickleness of mind and bring it to a state of steadiness. (89) Perform the outward-yogya after performing inward-Yogya. The worship of Hari and Hara should be done after purificatory ablution and the Sandhyaa. (90) For those who are outward oriented, the Path of Bhakti (devotion) is easier and that brings Mokshya to them. It is difficult to become inward looking for those who are having bodily attachment and arrogance. (91) Though Tapa, and Yoga and other methods, are also there for Mokshya, but for those who are attached to the changing world, the path of Bhakti to Me is far superior. (92) This conclusion on Bhakti Maarg has been arrived by the all-knowing Brahma and others, after having repeated deliberations of the Vedas and the Shastra, lasting for three periods. (93) Mind gets purified through Yagya and other act of worship. This leads to My Bhakti. Bhakti gives a reward due to which the receiver is never corrupted. (94)

Bhaktaa-anu-kampee bhagavaan saadhoonaam rakshanaay ch,
Aavir-bhavati lokeshu gunaeevaa-agyaiah prateeyate(95)
Evm vivekavatyaa yo buddhyaa snsheelayed hridi,
Bhakti-yogen santusht aatmaanm darshayed-ajah(96)
Tatah kritaartho bhavati sadaa sarvatraa niah-sprihah,
Ato-ahankaaram-utsrijy sa-anu-bandhe kalevare,
Chared-asango lokeshu svapna-praayeshu nirmamah(97)
Kv spapne niyatm dhairyam-indra-jaale kv satyataa,
Kv nityataa sharan-meghe kv vaa satym kalevare(98)
Adhidyaa-karma-janitm drishya-maanm chara-acharam,
Gyaatvaa-a-achaara-vashee yogee tatah siddhimavaapsyasi(99)
Karma-vibhasta-kaalushyo vaasu-deva-anu-chintayaa,
Buddhyaa vishuddhayaa mukto dhrityaa-a-atmaanm niyamy ch(100)
Shabda-adeen vishayaans-tyaktvaa raaga-dveshau vyudasy ch,
Vi-vikta-sevee laghvaashee yata-vaak-kaaya-saanasah(101)
Dhyaana-yoga-paro nitym vairaagym sam-upa-ashritah,
Ahnakaarm balm darpm kaamm krodhm pari-graham(102)

The Bhagwan, who is benevolent to Bhaktas, takes Avataar in the world for the protection of Saadhus and for the love for knower and virtuous. (95) The wise meditates about the Parma-atma again and again. It is due to the Bhakti that Ishwara appears before the Bhakt, pleased due to their devotion. (96) Then, the person becomes free from indulgence and is ever grateful. Therefore, rejecting the arrogance of possessions and body, overcoming the attachments to this dream-like world, one should lead an **Anaashakt** (detached) life. (97) Where do you find endurance in dreams, where is truth in magic, how can the rainy clouds be permanent, where is the eternity in the body? (98) Treating the flickering and visible world as untruth, the human being should focus on mastering over the sense organs. This would lead them to Mokshya. (99) It is by following the actions as prescribed in the scriptures and by the meditation of Vasudwa; that one can get rid of the impurities of body, mind, thought and speech. (100) By achieving purity of mind, relinquishing from **Raag-Dvesh** (attachment and aversion), cherishing solitude, having controlled diet and chastity over mind, body and speech; (101) Devotion to Yoga and meditation, an ascetic, can overcome the weakness of arrogance, power, greed, anger and sense of possessiveness; (102)

Vimuchy nirmamah shaanto brahma-bhooyaay kalpate
Atah parm nrinaam kritym na-asti kashyapa-nandan(103)
Aakaashe ch tathaa-a-akaashm sarva-vyaapi nishaakare,
Tatraa kaamas-tathaa krodhah kaaye panch-endriyaanai ch(104)
Ete taarkshyaa samaakhyaataa dehe tishthanti taskaraah,
Kaamah krodho hyahnkaaro manas tatrauv naayakah(105)
Snhaarash chaiv kaalo-asau punaya-paapen snyutah,
Panch-endriya-samaayuktah sakalair-vi-budhaiah sah(106)
Pravishet s nave dehe grihe dagdhe grihee yathaa,
Shareere ye samaaseenaah sarve vai sapt dhaatavah(107)
Visayaish-cha samaa-kraantm kaama-krodha-samaakulam,
Raga-dvesha-samaa-keernam trishnaa-durgama-taskaram(108)
Lobha-jaala-pari-chchhinnm moha-vastrona veshtitam,
Su-baddhm maayayaa chaital-lobhena-adhisthitm puram(109)
Etad-gunaa-samaa-keernam shareerm sarva-dehinaam,
Aatmaanm ye n jaananti te naraah pashavah smritaah(110)
Laabhas teshaam jayas teshaam kutas teshaam paraajayah,
Yeshaam-indeevara-shyaamo hriday-astho janaardanah(111)

By abdicating affection with things one can achieve divinity. O son of Kashyap, with this, one is redeemed thereafter. (103) The ether is absorbed in ether, while the mind which encompasses to other sense organ, is absorbed by Moon. There are lust, anger and five sense organs in the body. (104) The Lust, greed and arrogance are the chief smugglers staying in the body in the form of sense organs and the mind being their leader. (105) The body has an inbuilt element of decimation in it and along with Paapi and virtuous deeds and with five senses along with the mind; (106) The Atma of dead moves to another life just like a resident moves to new house once his house gets burnt. (107) Human being is engrossed in carnal desires, gripped by lust and anger, filled with love and aversion, and the longing for impermeable smuggler of greed; (108) Draped by the mesh of greed, enmeshed by the cloth of temptation in the city of deep delusion, tightly tied with Maya and this city is administered by greed; (109) The body of all living beings is filled with these elements. The one who does not understand this is just like an animal. (110) Where the heart is filled with the blue lotus like appearance of Krishna there is always benefit, victory lies with them; who can defeat them? (111)

Gyaana-hride satya-jale raaga-dvesha-mala-apahe,
Yah snaato maanase teerthe n s lipyet paatakaiah(112)
Evamaacharanam taarkshyaa karoti sukritee narah,
Snyogen ch mabhaktyaa moksm yaati sanaatanam(113)
Apavitraah pavitro vaa sarva-avasthaam gato-api vaa,
Yah smaret punadaareeka-akshm s bohya-abhyantarah shuchiah(114)
Vishnaur-maataa pitaa vishnaur-vishnauah sva-jana-baandhavaah,
Yeshaam-ev sthiraa buddhir-n teshaam dur-gatir-bhavet(115)
Tad gopitm syaad dharma-arthm dharmo gyaana-artham-ev ch,
Gyaanm tu dhyaana-yoga-artham-achiraat pra-vi-muchyate(116)

The one who has taken a dip in the reservoir of wisdom, which removes dirt of hatred and attachment, in the pilgrim place of mind, can never be touched by Paap. (112) O Taarkshya, the Sukriti (righteous) people who follow this behavior are liberated due to devotion to Me. (113) Whether a person is in a impure or pure state or even in any other conditions, if he remembers Bhagwan Vishnu, he becomes pure outwardly and inwardly. (114) For whom the mother is Vishnu and also the father is Vishnu and Vishnu is also friend and sibling, a person of this stable mind will never face Durgati (speed to untruth). (115) The one whose body is protected for Dharma, and Dharma is for self realization, and self realization is meditation of almighty and whose life is for emancipation, is destined to get liberated. (116)

Annadi-nidhano Devah Shankh Chakra Gadaa-dharah,
Akshayah pundree-kaakash Preta-mokshya-prado-bhav.

CHAPTER 16

MAYA (DELUSION), TRISHNA (LONGING), PRAGYA (WISDOM), MOKSHYA FROM SANSAAR (WORLD OF CHANGE) AND SO ON

GARUD UVAACH

Shrutaa mayaa dayaa-sindho hy-agyaanaaj-jeeva-snsritiah,
Adhunaa shrotum-ichchhaami moksh-opaaym sanaatanam(1)
Bhagavan   deva-dev-esha   sharana-agata-vatsal,
Asaare   ghora-snsaare   sarva-dukha-maleemase(2)
Naanaa-vidha-shareerasthaa hy-anantaa jeeva-raashayah,
Jaayante ch mriyante ch teshaam-anto n vidyate(3)
Sadaa dukha-aturaa ev n sukhee vidyate kvachit,
Ken-opaayen moksh-esh muchyante vad me prabho(4)

SHREEBHAGAVAANUVAACH

Shrinau taarkshyaa pravaksyaami yan-maam tvm pari-prichchhasi,
Yasy shravanaa-maatrona snsaaraat muchyate narah(5)
Asti devah para-brahma-svaroopee nish-kalah shivah,
Sarvagyah sarva-kartaa ch sarv-esho nirmalo-advayah(6)

GUARDA SAID O **Daya-sindhu** (ocean of compassion), I have heard about persons getting into the vicious circle of transmigration of Atma from one birth to another due to ignorance. I wish to hear the means of eternal Mokshya. (1) Hey Bhagwan, O **Devdevesh** (Ishwara of Deities), O **Sharanagat-vatsal** (compassionate to those who take your refuge), this meaningless terrible Sansaar is full of the multitude of miseries; (2) Numerous creatures, in various types of bodies, are born and perish endlessly and there is no end to it. (3) They are always in the misery and are never contented. O Prabho! Tell me the ways and means which will liberate them. (4) **BHAGWAN SAID-** O Taarkshya! Listen and I will explain to you on what you have asked. Merely by listening it, a person is released from the Sansaar. (5) The Divine Shiva, the form of **supreme Brahmn** (the ultimate reality) is complete, undivided, unaffected, all-knowing, all-doing, Bhagwan of all serene and **Advaj** (unique without second to him). (6)

Svaym-jyotira-na-ady-anto nir-vikaarah paraat-parah,
Nir-gunaah sachchida-anandas-tad-anshaaj-jeeva-sngyakah(7)
Anaady-avidy-opahataa yathaa-agnau visful-ingkaah,
Deha-ady-upaadhi-sambhin-na-aste karma-bhir-anaadi-bhiah(8)
Sukha-dukha-pradaiah punaya-paapa-roopair-niyantriaataah,
Tat-taj-jaati-yutm dehama-ayur-bhogm ch karmajam(9)
Prati-janm prapadyante yeshaam-api parm punah,
Su-sookshma-ling-shaareerama-amokshaad-aksharm khag(10)
Sthaavaraah krimaysh-cha-abjaah pakshinaah pashavo naraah,
Dhaarmikaas-tri-dashaastadvan-mokshinash-cha yathaa-kramam(11)
Chatur-vidha-shareeraanai dhritvaa muktvaa sahstrshah,
Sukritaan-maanavo bhootvaa gyaanee chen-mokshama-apnuyaat(12)
Tiryaktvm tamasaa jantur-vaasana-anugato-abudhah,
Maatur-labdhvaa punar-janm mriyate ch punah-punah(12.1)

Self-illuminated, without any beginning or end which is **Sat-Chit-Anand** (truth, conscience and bliss), beyond the beyond, without attributes. The **Jeeva** (creatures and humans) are also part of that almighty. (7) It is due to **Avidhya** (Maya), ignorance that **Jeeva** (creature) gets separated from Brahmn just like the sparks who flake out from the fire; and the Jeeva are encased in various bodies to experience their karmas. (8) Controlled by their happiness giving **Punya** (virtuous) Karmas and misery giving Paap karma, they are born in various types of species, bodies, ages and fortunes. (9) O Bird, there is a higher and more **Shukshyam Linga Sarira** (subtle body) which travels across births, uninterrupted till the Atma gets Mokshya. (10) One can be reborn according to their karma in this order (ascending order of importance)- the **Sthavar life** (trees, plants, etc.), worms, birds, animals, humans or thirty three Devi-devtas (Deities appointed by Ishwara to run His creation). These Devi-devtas are — Surya-dev for energy, Vayu-dev for air, Agni-dev for fire, Varun-dev for water and so on). (11) Having worn and cast aside the four sorts of bodies (Jiva is born into any of four categories 1. Swedaj or born of sweat, i.e. bugs; 2. Andaj -born of egg i.e. birds and reptitles 3. Udbhij- born of seeds, i.e. plants) and 4. Jaraayuj-born of womb, i.e. mammals) thousands of times, one become a human by **Sukriti** (good deeds), and attains Mokshya if becomes a **Gyani** (knower). (12) The ignorant, due to attachment to lusty desires, is born and dies again and again. (12.1)

Chatura-sheeti-lakshesu   shareeresu   shareerinaam,
N maanushm vinaa-anyatraa tattva-gyaanm tu labhyate(13)
Atraa   janma-sahstraanaam   sahstrair-api   kotibhiah,
Kadaachil-labhate jantur-maanushym punaya-sanchayaat(14)
Sopaana-bhoota-mokshasy maanushym praapy durlabham,
Yas-taarayati na-atmaanm tasmaat-paapataro-atraa kah?(15)
Narah praapy-ottamm janm labdhvaa ch-endriya-sausthavam,
N vetya-atma-hitm yastu s bhaved brahma-ghaatakah(16)
Vinaa   dehen   kasya-api   purushaartho   n   vidyate,
Tasmaad-dehm dhanm rakshet-punaya-karmaanai saadhayet(17)
Rakshayet-sarvadaa-a-atmaanamaatmaa sarvasy bhaajanam,
Raksanae yatnama-atisthej-jeevan bhadraanai pashyati(18)
Punar-graamah punah kshetraam punar-vittm punar-griham,
Punah shubha-ashubhm karm n shareerm punah punah(19)
Saaraa hi lokeshu bhavet trilokee dveepeshu sarveshu ch jambukaakhyam,
Desheshu sarveshv-api deva-deshah jeeveshu sarveshu manushy ev(20)

It is only the human birth in which one can acquire **Tattva Gyan** (knowledge of truth). (13) In thousands of crores of births, only rarely a being obtains human birth due to the accumulation of **Punya** (virtuous merits). (14) However, birth as humans, though is very rare to obtain, is the staircase of Mokshya. But after getting it, if one does not work for attainment of Mokshya then who is bigger Paapi than him. (15) A human birth is superior, because it has consciousness and sense organs. But despite this, if one does not think about his own welfare then he is treated as killer of human life. (16) But without the human body, no **Purusharth** (dharma, artha, Kama, Moksh) is possible nor can object of life be achieved. Therefore, one should protect the body like the wealth and keep earning **Punya** (virtuous merits). (17) One should guard the body as it is the mean for all the actions. Body should be carefully protected. The opportunities for doing good and bad deeds will keep coming provided the body remains in existence. (18) You may get a village again, a farm-land again, wealth again, a house again, perform auspicious and inauspicious Karmas again- but the body is not obtained again and again. (19) The essence of **Lokas** (realms) is the **Triloka** (three realms i.e Swarga, earth and nether world), the essence of islands is Jambu Dveepa, in all the countries, the country of Deva, where Trimurti is worshiped and the essence of all living creatures is the human being. (20)

159

Tad-gopitm syaad-dharma-arthm dharmo gyaana-artham-ev ch,
Gyaanm tu dhyaana-yoga-arthama-chiraat pra-vi-muchyate(21)
Aatmaiv yadi na-atmaanama-hitebhyo nivaarayet,
Ko-anyo hitakaras-tasmaada-atmaanm taarayishyati(22)
Ihaiv naraka-vyaadhesh-chikitsam n karoti yah,
Gatvaa nir-aushadhm deshm vyaadhisthah kim karishyati(23)
Vyaaghree-vaaste jaraa cha-ayur-yaati bhinna-ghata-ambu-vat,
Nighnanti ripu-vad-rogaas-tasmaach-chhreyah sam-abhyaset(24)
Yaa-van-na-ashrayate dukhm yaa-van-na-ayaanti cha-apadah,
Yaa-van-n-endriya-vaikalym taa-vach-chhreyah sam-abhyaset(25)
Yaa-vat-tisthati deho-aym taa-vat-tattvm sam-abhyaset,
Sandeepte konu bhavane koopm khanati dur-matiah(26)
Kaalo n gyaayate naanaa-kaaryaiah snsaara-sambhavaiah,
Sukhm dukhm jano hant n vetti hitama-atmanah(27)
Jaataanaartaan-mritaana-apad-grastaan drishtvaa ch dukhitaan,
Loko moha-suraam peetvaa n bibheti kadaachan(28)
Sampadah svapna-snkaashaa yauvanm kusum-opamam,
Tadaich-chapala-maayushym kasy syaaj-jaanato dhritiah(29)

Protect your life for duty; perform duty for knowledge; knowledge for the meditation and yoga—then one is released immediately. (21) If one does not protect the self against harm, who else will? Therefore, one should look after the self and become own well wisher. (22) If one does not take precaution against the disease called Narak, while remaining in human form (Karma-Yoni), what can one do when he is to take other births (like animal and others, which are Bhog Yonis) (23) Old age descends like tigress; life goes like water spilling out from a broken pot; diseases attack like enemy. Therefore, one should strive for the excellence. (24) So long as the misery does not strike, so long as the calamity does not befall, so long as the sense organs are not decayed, one should strive for the Noble deeds. (25) Till the body lasts, one should pursue truth. Only the stupid starts digging a well when a corner of the house is already ablaze. (26) Being busy in this world of change, one is not conscious about the arrival of death. Entangled between happiness and miseries, one has no time to think about own welfare. (27) Despite seeing someone getting born, someone dying and the afflicted, the one under calamity; they are not perturbed. The intoxication of worldly Maya has illusioned them. (28) Wealth is as unstable as a dream; youth is like a flower in a garden, life is as fickle as lightning. How can there be a discerning one who can still keep patience. (29)

Shatm jeevitam-aty-alpm nidra-alasyais-tad-ardhakam,
Baalyah-roga-jaraa-dukhair-alpm tad-api nish-falam(30)
Praarabdhavye nir-udyogo jaagartavye pra-suptakah,
Vishvastavyo bhaya-sthaane haa narah ko n hanyate(31)
Toya-fena-same dehe jeevenaakramy snsthite,
Anitya-priya-snvaase kathm tisthati nir-bhayah(32)
Ahite hita-sngyah syaada-dhurave dhurava-sngyakah,
An-arthe cha-artha-vigyaanah svam-arthm yo n vetti sah(33)
Pashyann-api pra-skhalati shrinavann-api n budhyati,
Pathann-api n jaanaati deva-maayaa-vimohitah(34)
San-nimajjaj-jagad-idm gambheere kaala-saagare,
Mrityu-roga-jaraa-graahairn kshchid-api budhyate(35)
Prati-kshanaa-maym kaalah ksheeya-maanao n lakshyate,
Aama-kumbh ivaambhah stho visheernao n vibhaavyate(36)
Yujyate vesthanm vaayora-akaashasy ch khanadaanam,
Grathanm ch tarngaanaamaasthaa na-ayushi yujyate(37)
Prithivee dahyate yen merush-cha-api vi-sheeryate,
Shushyate saagara-jalm shareerasy ch kaa kathaa(38)

Even a life lasting for hundred years is very short and half of it goes in sleep and idleness, and even the remaining is unfruitful owing to the fragile childhood, diseases, miseries and old age. (30) Not doing what is ought to be done, remain asleep when one should be awake, putting faith in a place where one should be fearful. Who can save such person from being stricken? (31) The body is as fragile as foam on water, but how can one who is attached to the worldly objects, which are temporary; remain free from fear. (32) The one, who treats the harmful things as beneficial, believes the temporary objects are permanent and treats the meaningless things as meaningful which will bring wisdom; how can such person get self-knowledge. (33) Stumbles despite seeing the stumbling stone; does not understand despite listening; though reading, does not know; bewildered by the divine Maya. (34) Does not realize that the universe is immersed in the ocean of death, disease and old age. (35) Age though wearing away with every moment without getting noticed just as an unbaked pot placed in water gets dissolved unnoticed. (36) It may be possible to siege the air, split the sky and bind the waves but the life cannot be made permanent. (37) The Earth is burnt away by time; even **Meru** (highest mountain) is reduced to powder; the water of the ocean is dried away;- what to talk of the fragile human body. (38)

Apatym me kalatraam me dhanm me baandhavaash-cha me,
Jalpantamiti martyaajm hanti kaala-vriko balaat(39)
Idm kritam-idm kaaryam-idamanyat-kritaa-akritam,
Evameehaa-samaayuktm kritaantah kurute vasham(40)
Shvaah kaaryamady kurveet poorva-ahne cha-aparahnikam,
N hi mrityuah prateekshet kritm vaa-apy-athavaa-akritam(41)
Jaraa-darshita-panthaanm prachanadaa-vyaadhi-sainikam,
Mrityu-shatraaum-adhishtho-asi traataarm kim n pashyasi(42)
Trishnaa-soochee-vi-nir-bhinnm siktm vishaya-sarpishaa,
Raaga-dvesha-anale pakvm mrityura-shnaati maanavam(43)
Baalaansh-cha yauvana-sthaansh-ch vriddhaan garbha-gataan-api,
Sarvaana-avishate mrityur-evm-bhootam-idm jagat(44)
Sva-deham-api jeevo-aym muktvaa yaati yama-alayam,
Stree-maatri-pitri-putra-adi-sambandhah ken hetunaa(45)
Dukha-moolm hi snsaarah s yasyaa-asti s dukhitah,
Tasy tyaagah krito yen s sukhee na-aparah kvachit(46)
Prabhavm sarva-dukhaanaama-alaym sakala-apadaam,
Aashraym sarva-paapaanaam snsaarm varjayet kshanaat(47)

A person who is deeply engrossed in "my wife, my husband, my offspring, my wealth, my relative, etc.," is suddenly slayed by the wolf of death like a lamb. (39) "This has been completed; this is to be done; whether this is done or not done". The death suddenly overpowers while one is involved in these thought. (40) "It must be done tomorrow; it must be done today in the forenoon or in the afternoon," but the death does not consider whether the work has been completed or not. (41) The enemy death, encounters through the route of old age and has the serious diseases as its soldiers, therefore, why not to take refuge of the savior. (42) Needle like **Trishna** (thirst or longings) and the serpent of lusty desires kill the human being and who is baked by the fire of **Raag-dwesh** (affection and aversion). (43) The children, young, the old, those in the embryo, death can attack anyone and such is the world of creatures. (44) When the Jeeva leaving the body goes to **Yamalaya** (abode of Yama) then for what are the association with wife, husband, mother, father offspring and others! (45) The root of misery is **Sansaar** (wondering in the cycle of birth and death due to desires and longings). The one, who is in it, is afflicted with misery. Only the one, who abandons it, becomes happy. There is no other way out. (46) The Sansaar is the source of all miseries, the home of all calamities, and the shelter of all Paap. Therefore, the attachment to it should be abandoned at once. (47)

Lauha-daaru-mayaiah paashaiah pumaan baddho vi-muchyate,
Putraa-daara-mayaiah paashair-muchyate n kadaa-chan(48)
Yaa-vantah kurute jantuah sambandhaan manasah priyaan,
Taa-vanto-asy nikhanyante hridaye shoka-shankvah(49)
Vanchitiaashesa-vishayair-nitym loko vinaashitah,
Haa hant vishaya-ahaarair-dehasth-endriya-taskaraiah(50)
Maansa-lubdho yathaa matsyo loha-shnkum n pashyati,
Sukha-lubdhas-tathaa dehee yama-baadhaam n pashyati(51)
Hita-ahitm n jaananto nityam-unmaarga-gaaminah,
Kukshi-pooranaa-nishthaa ye te naraa naarakaah khag(52)
Nidra-adi-maithuna-ahaaraah sarveshaam praanainaam samaah,
Gyaana-vaan-maanavah prokto gyaana-heenah pashuah smritah(53)
Prabhaate mal mootra-abhyaam kshuttrid-abhyaam madhyage ravau,
Raatrau madana-nidra-abhyaam baadhayante moodha-maanavaah(54)
Sva-deha-dhana-daara-adi-nirataah sarva-jantavah,
Jaayante ch mriyante ch haa hanta-agyaana-mohitaah(55)
Aatmaanm rathinm viddhi shareerm ratham-ev tu,
Buddhim tu saarathim viddhi manah pragraham-ev ch(55.1)

It is possible to get released from the chains made of iron or wood but not from the **Moh-pash** (rope of enchantment) of wife, husband and offspring. (48) As long as the being is mentally attached to worldly Maya so long shall the thorns of sorrow pierce his heart. (49) This world is destroyed every day by the desire for objects. Ah! The man is killed by the desires of bodily sense organs working like smugglers. (50) Just as the fish, does not see the iron hook due to temptation for flesh. Similarly, the embodied due to temptation of pleasure, does not see the torments of Yama. (51) O Bird, the people who do not understand what is in their interest and what is not in their interest, who constantly pursue evil courses, and only are concerned with filling of their belly, are destined to go to Narak. (52) Sleep, mating and eating are common in all creatures. But the one who possesses knowledge, is called a human and the one devoid of it, is called animal. (53) Foolish people are bonded by nature's calls in the morning, by hunger and thirst in the noon and by passion and sleep in the night. (54) Alas! All those beings who are obsessed with their bodies, wealth, life partner and other things, are born and die of ignorance. (55) Treat the Jeev-Atma as the **Rathee** (the owner of chariot), body as **Rath** (chariot), and intellect is like **Saarathi** (charioteer) and mind is the bridle which acts as controller of **Indriyan** (sense organs). (55.1)

GARUD PURAAN

Indriyaanai hyaana-ahur-vishayaansteshu gocharaan,
Aatm-endriya-mano-yuktm bhoktetyaahur-maneeshinaah(55.2)
Yastu vigyaana-vaan bhavati samanaskah sadaa shuchiah,
S tu tat-padamaapnoti yasmaad bhooyo n jaayate(55.3)
Indriyaanai paraanaya-ahur-indriyebhyah parm manah,
Manasastu paraa buddhiryaae buddheah paratastu sah(55.4)
Evm buddhe parm buddhvaa snstabhya-atmaanama-atmanaa,
Jahi shatraaum mahaa-baaho kaama-roopm duraasadam,
Kshurasy dhaaraa pishitaa duratyataa durgm pathastatkavayo vadanti(55.5)
Indriyaanai mano buddhirasya-adhisthaana-muchyate,
Etair-vimohayatyesh gyaanama-avrity dehinam (55.6)
Tasmaat-sngah sadaa tyaajyah sarvas-tyayuktam n shakyate,
Mahadbhiah sah kartavyah santah sngasy bheshajam(55.7)
Satsngsh-cha viveksh-cha nirmalm nayana-dvayam,
Yasy na-asti narah so-andhah kathm n syaad-amaargagah(56)
Sva-sva-varna-ashrama-achaara-nirataah sarva-maanavaah,
N jaananti parm dharmm vrithaa nashyanti daambhikaah(57)

The wise have termed the sense organs as horse which pulls the chariot of body; the sense organs are means for movement on the path. The **Atma** (pure consciousness) which is accompanied by sense organs and mind has been treated as the user of the body by the **Manishis** (knowers). (55.2) The one who is **Vigyanvaan** (dispassionate scientist) and **Viveki** (discerning), who has his mind under control (**Sam-manask**) and ever pure, leads to the **Parampad** (supreme state) forever. (55.3) Sense organs are superior to body, and **Mana** (mind) is superior to sense organs, **Buddhi** (Intellect) is higher then the mind and that which is beyond the mind, is called **Atma**. (55.4) The sense organs are outward oriented; therefore, they get attracted to the outside objects and do not look towards the **Anter-aatma** (Inner spirit). It is only the wise who, with a auspicious desire for immortality, turn the sense organs to inward looking and are able to see the inner spirit. (55.5) The sense organs, heart and wisdom are the abode of **Kama** (lust). This Kama, engulfing the knowledge, illusions the Jeevatma. (55.6) Therefore, always discard the lust. In case of difficulty, keep the company of sant. The company of Sants is the medicine in the ocean of Sansaar. (55.7) **Satsang** (Company of truthful persons) and **Viveka** (capacity to discern the truth from untruth) are the two serene eyes; and whoever lacks them is a blind who, therefore, is bound to tread on a **Kumarg** (wrong path). (56) Those engrossed in the ideas of Varna and Ashram are the snobs who are ignorant about the supreme dharma and are actually wasting their life in vain. (57)

164

Kriyaayaasa-paraah kechid vrat-acharya-adi-snyutaah,
Agyaana-snvrita-atmaanah sncharanti pra-taarakaah(58)
Naama-maatrona santustaah karma-kaanadaa-rataa naraah,
Mantr-ochchaaranaa-homa-adyair-bhraamitaah kratu-vistaraiah(59)
Eka-bhukt-opavaasa-adyair-niyamaiah kaaya-shoshanaaiah,
Moodhaah paroksham-ichchhanti mam maayaa-vi-mohitaah(60)
Deha-danadaana-maatrona kaa muktir-aviveki-naam,
Valmeeka-taadaanaadev mritah kutraa mahoragah(61)
Jataabhaara-ajinair-yuktaa daambhikaa vesha-dhaarinaah,
Bhramanti gyaani-valloke bhraamayanti janaan-api(62)
Snsaaraja-sukha-asaktm brahmagyo-asmeeti vaadinam,
Karma-brahm-obhaya-bhrashtm tm tyajed-antyajm yathaa(63)
Griha-aranaya-samaa-loke gata-vreedaa dig-ambaraah,
Charanti gardabha-adyaash-cha virakta-aste bhavanti kim(64)
Mrid-bhasmod-dhoolanaadev muktaah syur-yadi maanavaah,
Mrid-bhasma-vaasee nitym shvaaan kim mukto bhavishyati(65)

Some indulge in fasts and performance of rites and some into daily rituals; these imposters are ignorant of reality. (58) They are engaged into karamkanda satisfied just by name, engrossed into elaborate ceremonies. These illusioned people have a belief that by repeating **Mantras** and performing Homa they will achieve Swarga. (59) Captivated and bewildered by Maya, these fools think that by fasts and restraints and taking food once a day, remaining thirsty and torturing the body will lead them to Mokshya. (60) Of those who have no **Viveka** (capacity to discriminate), what Mokshya can there be by bodily tortures alone? Can the dreaded serpent be killed by beating the anthill (around which it lives) alone? (61) Keeping a heap of matted hair on the head and wearing antelope skin, these imposter hypocrites are not only delusioned themselves but they deluse others also. (62) Those enamored to worldly comforts; those who keep on repeating "**Aham Brahmn-asmi**" (I am Brahmn); who are strayed from both Karma and Gyana path of devotion; should be abandoned treating them ignorant. (63) Wandering like the donkey among the people, around houses, forests, without wearing cloths, how can they be treated as virakt (recluse). (64) Had the Moksh been attained by putting ashes and clay on the body, the stray dog, which always remains in the dust and ashes, should be getting Mokshya. (65)

165

GARUD PURAAN

Trinaa-parna-odaka-ahaaraah   satatm   vana-vaasinah,
Jambukaa-a-akhu-mriga-adyaash-cha taapasa-aste bhavanti kim(66)
Aajanma-marana-antm   ch   gnga-adi-tatinee-sthitaah,
Manadaooka-matsya-pramukhaa yogi-n-aste bhavanti kim(67)
Paaraa-vataah shilaa-haaraah kadaachid-api chaatakaah,
N pibanti mahee-toym vrati-n-aste bhavanti kim(68)
Tasmaad-itya-adikm   karm   loka-rnjana-kaarakam,
Mokshasy kaaranam saakshaat tattva-gyaanm khag-eshvar(69)
Shada-darshana-mahaa-koope patitaah pashavah khag,
Parama-arthm n jaananti pashu-paasha-niyantriaataah(70)
Veda-shaastra-arnaave   ghore   uhyamaanaa   itastatah,
Shadaoormi-nigraha-grastaas-tishthanti hi ku-taarkikaah(71)
Veda-agama-puraanaagyah   paramaarthm   n   vetti   yah,
Vidaambakasy tasy-aiv tat-sarvm kaaka-bhaasitam(72)
Idm   gyaanam-idm   gyeyam-iti   chintaa-samaa-kulaah,
Pathanty-ahar-nishm shaastrm para-tattva-paraan-mukhaah(73)

(Had the Moksh been attained by eating grass, leaves, etc.).
The jackals, rats, deer and others, who always eat grass, leaves
and water and always live in forests, become ascetics? (66) (In
case Mokshya could have been attained by taking bath in holy
Ganga, then) do the frog, fishes and others who right from birth
till death, dwell in the waters of Ganga, become Yogis? (67)
The pigeons, at times, eat stones, and Chaataka birds do not
drink water from the earth, but can they be called observers of
vows? (68) O Garuda, the conduct of Varna-Ashram practices
and daily ritual practices are enough only for the Lok-ranjan
(showmanship) in society, but the Moksh can be obtained only
by **Tatva-Gyan** (knowledge of element or reality). (69) O Bird,
the people entangled into the deep well of the six
philosophies, does not understand that what is the supreme
truth- the Brahmn and remain bound by the animal rope.
(70) Lost in the deep ocean of Veda-Shastras; making endless
arguments, reasoning, and caught in the six waves, they
remain sophists. (71) The one who knows the Vedas, the
Shastras and the Puranas, but does not know the **Parmarth**
(ultimate truth) is the imitator, repeating the shastras just
like the screech of a crow. (72) "This I know" and "this I need
to know," lost in this anxiety of finishing the reading of the
scriptures, they lose the track of ultimate truth. (73)

Vaakya-ch-chhando-nibandhen kaavya-alnkaara-shobhitaah,
Chintayaa dukhitaa moodhaas-tisthanti vyaakul-endriyaah(74)
Anyathaa paramm tattvm janaah klishyanti chaa-anyathaa,
Anyathaa shaastr-sadbhaavo vyaakhyaam kurvanti chaa-anyathaa(75)
Kathayantyunmanee-bhaavm svaym na-anubhavanti ch,
Ahnkaara-rataah   kechid-upadesha-adi-varjitaah(76)
Pathanti veda-shaastraanai bodhayanti paras-param,
N jaananti parm tattvm darvee paaka-rasm yathaa(77)
Shiro   vahati   puspaanai gandhm jaanaati   naasikaa,
Pathanti veda-shaashraanai durlabho bhaava-bodhakah(78)
Tattvama-atmasthama-gyaatvaa moodhah shaastreshu muhyati,
Gopah kukshi-gate chhaage koope pashyati dur-matiah(79)
Snsaara-moha-naashaay shabda-bodho n hi kshamah,
N   nivartet   timirm   kadaachid-deepa-vaartayaa(80)
Pragyaa-heenasy pathanm yatha-andhasy ch darpanaam,
Atah pragyaa-vataam shaastraam tattva-gyaanasy lakshanaam(81)

A fool who is anxious and concerned about the figure of speech, decoration of verses of the scriptures, how can he understand the deep meaning of Shastras. (74) The ultimate truth is somewhere else but they look for it elsewhere. The scriptures say something and they interpret something else. (75) They teach about the highest experiences which they themselves have never realized. Some have stopped preaching being engrossed in ego. (76) They read Vedas and Shastra and argue with one another, but they do not understand the highest truth. It is just like the spoon does not recognize the flavor of the food (though it remains in the food). (77) The flower is placed on the head but it is the nose which can feel the aroma. Similarly, so many people read the Ved-Shastra but rare are the wise who understand the essence of it. (78) Vedas tell that the ultimate reality is in you as your Atma, but the silly is tracing it in the scriptures, just like a shepherd holding the lamb in his lap but searching for it in the well (due to reflection). (79) As the darkness does not disappear just by talking about a lamp, similarly knowledge of vocabulary is not enough to destroy the Maya of Sansaar. (80) Study of scriptures by the one devoid of wisdom, is like showing mirror to a visually impaired; hence only the wise can obtain wisdom. That is why the wise are termed as the knower of the reality. (81)

Idm gyaanam-idm gyeym sarvm tu shrotum-ichchhati,
Divya-varsha-sahstraayuah shaastra-antm naiv gachchhati(82)
Anekaani ch shaastraanai svalpa-ayur-vighna-kotayah,
Tasmaat saarm vijaaneeyaat ksheerm hns ivaambhasi(83)
Abhyasy veda-shaastraanai tattvm gyaatva-ath buddhi-maan,
Palaalam-iv dhaanya-arthee sarva-shaastraanai santyajet(84)
Yathaa-amriten   triptasy   na-ahaarena   prayojanam,
Tattva-gyasy tathaa taarkshyaa n shaastrona prayojanam(85)
N veda-adhyayanaan-muktir-n shaastraa-pathanaad-api,
Gyaanaadev hi kaivalym na-anyathaa vinata-atmaj!(86)
Na-ashramah kaaranan mukter-darshanaani n kaaranaam,
Tathaiv sarva-karmaanai gyaanamev hi kaaranaam(87)
Muktidaa guru-vaag-ekaa vidyaah sarvaa vidaambikaah,
Kaastha-bhaara-sahstreshu hyekm snjeevanm param(88)
Advaitm hi shivm proktm kriyaayaasa-vi-varjitam,
Guru-vaktrona labhyet na-adheetaagama-kotibhiah(89)

"This is known, this must be known and this all I desire to listen", but there is no end. Even, if one lives for a thousand celestial years, he cannot complete reading of Shastra. (82) The Shastra are numerous but life is short; and there are tens of millions of obstacles; therefore, the essence of Shastra be taken out just like the swan takes the milk out of the water. (83) Having practiced the Vedas and Shastra and having known the Truth, the wise would abandon all the scriptures; just as one abandons the straw after taking out the grains. (84) O, Taarkshya, just as there is no necessity of food to the one who is satiated with nectar, so there is no use of the scriptures to the knower of the truth. (85) O son of Vintaa, it is not by the study of Vedas or repeating of scriptures, rather the **Kaivalya** (Mokshya) is achieved by gaining the knowledge alone. (86) Moksh is attained neither by following the stages of Ashrama nor by following the Darshans, rather the knowledge alone is the cause of all actions. (87) All learning is like masquerade, the words of Satguru are liberating. It is like the **Sanjivini** (herb for reviving life) which is best among the thousands of Plants. (88) It is Shivam (auspicious) to have faith in **Adveta Darshan** (non-dual meaning oneness of a person's Atma and universal power-Parmatma-meaning Brahmn). But what cannot be obtained through crores of scriptures, can be obtained from the word of Guru. (89)

Aagam-oktn vivek-otthm dvidhaa gyaanm prachakshate,
Shabda-brahma-agama-maym para-brahma-viveka-jam(90)
Advaitm kechid-ichchhanti dvaitam-ichchhanti cha-apare,
Samm tattvm n jaananti dvaita-advaita-vi-varjitam(91)
Dve pade bandha-mokshaay mameti n mameti ch,
Mameti badhyate janturn mameti pramuchyate(92)
Tat-karm yan-n bandhaay saa vidyaa yaa vimuktidaa,
Aayaasaayaaparm karm vidyaa-anyaa shilpa-naipunaam(93)
Yaa-vat-karmaanai deeyante yaa-vat-snsaara-vaasanaa,
Yaa-vad-indriya-chaapalym taa-vat tattva-kathaa kutah(94)
Yaa-vad-deha-abhi-maansh-cha mamataa yaa-vad-ev hi,
Yaa-vat-prayatna-vego-asti yaa-vat-snklpa-kalpanaa(95)
Yaa-van-no manasa-sthairym n yaa-vach-chhaastr-chintanam,
Yaa-van-n guru-kaarunaym taa-vat tattva-kathaa kutah(96)

Knowledge is said to be obtained from two sources: through **Aagam** (Shruti and Smriti) scriptures and **Viveka** (discrimination). The knowledge obtained from Aagam is known as **Shabd Brahmn** and the one achieved through Viveka is known as **Par-Brahmn**. (90) Some prefer the Advaita (Atma is the part of Param-atma) other prefer the Devaita (meaning the individual Atma has a separate existance from Parm-atma) but they do not know the one reality, which is beyond the dual and non-dual. (91) There are two phrases which are indicative of bondage and Mokshya- "mine" and "not mine". The word 'mine' puts into bondage whereas the world 'not mine' is liberating. (92) Karma is that which does not put in bondage; knowledge is that which liberates. The rest of the Karma is nothing but labor and rest of the knowledge is nothing but good craftsmanship. (93) So long as karma (the type of karma which put in bondage) are performed; so long as the worldly longings remain, so long as the senses are fickle; till than how can there be narration of the story of truth. (94) So long as there is pride of body; so long as there is the feeling of 'me and mine', so long as there is excited striving; so long as there are longing for unrealized resolutions; (95) So long as there is no stability of mind; so long as there is no contemplation upon the Shastra, so long as **Kripa** (grace) of Guru is not realized; where is the consideration of **Tatva-Gyan** (knowledge of the element); (96)

Taa-vat tapo vratm teerthm jap-homa-archana-adikam,
Veda-shaastra-agama-kathaa yaa-vat-tattvm n vindati(97)
Tasmaat sarva-prayatnen sarva-avasthaashu sarvadaa,
Tattva-nishtho bhavet taarkshyaa yade-echchhen-mokshama-atmanah(98)
Dharma-gyaana-prasoonasy svarga-moksha-falasy ch,
Taapa-traaya-adi-santaptash-chhaayaamm moksha-taroah shrayet(99)
Tasmaat gyaanena-atma-tattvm vigyeym shree-guror-mukhaat,
Sukhen muchyate jantur-ghora-snsaara-bandhanaat(100)
Kshiprm nashyati dharmagy jalaa-naam sharado yathaa,
Aneka-janma-janitm paatakm saadhu-sngame(101)
Tattvagyasya-antimn kritym shrinau vakshyaami te-adhunaa,
Yen mokshama-vaapnoti brahma-nirvaanaa-sngyakam(102)
Anta-kaale tu purush aagate gatasaadhvasah,
Chhindyaada-snga-shastrerna sprihaam dehe-anuye ch tam(103)

So long as one does not attain Tatva-Gyan, so long should one do **Tapa** (austerities), **Vrita** (vows), pilgrimage to **Teerth** (sacred places), **Japa**, **Homa** (oblations to fire), worship and **Kathaa** (narration) of the prescribed texts of the Vedas and Sastras. (97) But O Taarkshya, one desirous of Moksh for self, should always and under all circumstances be **Tatva-nisht** (fully absorbed to the truth). (98) The one who is agonized by three - **Taap** (Daihik, Devik, Bhotik miseries associated with body, Devta (deity)- natural calamities, etc., and physical existence) should take the rest and the shelter under the shade of the tree of Mokshya. Dharma and Gyana are the flowers of this tree and Swarga and Mokshya are its fruits. (99) Therefore, the knowledge of Atma-tatva is known from the mouth of the blessed Gurus. By knowledge, the being is easily released from the awful bondage of the **Sansaar**. (100) The company of Saadhus and of **Dharamgya** (knower of Dharma) quickly washes away the Paap accumulated from various births,; just as the Rainey season washes away the litter accumulated during autumn. (101) Listen now! I will tell you about the final actions of the **Tatva-gyani** (knower of the reality), by which one obtains Mokshya also known as the Brahmn Nirvana. (102) Seeing the last time approaching, the person should rid himself of fear, and should cut off the desires associated with the body and the worldly attachments with the sword of unattachment. (103)

Grihaat pravrajito dheerah punaya-teertha-jala-aplutah,
Shuchai vivikt aaseeno vidhi-vat-kalpita-asane(104)
Abhyasen-manasaa shuddhm tri-vrid-brahma-aksharm param,
Mano yach-chhej-jit-shvaaaso brahma-beejama-vismaran(105)
Niyachchhed-vishaye-bhyo-akshaan-manasaa buddhi-saarathiah,
Manah karma-bhira-akshiptm shubha-arthe dhaarayed-dhiyaa(106)
Ahm brahm parm dhaam brahmaahm paramn padam,
Evm sameekshy cha-atmaanama-atmanyaa-dhaay nishkale(107)
Om-ity-eka-aksharm brahm vyaaharan-maam-anusmaran,
Yah prayaati tyajan dehm s yaati paramaam gatim(108)
N yatraa daambhikaa yaanti gyaana-vairaagya-varjitaah,
Sudhiyastaam gatim yaanti taanahm kathayaami te(109)
Nirmaana-mohaa jita-snga-doshaa adhyaatma-nityaa vi-nivritta-kaamaah,
Dvand-vair-vi-muktaah sukha-dukha-sngyair-gachchhantya-moodhaah padama-vyaym tat(110)

Steady and self possessed, venturing out of home, perform ablution in the water of the holy Teerth, sitting alone on a pure **Asana** (seat) prepared as prescribed, (104) With mind concentrated and pure, should carry out Jaap of "Om" mentally; the supreme three-fold pure name of Brahmn; with breath controlled, mind restrained, not forgetting Om the Brahmn **Beej** (seed) mantra. (105) With the help of intellect, which is a charioteer, one should control the mind and pull out the sense-objects from longing of desires and withdraw from engagement of karma (mental and physical actions), with the help of mind, and fix the mind upon the pure Brahmn. (106) "I am Brahmn, I am the Supreme Abode, the Brahmn, I am the highest seat-the Brahmn"; having realized this, making Atma as **Niskal** (without any position, status, designation) and placing the mind in Ishwara, one should meditate. (107) The one who, when leaving the body, remembering me (Ishwara) utters 'Om' the one syllable Brahmn (highest Goal); attains the Mokshya. (108) The hypocrites, devoid of Gyan-Vairagya (knowledge of truth and asceticism), do not reach there. I will tell you about the **Sudhee** (sensible) who attain that goal. (109) Those who are free from **Moha** (longings) and **Maya** (delusion), who have conquered the evils of attachment, always dwelling in the meditational stage of Higher Self, having overcome the lusty desires, released from the dichotomy of pleasure and pain, they go, undiluted on that eternal path. (110)

Gyaana-hrade   satya-jale   raaga-dvesha-malaapahe,
Yah snaati maanase teerthe s vai mokshama-vaapnuyaat(111)
Praudhm vairaagyama-asthaay bhajate maam-ananya-bhaak,
Poornaa-drishtiah prasanna-atmaa s vai mokshama-vaapnuyaat(112)
Tyaktvaa grihm ch yas-teerthe nivasen-marana-otsukah,
Mriyate mukti-kshetroshu s vai mokshama-vaapnuyaat(113)
Ayodhyaa mathuraa maayaa kaashee kaanchee hyavantikaa,
Puree dvaaraa-vatee gyeyaah saptaitaa moksha-daayikaah(114)
Iti te kathitm taarkshyaa moksha-dharmm sanaatanam,
Gyaana-vairaagya-sahitm shrutvaa mokshama-vaapnuyaat(115)
Mokshm gachchhanti tattvagyaa dhaarmikaah svargatim naraah,
Paapino durgatim yaanti snsaranti khagaadayah(116)
Ity-evm sarva-shaastraanaam saar-oddhaaro niroopitah,
Mayaa te shodaasha-adhyaayaiah kim bhooyah shrotum-ichchhasi?(117)

The one who washes the dirt of **Raag-dvesha** (affection and aversion) in the Teerth of Gyana, from the water of truth, on the **Jalkund** (water-pool) of mind; gets Moksh. (111) One who has firmly developed the quality of **Vairagya** (renunciation from Maya), who is fully devoted to non-other than Me (Bhagwan), one who is having complete vision and tranquil state of mind, obtains Mokshya. (112) One, who is expecting his death, leaves home and dwells at a Teerth or dies in a place of emancipation, verily attains Mokshya. (113) Ayodhya, Mathura, Gaya, Kasi, Kanchi, Avantika, Dwaravati are the seven cities which are known as the givers of Mokshya. (114) O Taarkshya, this eternal Path of Mokshya has been described to you. Whoever hears it with knowledge and dispassion attains Mokshya. (115) The **Tatva-gyanis** (knowers of truth) attain Mokshya; those who are committed to Dharma attain Swarga; Paapi go to face the Durgati and obtain the birth of animals, birds and others. (116) Thus, in sixteen chapters, I have depicted to you the essence of all the scriptures. What else do you wish to hear? (117)

SOOT UVAACH

Evm shrutvaa vacho raajan garudo bhagavan-mukhaat,
Krita-anjlir-uvaachedm tm pranaamy muhur-muhuah(118)
Bhagavan deva-devesh shraavayitvaa vacho-amritam,
Taarito-ahm tvayaa naath bhava-saagaratah prabho(119)
Sthito-asmi gata-sandehah kritaartho-asmi n snshayah,
Ity-uktvaa garudas-tooshnaeem sthitvaa dhyaana-paro-a-bhavat(120)
Smaranaad-dur-gati-hartaa poojana-yagyen sad-gater-daataa,
Yah parayaa nija-bhaktyaa dadaati muktim s maam hariah paatuah(121)

SUTA SAID O king, having thus heard these words from the mouth of the Bhagwan, Garuda repeatedly prostrating himself, said this, with hands folded together (118) "O Bhagwan, O **Devadhi-dev** (Eternal Lord of Deities), having heard these nectar like words, I have been helped to cross the **Bhavsagar** (ocean of existence), O Naath (Bhagwan), O Prabho". (119) I am obliged and now completely free from doubts and feel fulfilled. Having said this, Gaurda became silent and submerged in meditation. (120) May Hari, whose remembrance dispels **Durgati** (speed towards Narak or bad condition) and whose worship and performance of Yagya, bring **Sad-gati** (speedy elevation to truth), who bless the devotees with Mokshya, May such benevolent Shri Hari Vishnu protect us. (121)

Annadi-nidhano Devah Shankh Chakra Gadaa-dharah,
Akshayah pundree-kaakash Preta-mokshya-prado-bhav.

173

Ath Shruti-Phal

LISTENING OF GARUD PURAAN WITHIN TEN DAYS AND THE REWARDS OBTAINED BY THE PERFORMER AND MOKSHYA TO THE DEPARTED.

SHREEBHAGAVAANUVAACH

Itya-akhyaatm mayaa taarkshyaa sarvam-ev-aurdhva-daihikam,
Dashaaha-abhy-antare shrutvaa sarva-paapaiah pra-muchyate(1)
Idm chaamushmikm karm pitri-mukti-pradaayakam,
Putraa-vaanichhatadm chaiv paratroh ch sukha-pradam(2)
Idm karm n kurvanti naastikaa ye nara-adhamaah,
Teshaam jalam-apeym syaat suraa-tulym n snshayah(3)
Devataah pitarsh-chaaiv naivm pashyanti tad-griham,
Bhavanti teshaam kopen putraah pautraash-cha durgataah(4)
Braahmanaaah kshatriyaa vaishyaah shoodraash-chaiv-etare-api ch,
Te chaanadaala-samaa gyeyaah sarve preta-kriyaam vinaa(5)
Preta-kalpam-idm punaym shrinaoti shraavayech-ch yah,
Ubhau tau paapanir-muktau dur-gatim naiv gachchhatah(6)
Maataa-pitrosh-cha maranae sau-parnam shrinaute tu yah,
Pitarau muktima-apannau sutah santati-maan bhavet(7)

BHAGWAN SAID- I have described everything about Aurdhva-dehik rites. Listening Garud Puraan within ten days of the death absolves one from all his Paap. (1) Performance of the Aurdhva-dehik rites is liberating to the Pitr, fulfills the wishes for having offspring and bestows happiness in this world and also in the other world. (2) It is not worth even to take water from the house of the Nastik and banal who do not perform this rite, because this water is like poison, no doubt about that. (3) The Devta and Pitr do not even look at their homes and due to their anger even children and grandchildren face Durgati (speed to untruth). (4) The one who narrates Pret-kalp to others or the one who listens the narration is released from the Paap. (5) Brahmin, Kshtriya, Vaishya or Shudra and others who do not perform the Pret-kriya, are all like demons. (6) The couple, who listen this on the death of their parent, would bestow Mokshya parent while it would bless the couple with offspring. (7)

N shrutm gaarudam yen gayaa-shraaddhm ch no kritam,
Vrish-otsargah krito naiv n ch maasika-vaarshike(8)
S kathm kathyate putraah kathm muchyet rinaa-traayaat,
Maatarm pitarm chaiv kathm taarayitum kshamah(9)
Tasmaat sarva-prayatnen shrotavym gaarudam kil,
Dharma-arth-kaam-mokshaanaam daayakm duahkha-naashanam(10)
Puraanam gaarudam punaym pavitraam paapa-naashanam,
Shrinavataam kaamanaa-poorm shrotavym sarva-daiv hi(11)
Adhyaaya-menm sukritasy saarm shrinaoti gaayaty-api bhaava-shuddhyaa,
S vai kuleenah s ch dharma-yukto vishva-aalaym yaati parm s noonam(12)
Yshchedm shrinauyaan-matyon yshchas-api parikeertiyet,
Vihaay yaatanaam ghoraam bhoota-paapo divm vrajet(13)
Y idm shunauyaan martyo yo vaapyabhidadhaati ch,
Ihaa-amutraa ch loke s yarvatraa sukhama-apnuyaat(14)
Bhajat jita-hriseekaah krishnaamenm muneeshm,
samajani bat yasmaad geeah sudhaa-saara-dhaaraa,
Prisatam-api yadeeym varnaa-roopm nipeey,
shruti-puta-chuluken praapnu-yaada-atman-aikyam(15)
Vrajatah snyamanyaam yad duahkhamatraa niroopitam,
Asy shravanaatah punaym tan-mukto jaayate tatah(16)

Who neither hear Garuda Puraan and perform Shraddh at Gaya nor perform the Varsho-utsarg nor the monthly and annual Shraddh; (8) How can he be called son and how would he be freed from the three debt (Tri-rina) he owes. How would he be able to ferry (liberate) mother and father. (9) Therefore, with all efforts one should listen the narration of Garud Puraan. This bestows Dharma, Artha, Kama and Mokshya and annuls the Paap. (10) The Gaurd Puraan brings chastity, gives Punya and destroys Paap, hearing it is wish fulfilling, therefore, should always be listened. (11) The Sukriti (noble doer) who reads it with devotion or narrates for others, that Dharmik and noble person is liberated and becomes part of Brahmn. (12) The one who internalizes it and helps others to know this truth is absolved from the terrible tortures of Yam and goes to Swarga and becoming Nis-paap (sinless). (13) The person who listens to it or narrates it to others, he will enjoy happiness in this world and in the Par-lok (other world). (14) O Jitendriya! (One who has achieved victory over sense organs), you all worship the Krishna, Lord of Munis, from whom we received the nectar like words, listening even a drop of that merges one with Ishwara. (15) Listening, with devotion, the miseries narrated in this Purana about Yampuri, one is absolved from such miseries and is freed from the pains of this world. (16)

175

SHOK SABHA AND
SHRADDHANJALI

(THE MODEL SPEECH FOR ACHARYA PUROHIT)

**"Asato maa sada-gamayah,
tamaso maa jyotir-gamayah,
mrityormaa. Amritam gamayah"**

(O Ishwara! Lead me to truth from ignorance, lead me to light from darkness and lead me to immortality from the death).

AIM OF SHOK SABHA AND SHRADHANJALI: The immediate aim of the condolence meeting, prayer, homage or tribute is to pray Ishwara for Sad-gati (Speedy Elevation to Truth) of the departed and also to give strength to the bereaved family by expressing solidarity, so that they are able to bear the sorrows. However, in the long run the aim is to motivate people to follow the path of Dharma and Purusharth (human endeavor). As per Garud Puraan, this is a suitable time to impart the message of Dharma and faith (Garud Puraan 6.27). People should be made to realize that human birth is a rare opportunity to earn Punya (merits) and achieve Mokshya by following the paths of Karma, Bhakti and Gyan.

DHARMA, KARMA, DAAN: The Pravachan (speech) should start by praying to Lord Vishnu, the liberator. Thereafter, seek blessing for Mokshya of the departed by reciting the Stuti: **Anaadini dhano devah sankh-chakra-gadaa-dharah aksayah punadaree-kaaksahya preta-mokshya-aprado bhav**. Emphasis should be on the importance of human birth aim of life and how to make it purposeful (2/34). Similarly, the importance of Purusharth (Dharma, Arth, Kama,

176

Mokshya), Daan and Sat-karma (good deeds) in life may be highlighted. Further, how one can conquer over desires, anger, greed, attachment, fear, hatred and how to lead a life of Karma-Yogi, should be emphasized.

People should take care of their body because body is the only mean to do Purusharth and achieve Mokshya. Aim of life is liberation of self and welfare of the world **(Atmano Mokshyartham Jagat Hitay Ch**-Rig-veda).In Ramcharitmanas Goswami Tulsidas wrote **"Saadhan-Dhaam mokshya kari dwaaraa, paii n jehi paralok snvaaraa"**.

There is reference in Garud Puraan (10/56-59) that when the relatives sit on the clean ground after the cremation then the priest or any knowledgeable person sitting along with them, should recite the Suddhi Mantra **"Om Apavitrah Pavitro Vaa Sarva-Avasthaam Gato-pi Vaa Yah Smaret-Punnddarii-kaakssam Sa Baahya-Abhyantarah Shucih"**. Thereafter, start the sermon on instability of Life and that only the Truth is permanent. Speaking about the instability of the world, will help bereaved family in relieving the sorrow. He may say, "Anyone who tries to find essence in the human body, which is like content less banana stem or water bubble, is a fool." If the body, made of five elements, merges with the original five elements, why to repent. The land gets destroyed, ocean is also destroyed, the deities are also not immortal, how then the foam like creatures of this earth, will not get destroyed.

This means the body, mind, wealth, youth and life, all are flickering but the one, who has achieved the glory during life only has lived. The Acharya should quote Shloka on these lines.

Due to the death of a relative, the whole of family feels shattered and is in the deep ocean of sorrow, therefore, it is the duty of Acharya, to underline the instability of life and the death being the universal truth. He should keep on consoling the bereaved family, particularly, at the time of cremation of the departed, at the time of collection of mortal remains, on the fourth day's rites, at Dashgaatra karma and at the time of last condolence meeting.

177

According to **Kishkandha Kand** of **Ramcharitmanas** (11/2-3), when Tara, the wife of Bali, started crying on seeing the body of her departed husband, Bhagwan Ram consoled Tara, by underlining the transitory nature of life. He told her that it is the destiny of body to dissolve with the source elements. He said, O Tara! If you are weeping for the perishable body of Bali, then that is lying before you, and if you are weeping for his Atma, that is still alive. Atma does not die as it is immortal, undestroyable, and is perpetual. Therefore, for what you are bereaved? In this scriptures also there are many Shloka relating to this aspect (8/45-A-B).

GRIHAST SHOULD BECOME KARMA-YOGI: Out of 8.4 Million births, only the human birth is Karm Yoni. All other births are for experiencing the result of Karma. Therefore, the human birth is obtained for doing "Purusharth" and "performing Dharma". (Katho. 1.2.6). The service of humanity is inherent in the concept of **Karmyog**.

FOCUS ON GOOD DEEDS OF DEPARTED: The Acharya should further deliberate that it is the contribution of a person which remains permanent **"Chalm vittam chalm chittam chale jeevita-yauvane Chalaa-challa-midam sarvam keertiryasya s jeevati".** Here the good deeds done by the departed and his or her contribution to society, family, nation, Dharma, etc., must be highlighted so that his offspring and other people are motivated to follow the right path. The Acharya may recite various original Shloka which can improve the knowledge of listener on Dharma, Karma, Bhakti and Mokshya.

IMMORTALITY OF ATMA: The Acharya may make special emphasis on the immortality of Atma, how it acquires new body in accordance with deeds, similar to a person wearing new clothes after discarding the old worn out ones- Vasamsi Jirnaani Yatha Vihaya (Gita 2.2).

The speaker may deliberate on the aim of human life? Importance of service to human beings and other creatures, Daan, mercy, and victory over desire, anger, attachment and fear (8/93,94) and efforts to achieve victory over the vices.

In the Garud Puraan itself and other scriptures there are many Shloka which motivate the people towards doing the good deeds. Living a Dharmik life (2/34 & 40), how to do Purusharth (18.47, 5/29), (Shrimadbhagwat-3/25/21); Sat-asat, Paap-Punya (2.41) and the importance of keeping a healthy body (8/85), (16/17-19,21); impermanence of the body (10/55-59), (16/34-38); the transmigration of Atma and immortality (9/45-47) and Karma (2/33), (5/4), (Katho-1.2.18,2.2,7), (Gita 2.12-13); death as the universal truths (8/91), preservation of environment (8/106.2), the body being the chariot of Atma (16/54,55), etc., may highlighted suitably.

Quoting from this and other scriptures on the human values like mercy, love, affection, human sensitivity and inspiration to live a vibrant life- should be emphasized. The preaching on Niskaam Karma and Saakshi Bhaav in Gita may be highlighted. Every human being is performing his or her own separate journey (5/3), the preaching from Garud Puraan on study of Ved-Puraan (8/9-8) may also be utilized. But the substance presented in the condolence meeting is not to be treated as substitute for the narration of Garud Puraan or Nasket, rather within ten days of death the reading of Garud Puraan and Nasket should performed as per procedure as that is very rewarding (destroys Paap, fulfill the wishes and acts as consolation to bereaved family and friends, and bestows Sad-gati to departed). (Shrutiphal-1).

The Ishwara is compassionate and loving (15/95), may He shower peace and happiness on all. After making the prayer tell the people to take the refuse of the Krishna (Gita 18.66). At the end **"Sarve bhavantu sukhinah sarve santu niraamayaah sarve bhadraanai pashyantu maa kashit-Dukh-Bag-Bhavet"**

"Om visvaanidev saviturar-duritaani paraashuv, yadbhadrm tanna aasuv". These Mantras should be recited collectively and, thereafter, the Shanti Paatha **"Om dyauah shaanti antarikcn shaantiah prithivee shaanti raapah shaanti-ausadhayah shaantiah vanaspatayah shaanti, shaantir-vishve-devaah shaanti brahm shaantiah sarvn shaantiah shaantirev shaantiah saa maa shaanti redhi: Om Shanti Shanti Shanti"**

At the conclusion of the condolence meeting, the priest may pray to Ishwara to give refuge to the departed in His holy feet, may the departed attain Sad-gati and also may give strength and wisdom to the bereaved family to be able to bear the loss.

While delivering the speech the factors like type of audience, time allowed, size of gathering and other factors should be kept in mind. The people gathered may also be allowed, to make the condolences speech.

(The above modal speech of condolence meeting is only indicative and directed towards the beginners only and not for the Pandits.)